THE
Landlord's Kit

REVISED EDITION

A Complete Set of Ready-to-Use Forms, Letters,
and Notices to Increase Profits, Take Control, and Eliminate the
Hassles of Property Management

Jeffrey Taylor, Certified Professional Landlord
Founder of MrLandlord.com

KAPLAN PUBLISHING

Vice President and Publisher: Maureen McMahon
Editorial Director: Jennifer Farthing
Acquisitions Editor: Mary B. Good
Interior Design: Lucy Jenkins
Cover Design: KTK Design Associates
Typesetting: Sokie Lee

Published by Kaplan Publishing, a division of Kaplan, Inc.
1 Liberty Plaza, 24th Floor
New York, NY 10006

Printed in the United States of America

January 2008
10 9 8 7 6 5 4 3 2 1

ISBN-13: 978-1-4277-5468-4

Kaplan Publishing books are available at special quantity discounts to use for sales promotions, employee premiums, or educational purposes. Please email our Special Sales Department to order or for more information at kaplanpublishing@kaplan.com, or write to Kaplan Publishing, 1 Liberty Plaza, 24th Floor, New York, NY 10006.

DEDICATION

This book is dedicated to my wife, best friend, life and business partner, Dot Taylor, for her 25+ years of love, business savvy, support, and the valuable balance (fun) she brings to my life. Together, we have worked as rental property owners, and she has literally traveled the entire country (and I mean entire), from town to town, as I've spoken to real estate associations nationwide, sharing our landlording experiences and management strategies, tips, and forms. If the truth be told, she was the one who actually found our first fixer-upper and did most of the fix up. As a young married couple, we were just trying to buy a home that we could afford. Neither of us had any idea that we were actually laying the groundwork for a future of real estate investing and much, much more. To my two sons, Jeffrey and Justin: My hope is that I continue to inspire you to reach for your dreams and strive to be the best at whatever you do. In memory of my mentor, Nick Koon, the hard-nosed landlord, who first allowed me to learn up close from a real landlord, millionaire, author, and coach. He took me under his wing. And most of all I give praise and thanksgiving to God for the opportunities, assets, and grace I've been given.

Contents

PART THREE

COLLECTION AND VIOLATION NOTICES   111

PART FOUR

MAINTENANCE AND MANAGEMENT   153

PART FIVE

RETENTION, TURNOVER, AND ADVERTISING   203

Bonus Record Keeping forms! For your bonus record keeping forms, please go to
kaplanpublishing.com/landlordskit
To access the site, you'll need to have a password from the book.
The site will tell you what page to look for and what word to put in.

Foreword

As a real estate attorney and consultant, investors and landlords seek my advice for real estate investing and asset protection. However, when they need help with landlording or property management, I point them in the direction of Jeffrey Taylor, "Mr. Landlord." There is no other person on the planet who has more proven or better ideas on how to communicate (both verbally and in writing) with tenants so that you get the most income possible from your rentals, and keep your residents longer, happier, and cooperative.

I've known Jeffrey for over ten years. He totally blew me away when I first heard him speak on landlording. He was talking about developing win-win relationships with residents and how they will actually ask you if they can pay more money or stay longer. He taught about incorporating marketing, customer service, customer retention, and collection ideas from other industries, ideas that up to that point I had never seen used in the real estate arena and I had never heard any landlording speaker or coach talk from such perspectives. He likewise incorporates those ideas into his book, *The Landlord's Kit.*

Up to the time of hearing Jeffrey, I was the typical investor who dreaded the landlording part of the real estate business. In fact, I once shared with him that I'd sometimes let a place sit empty for a few months until it sold (for a big profit mind you), rather than deal with the challenges that come with landlording and tenants. However, after listening to Jeffrey, my mindset totally changed. I was so impressed with his teachings, trainings and "Mr. Landlord" newsletter, that I purchased his books, newsletter subscription and complete training materials and resources.

I have to say that his ideas work. My cash flow has greatly increased and my management headaches have been reduced, because my tenants now stay longer and follow the programs I have put into place thanks to Jeffrey and the rental forms he provides.

Annually I host a major real estate convention. For the last several years, I have made it a necessity to invite Jeffrey as one of the featured instructors, because I am convinced that every landlord can benefit tremendously from the forms and principles he shares. I also encourage members of my local real estate association, which I oversee, to purchase his bestselling book, *The Landlord's Kit,* and go to his website MrLandlord.com for additional ideas, resources, and landlording services to help them be successful. The credit check on his website is easy to use, he provides a listing of real estate associations nationwide and he has links to landlord-tenant laws for every state. Those are just a few of the resources that make his website the most visited place on the Internet for do-it-yourself landlords. Not to mention, his awesome Q&A Forum where thousands consult daily to learn from the questions posted by other landlords. It's like having your own personal landlord board of advisors 24/7.

With his over 100 rental forms, included in this book, and other resources, Jeffrey Taylor really provides everything a landlord needs to take control of his rental business. And on top of all that, he is a decent guy with integrity and strong moral convictions. I know when I invite him to speak for my three-day conferences, I can't schedule him for Sunday. That day he keeps free so he can attend his local church, where he and his wife oversee the business owners and professionals association. I've met his wife Dot, who runs the MrLandlord.com conferences and cruises, which they have been doing for eighteen years. She too teaches to real estate investors and business owners. Together, they make a powerful real estate couple and business pair.

The Landlord's Kit is the result of lots of research and the school of hard knocks, as well as formal training in the area of communication, plus consulting with landlords, managers, and attorneys over the last 25 years. Jeffrey has learned a lot over time, not only to help make him successful, but he has literally coached tens of thousands of other landlords, including myself, to be more successful. Utilize the forms in this book to improve your communication and landlording effectiveness and increase your cash flow. There is a form here for almost every kind of landlording situation you may face. Equally important, Jeffrey always addresses those situations in a proactive, positive, and professional manner so that you can stay in control of your rental business.

—William Bronchick, attorney, consultant, founder of LegalWiz.com and author of *Wealth Protection Secrets of a Millionaire Real Estate Investor*

Preface

This book contains rental forms, letters, checklists, scripts, and notices to be used by landlords and rental managers. In addition, this updated edition includes not only revised forms from the first edition, but nearly three dozen new and unique rental forms to help you take greater control of your rental business. Just one of the new forms alone is worth getting a copy of this new edition. If you own and rent homes or apartments (one to one hundred), this book is for you! This book is purposely designed so that you can tear out and copy these forms for your rental business. Hey, for the low cost of this book, I'd suggest buying more than one copy (you're time is worth far more than the time it would take to make copies of all the forms you will need).

The main benefit of this book, however, is to provide you with a complete set of forms that can serve as a reference or starting point to create or modify for use anytime you need to communicate with a resident. This kit has practically every rental form or letter you need! (Also refer to the special offer at the back of the book, which allows buyers of this book to obtain all the forms herein on CD at a special half-price offer.)

To best understand the use of some of the forms, landlords should first read the text that precedes each set of forms in this book. Also note that rental laws vary from state to state. While the forms and letters communicate universally sound business, marketing, and management concepts, certain notices or agreements may require wording specified by state or locale.

My goal is to coach and challenge you to communicate effectively with rental residents. While the forms in this book are based on tried and tested concepts, many of them are innovative for the landlording profession. I am quick to recommend that you always seek professional advice if or when faced with legal challenges by your residents. Do not do as many landlords have and try to make all your decisions without considering the counsel of professionals. While I serve as a coach and mentor, your primary source of advice must start with local, competent, professional advisors. As a landlord, it is to your great advantage to have a good working relationship with a local attorney, accountant, financial advisor, and real estate broker, preferably ones who own rental real estate themselves. Good advice will always pay for itself with increased cash flow and prevention of enormous losses.

To increase your chances of exposure to good counsel, join a local rental owner's association. Go to *www.realestateassociations.com* to find a local association near you. There you should be continually exposed to the ideas of professionals and colleagues with years of experience. Don't be an independent or cheap landlord who makes very costly decisions by not seeking competent advice.

Especially seek the advice of long-time (seasoned) rental owners. One of the absolute best resources available to landlords is the companion website to this publication, MrLandlord.com. As a buyer and reader of this book, you will learn of access to additional bonuses and resources available to you. On our website is a nationwide question and answer forum, where you can ask questions related to the forms and ideas discussed in this book or any other landlording-related question and receive answers within the hour. *landlordingadvice.com*

Throughout this book I promise to coach you, motivate you, provoke you, and unrelentingly expose you to innovative and effective landlording forms and letters. But you must promise to always seek professional advice before making important legal decisions. And thanks for letting me (and this book) be part of your real estate success team.

Acknowledgments

My appreciation and gratitude to all those who have provided inspiration and support to me and this publication. I wish to especially thank the following:

Readers of the first edition of *The Landlord's Kit*, my "Mr. Landlord" newsletter and landlords who visit the MrLandlord.com website. I want to recognize the hundreds of thousands of "do-it-yourself" landlords and landladies who daily face challenges to survive and succeed in managing rental properties, while providing a tremendous and often thankless service for millions, with little, if any, recognition. I salute you!

Georgie Gregory, who has served faithfully as an assistant editor to my newsletter and publications. My son Justin Taylor, a published writer in his own right, who also assisted in the editing of this edition, developed the "laundry" form, and he oversees the laundry machines in our rentals.

Leigh Robinson, author of the bestselling book, *Landlording*, whom I count it a privilege to be a friend and whom I look to as a role model in business. Thanks for your friendship and professional support.

The many business associates and fellow real estate authors and speakers whom I have had the opportunity to work with and learn from.

Real estate associations throughout the United States that have welcomed me into their meetings and allowed me to share landlording ideas and concepts with their members.

Mary Good, Sandy Thomas, Michael Sprague, and the other Kaplan/Dearborn Trade Publishing staff who prompted, assisted, and kept me on track throughout this project.

Finally, my mom and dad, whom I don't thank enough for never discouraging me from reaching for greater possibilities and whom I now wish to encourage to never give up on all life has for you!

Introduction

My wife and I got into the rental business by accident. After getting married, we purchased a home that was more than we could afford. Refusing to let this situation overwhelm us, we purchased a more affordable home; a "fixer-upper" would be putting it positively. We decided not to sell our first home but instead rented it out. So began our life as landlords. We are thankful that our first residents paid on time and took care of the property. They were such great residents that they gave us a false sense of security. We went on to purchase several dozen rental units, and quickly learned the hard way that not all residents are created equal. There were some who did not pay rent (let alone pay on time), called us at all hours, damaged our properties, left in the middle of the night, and created all kinds of management headaches.

Again, we refused to get overwhelmed. Instead we sought education, which at the time was extremely hard to come by. Back then, there was no MrLandlord.com or "Mr. Landlord" newsletter (see the free subscription offer at the back of this book). I'm the type of person who believes that the "buck stops here!" I don't wish to blame others for my problems, even if I could be justified in doing so. When you put the fault for your problems on others, you put the power to control the outcome of your success in someone else's hands. I knew that if I was going to be successful as a landlord, I wanted to always take control and not have my financial fate determined by my residents. Because of this line of thinking, I have constantly asked myself, "What could I have done or communicated differently that would have produced better results?"

Over the past 20 years, I have looked at how many other industries (including airline, fast food, and retail) have developed programs to improve customer satisfaction and net profits. I have discovered that it is most often what you communicate to prospective and current customers that is the key and makes the difference between a very successful company and one that is fighting to survive. So I've sought to incorporate what successful companies communicate to their customers into my relationships with rental residents. As a result, I've learned that 99 percent of the *tenant* problems I used to have were really created because of *my* lack of effective communication of my policies to residents. When I talk of communication, it is *far* more than just telling residents what I expect them to do. Effective communication includes knowing how and when to present information, and in such a way that the residents embrace your policies. I dare say to all landlords, as I teach throughout America and provide the forms and checklists included in this book, that 99 percent of the *tenant* problems you now experience can be eliminated (or greatly reduced) if *you* learn how, when, and what to communicate to your residents. I challenge you never to put the blame for your rental problems on your residents. That will only add to your frustrations. Instead, always look to improve your communication tools, and that will add to your success. With *The Landlord's Kit,* you too can take or stay in control of your real estate and financial future.

Let me explain what this book is *not*. If you are looking for a set of legal forms for evicting tenants or to take them to court, you will need more than these forms. Instead, you should seek local legal counsel and a local real estate association near you, which likely can provide you directly or indirectly with state-specific forms and enforceable notices needed for eviction.

These forms are meant to provide rental owners with letters, notices, and checklists that clearly communicate rental policies. The single most important activity of a rental owner is what he or she communicates to residents. With these forms, you can take total control of every rental situation, generate more monthly cash flow, and eliminate headaches.

Most importantly, and what makes this collection of forms unique and valuable, is that many of the forms interweave powerful marketing and proven business strategies from other industries. By using these forms, you can:

- Fill vacancies faster
- Keep residents longer
- Generate more rental profits
- Foster greater resident cooperation
- Begin and end relationships positively

In other industries, consultants and coaches charge thousands of dollars to assist clients with implementing the very same marketing and business strategies that have been interwoven into many of these forms. This powerful landlord's kit has been in continual development and revision over the last 15 years. This book introduces rental owners to some of the most powerful marketing and business strategies that until now have been seldom used in the rental industry. At the beginning of each section of this book, you will be introduced to several innovative marketing, business, or management concepts. The introduction to each set of forms points out valuable management tips and costly business mistakes made by most landlords. Thus, *The Landlord's Kit* is much more than just a collection of forms. It is also a mini-training manual for landlords, teaching concepts to improve rental success and how to avoid costly mistakes. The training starts with what to communicate in the very first phone conversation, and it is all aimed at significantly increasing rental profits and eliminating management headaches.

PART ONE

Application and Verification

Forms to Screen and Select Ideal Residents

THE PHONE CALL

■ *Tip Number* **1**

Take control from the start.

The time to take control of the landlord-tenant relationship is not when you are having a move-in discussion with an approved applicant. Take control right from the start when a prospective resident first calls you inquiring about a possible rental. Do this by asking questions of every prospect, not only to prescreen potential residents, but also to identify ways to maximize your potential income and immediately gain control of the relationship. I want to take you through a possible scenario of your first contact with a prospective resident and give you suggestions for the actual dialogue to use. Take careful note, because these key questions will help you distinguish between potentially ideal residents and unacceptable residents, by the answers that prospective residents may provide. Their answers can serve as red flags or green lights. The prospective resident usually starts the dialogue with a question, but after that you take control. Here's how!

A prospective resident starts with the question usually asked of all landlords.

Prospect: "Hello, how much is the home or apartment on _____?"

Landlord (LL): "My name is _____. I'm one of the rental managers." Say it that way even if you just operate a mom and pop operation. "I'll be glad to help you. To whom am I speaking?"

Answer: "_____."

LL: "Hello, _____. I am happy to assist you. Tell me, about how much are you looking to spend on the next rental that meets your needs?"

Answer: "_____."

LL: "Our rental is right within your price range. "Please note: Do not quote a specific price over the phone. Make the suggested statement and jot down the price the prospect may be willing to pay. If the price the resident suggests is too low, you respond by saying that you do *not* have anything within that price range. A figure higher than the rental price you had in mind may provide helpful feedback that prompts you to set a higher monthly rental rate, and thus the opportunity for more cash flow. Not quoting a price leaves room for another prospect who calls and is willing to pay a slightly higher price. In order to avoid residents preset on a price when calling, none of your advertisements or classified ads should state a specific rental price, but instead include a price range; for example, $495 to $595, $645 to $775, or $845 to $995. Understand that the responses from prospective residents is simply one additional way of testing the market to help you determine what prospects many be willing to spend before you set the rental price.

■ *Tip Number* **2**

Schedule small "group" showings.

Schedule to meet more than one person at the same time when showing your rentals. If at all possible, do not show your rental to only one person at a time, preferably three or four persons. That way if one does not show up, you have not wasted your time. Another big benefit of group showings is that you create a spirit of competition, which makes the rental seem like it is in demand, and applicants are more likely to take immediate action and fill out the application, so they don't lose out to others wanting the same place. Applicants are also less likely to ask dumb questions, like, "do you need all the deposit upfront." They are more likely to ask, "can I please fill out the application, I was here first."

You will set the price at the first group showing of the rental, which if you schedule according to the suggestion here, there will be more than one applicant present. Once the applicants show up, set the price based on the lowest "acceptable" price of those who come to the showing. For example, if you wanted at least $795 in rent, and three people came to the first showing, here's how you set pricing. If one had stated over the phone they were looking to spend $700, another said $850 and one said $900, in this scenario, you set the price at $850, not $900. Obviously, you don't go with $700, because that is lower than what you wanted. Do not

be greedy, however, and set the price based on the $900 response. Why? Because you will make the person who said $845 feel like you misled them. And why turn off that individual if all you wanted was at least $795. When you announce the price at the group showing for $845, the person who had stated that figure over the phone is okay with that price and the one who had stated $900 over the phone is absolutely thrilled and practically ready to sign up now, thinking they will get better than what they hoped. Now once you set the price, that's the price. Your price testing is over. Do not go up and down in price once you have stated a price to the first set of prospective residents. Once the price is set, offer that same price to all applicants from that point forward.

LL: "Is there any particular feature you would very much like included in your new home?" Hopefully, the response is something you offer (or can offer) and that will serve as part of your pitch when showing the rental, perhaps as part of a "custom" rental home—more on that later.
Answer: "_____."

LL: "Mr./Mrs._____, when are you looking to move in, if our rental does meet your needs?"
Answer: "_____."

LL: "You'll be glad to know that we offer all new residents a 30-day money back guarantee that they will be satisfied with our rental. By the way, will you be giving your present landlord a one-week or 30-day moving notice?" Your screening has begun. A responsible resident would give at least a 30-day notice to the current landlord.
Answer: "_____."

LL: "How many people will be living in the home or apartment, counting everybody?"
Answer: "_____."

LL: "And who else may join you?" Pause for response, then continue. "Anyone have other relatives or friends who may live there as well at some point in the future?"
Answer: "_____."

LL: "How many pets will be staying with you?" Pause for response, then continue. "Even if only for a short period?"
Answer: "_____."

LL: "Any birds, reptiles, fish, or animals, large or small, of any kind?"

Answer: "_____."

LL: "What is your reason for moving from your current residence?"
Answer: "_____."

LL: "Did you have any problem with your present landlord?" The answer may be most revealing. A resident who has a bad attitude about their current landlord will most likely have a bad attitude about you. This question may even help you discover that they considered suing a former landlord or ran into problems with lead paint or mold.
Answer: "_____."

LL: "One thing you should know, our company offers a maintenance guarantee. But let me ask you, what is most important to you about the next rental you select?"
Answer: "_____." This answer will also give you additional information to tailor your presentation at the showing.

LL: "__(Prospect's name)__, I believe our rental has what you want and you do not have to look any further for your next home. Our place is your answer. Let's set up an appointment so you can see if I'm right. Our next showing is on _____. I will meet you promptly at _____. We ask that you please be on time, because we have several other appointments that day and if you are late, we will miss you. Will that time work for you?"
Answer: "_____."

LL: "Let me get your phone number just in case anything comes up, because I would not want to stand you up if an emergency prevented me from being there, and I ask that you please give me the same courtesy. Your number is _____?" This question is to see if they are responsible enough to have a currently working phone number, and it also emphasizes the importance of being at the appointment and notifying you if they cannot make it.
Answer: "_____."

LL: "Is this home or work?"
Answer: "_____". This is almost always home.

LL: "What is your work number?" A polite way to find out if they work.
Answer: "_____."

LL: "What is the name of the company?"
Answer: "_____." A possible indication of income reliability.

LL: "And your position?"

Answer: "_____." An indication of amount of income.

LL: "Should you like our home, and I really think you will, to process your application and get you in by your move-date, we will need $_____ holding deposit and $_____ application fee at the time we meet. Will you have those funds available at that time?"
Answer: "_____."

LL: "Very well, we look forward to meeting with you on _____. Oh, will you need a refrigerator, microwave oven, or vacuum cleaner or will you provide your own?"
Answer: "_____." You may choose to offer these items or others as part of the rental custom "package" and charge extra (more on this later). Also, if they have their own, that may influence your selection or allow you to transfer items to another rental that may need them.

LL: "One final thing, Mr./Ms. _____. We look forward to meeting you, and please remind me or the manager who meets you to be sure to tell you about the free gift we give to all applicants who move in." This teaser will double the percentage of prospects who actually show up for your next renter's open house.

Reminder: The above dialogue should come across as a friendly conversation, not an interrogation. Remember to smile, even though the prospect can't see you, because smiling can be "heard." Smiling affects the tone of your voice and how your friendliness is conveyed. Also, while talking with any prospective resident, fill in the Daily Phone Summary form provided in this section. And review your notes before showing the property. If prospective residents ask questions during the phone conversation, refer to the Rental Availability Hot Sheet for what homes and features are currently available.

MEETING THE APPLICANT

Have you been shopping for a high-quality car lately? The effective dealer is prepared to persuade you to buy in a different manner than the average run of the mill dealer at the used car lot around the corner. One of the major differences is that the dealer with high-quality vehicles is ready and able to give you *tangible* evidence (pamphlets, brochures, testimonials, technical specifications, features, warranties, options, and so on) to help convince you of the value of their product and get you to commit right then to a large investment.

Mr. and Mrs. Landlord, if you are attempting to fill your vacancies fast, increase your cash flow in your properties, attract better quality residents, or all three, please consider the proven idea of being prepared and able to give prospective residents tangible evidence (handouts) of the high value of your property. By the way, high value can be found in low-income economy rentals as well as high-priced deluxe rentals, so whatever type rentals you own or manage, keep reading.

■ *Tip Number 3*

Give tangible evidence to prospective residents.

The following Super Handout suggestions can work extremely well for all type rentals. The handouts do not have to be fancy, professionally typeset on four-color, eight-page brochures. If you simply use neatly done flyers printed from your computer or duplicated at your local quick copy shop, you and your properties will stand out in the minds of your prospective residents far above 99 percent of all other rentals and landlords in your area.

Super Handout 1: Testimonies Testimonies of former and current residents are more persuasive than anything you can say. Approach current residents and always ask exiting residents (especially when they are asking you for a reference) to write a sentence or two about what they like about the rental, the neighborhood, or you/your company and services. Then list five to ten of the good comments on a handout with the heading Look What Our Residents Have Said about Our Homes/ Rentals.

Super Handout 2: Utility Expenses How many times has someone asked you. "What do the utilities cost for this apartment?" About the only thing most of us say is "Well, it depends on how you use them." Prospects get so tired of hearing that. They consider it a cop-out. They want specific answers. Here's how you give them just that.

First, ask the utility company to provide the average bill amount for the last twelve months and the highest and lowest bill. Not all utility companies are cooperative in this regard. If the utility company won't provide the information, ask your residents if they will make copies of their bills during the tenancy (maybe offer a small incentive to do so). When you are asked the question about utility expense, if your building has relatively low ex-

penses, you can show this in black and white in the form of a handout.

Super Handout 3: Property/Neighborhood Features List everything good you can think of about the rental, the services you provide, and the neighborhood. Put each feature on a separate line or paragraph, and place a space between each point. Put a large asterisk, star, check, or symbol before each feature.

Super Handout 4: Deluxe Options Available Offer extra features for your rentals that residents may choose. With the handout, you let them know about these options up-front, while they are deciding and comparing your rental. Examples of extras offered by other "Mr. Landlord" subscribers include ceiling fans, window coverings, mini-blinds, TVs and/or VCRs, tub enclosures, appliances (washers/ dryers, microwaves), and garages. Decide if you want to charge extra rent for these options. In a slow market, when attracting or persuading a high-quality prospect to rent from you, throwing in her choice of an extra may well be worth the added initial expense. If demand is high and few rentals are available, charge extra for the options and increase your monthly cash flow.

Start using variations of these handouts (see forms Most Popular Upgrades and Utility Expenses here, and Welcome to the Neighborhood in Part Two) as tangible evidence and you will be more effective in filling vacancies. Make sure that all tangible handouts have your name, business address, and phone number, because at least half of all prospective residents do not make decisions the first time they see the property. When these prospective residents walk away from your properties, they will have persuasive reasons to remember and continue considering your properties as they look and compare others. Most importantly, they will also know how to get back in touch with you.

Even if the original prospects decide not to rent from you, your handouts may still end up in the hands of a coworker, friend, or relative who is also looking for a place, simply because your original prospect had something tangible to give when the subject of apartment hunting came up. In fact, to increase the longevity of your handouts before they hit someone's round file, put the following words at the top of each handout: Save This Flyer for Comparing Other Rentals, Then Pass on to a Friend.

THE APPLICATION: YOUR BEST CASH FLOW TOOL

Your application is one of the most vital landlording tools, but it is often taken for granted. A good application can literally add thousands of dollars to your bottom line. This subject matter deserves your utmost attention. I want to spark enough interest in you so that after reading this section of the book, you'll pull out your application and consider adding suggested questions found in our sample Rental Application to make your application far more effective.

■ *Tip Number 4*

Ask questions that will help you recover money if necessary.

Your key concern should not just be getting responses to determine if an applicant is qualified now. You must also ask questions that will *help you recover all money due* should the now-qualified applicant have financial difficulty later.

Always ask for a Social Security number and a complete name. Don't stop there. Ask for maiden name or other last names they have used or that may show up on a credit report. Do not feel odd in asking. Terrible credit may not show up simply because you failed to get a full or correct name. If you get a judgment later in a name that's not complete or correct, it's doing no credit damage as far as your resident is concerned. Therefore, he or she has no incentive to pay off.

Ask applicants if they currently rent or own. If they do own, who is the mortgage with? Many landlords have discovered homes to buy cheap by asking these questions. Ask if parents or another relative will be willing to help with payments in case of financial hardship. If so, immediately follow up with a cosigner agreement.

RENTAL HOLDING DEPOSIT RECEIPT

Many rental owners mistakenly think that a deposit receipt given to a resident at the time of application is nothing more than proof that a payment was made. A major purpose of the deposit receipt is to summarize all the features the applicants will receive in their new "custom" home.

The deposit receipt is the last thing you give over to the applicant, and it provides one more opportu-

nity to remind, "sell," the applicant on the good decision he or she is making by pointing out home features and/or upgrades that are included. This final summary of good points makes a resident feel good about his decision and he does not have to keep looking at other rentals. Summarizing good points helps to create a more positive attitude with residents as they prepare to move into their new home. An example of a Holding Deposit Receipt is included in the forms in this section.

■ *Tip Number 5*

Do not call money given before move-in a security deposit.

It is also important not to call any deposit received before move-in a *security deposit.* Call it a *holding* or *reserve deposit* to hold the property exclusively for the future resident until move-in. Should the applicant back out of the deal after being accepted, a holding deposit can be forfeited to cover rental losses you may incur by having taken the property off the market.

However, landlord-tenant laws regarding security deposits in many states only permit landlords to withhold money given as security deposit for certain reasons, and keeping the deposit because prospective residents changed their mind is not enforceable in court. On the other hand, a holding deposit form in which the landlord clearly outlines the conditions of forfeiture and the applicant willingly signs is an enforceable practice.

VERIFICATION FORMS

Based on a survey of "Mr. Landlord" subscribers, the number one biggest mistake made by over 50 percent of the landlords, that they later regretted, was *trying to take shortcuts in screening* when accepting new residents. Before accepting any applicant, check all references listed on the application. Be sure the applicant signs the rental application, authorizing you to verify the information provided, including credit history.

■ *Tip Number 6*

Check and verify all references. Don't take shortcuts!

The application in this book provides an authorization statement. Because some property managers, employers, law enforcement agencies, and banks may require to see a separate authorization form, we include a complete series of verification forms that can be used to obtain verification for specific needs, including law enforcement, employer, landlord, bank references, and credit history. Also provided is a one-page authorization consent form that addresses all references, which can be copied and sent as needed.

Many professional deadbeats count on landlords taking all information at face value and not verifying anything. If you need assistance running a tenant credit report, a low-cost nationwide tenant check service is available at *www.mrlandlord.com*. Also check with your local real estate association: Many work with companies that offer credit check services to their members.

ACCEPTING AN APPLICANT

To avoid or reduce the chances of a discrimination accusation against you, there are several steps you can follow. You should start by having a written list of minimal objective criteria (see the New Resident Checklist) for selecting and determining whether an applicant is qualified. You are running a business that is being watched by numerous governmental agencies, and you cannot make your rental decisions without staying informed of the ever-changing rules of fair play you must follow. And don't think residents will continue to go along with whatever you ask, dictate, or reject. If you don't follow the proper rules in selecting new residents, you are putting yourself at high risk of having a discrimination accusation made against you by a tenant population that is growing more and more sophisticated and educated. They are encouraged daily to exercise their right to sue by attorneys and legal aid services ready to help prove their case.

■ *Tip Number 7*

Select the first qualified applicant.

Along with having a list of legal or fair criteria for qualifying residents, it is a good business practice to keep records on all applicants you turn down. Note the legal or fair criteria each rejected applicant did not meet. Keep this information in your records for up to two years. Countless landlords are getting in trouble for turning people down for invalid or unfair reasons. In fact, I encourage you to even stop asking about the sex, age, and marital status of your applications. Simply

asking these questions can be seen as possible grounds for discrimination. It really is a lot to be aware of, I know. But you must educate yourself in the fair housing area. It has become one of the biggest traps and horror stories for landlords.

WRITTEN CRITERIA

■ *Tip Number 8*

Develop a point system for selecting residents.

Do you have a list of written criteria for selecting residents? It is something that can save you thousands—possibly hundreds of thousands—of dollars!

A poll was taken at a rental owner's dinner meeting on how many members had their criteria written down. Out of 40 present, only three said they did! This is a shocker! Most landlords know better. We've been repeatedly advised of the benefits.

Are you negligent in this area of your rental management? Don't ignore such a crucial aspect of your rental operation. Everything starts with the resident you select. And the wrong resident can cost you dearly. In addition, if you are not consistent in your selection process, (which can easily occur if you don't have written criteria you always refer to) you can end up losing a fair housing lawsuit, which may cost you tens of thousands of dollars. Some landlords have been fined millions of dollars for turning down applicants for the wrong criteria. And please don't be naive to think it cannot happen to you.

In case there is any question, written criteria means it must be (1) in writing, (2) in your file, and (3) dated! Should you change your criteria, write it down, date it, sign it, and file it. The list of your criteria should include everything you rely on to determine qualified residents and a list of your objective and legally acceptable reasons for denial.

Treat all applicants alike, per your criteria, and you'll go a long way toward avoiding a lawsuit.

We give you absolutely no excuse for not having a written set of resident selection criteria. If you need help with what to write down as your criteria, refer to the New Resident Checklist. Use that form as a starting point for developing your own set of selection criteria.

I like using a point system with my written qualifying criteria. Applicants receive one point each time they meet one of the criteria. Once applicants get so many points, they qualify. This system allows me to be consistent in how I evaluate every resident.

This point-system approach is similar to what banks or loan companies do in determining whether to extend credit to an applicant. Banks and loan companies also give added value, weight, or points to those who have demonstrated long-term stability. Likewise, I give added points to those who have a longer track record in their rental history and source of income. In practical terms, on rental applications, I ask all prospective residents to give their last two addresses and dates of residency. I also ask for source of income, and for how long. Then I give the prospective resident 1, 2, or 3 points for residency or source of income corresponding to the number of verifiable years with the same (e.g., two years equals two points). Residing less than one full year earns 0 points for that criteria. Poor or no payment record also will cause a mark of 0 points. For example, if the applicant lived somewhere, but was not responsible for payment at the former address (e.g., living with relatives), that earns a 0 mark. This can be offset if the responsible person at the address (e.g., a parent) is willing to serve as a cosigner.

Additional note: Some landlords make a big mistake by neglecting to request permission to obtain a credit report on the rental application. Be sure to do so. The credit report can expose or verify addresses and dates over the past seven years.

COSIGNER AGREEMENT

An owner takes a risk each time he or she leases a property. The prospective resident may not pay the rent or may damage the premises. Even if the court grants you a judgment for unpaid rent or damages, the judgment is often difficult to collect. Some of the risk can be reduced by requiring a cosigner to personally guarantee the rental agreement.

■ *Tip Number* **9**

Reduce your risk by asking for a cosigner.

A cosigner, or guarantor, is typically more creditworthy than the resident and agrees to be liable for the lease terms agreed to by your resident. The cosigner promises to pay if the resident does not. You, as the rental owner, should check the creditworthiness of the cosigners just like you do for rental applicants, meaning you must get permission to check their credit history. You also will want

the cosigner to fill out a cosigner agreement *before* accepting and moving in the resident. A sample cosigner agreement is included in this section.

On signing of the cosigner agreement (guaranty), the cosigner becomes liable for all unpaid rent, property damages, other expenses, and legal fees to the same extent the resident is responsible for them under the terms of the rental agreement. I recommend that any notice regarding payment obligations served to the resident should also be served to the cosigner. For example, a notice to pay or quit should be served to both the resident and the cosigner. This gives the cosigner an opportunity to assist the resident before going to court, which could save all parties additional money.

ACCEPTING AND REJECTING APPLICANTS

The best way to eliminate deadbeats is to never begin renting to them in the first place. It is extremely important that you screen all prospective residents so that eviction occurs at the beginning of the rental process and not at the end. This book also includes a Reason for Nonacceptance letter with legal reasons for refusing an applicant.

■ *Tip Number* **10**

Evict deadbeats before they move in.

A couple of sample acceptance letters and a couple of sample rejection letters are included in the last few forms in this section. Depending on the situation, you can use the one that is appropriate. One acceptance letter is for a new resident. A second acceptance letter is for a new, additional resident or roommate who has been accepted and permitted to be added to the lease. One sample rejection letter is to be used if you simply are turning down an applicant based on your review of his or her application. A second rejection letter provides a reason for not accepting an applicant and is recommended to be used if the applicant requests a reason for denial or if the applicant was turned down based on information from a third party other than a credit reporting agency. If you do not rent to someone because of information provided on a credit report, you are required by law to give the prospective resident the name and address of the agency that furnished the report. The third sample denial letter (the final form in this section) includes such wording plus other required language.

RENTAL AVAILABILITY HOT SHEET TO ALL PROSPECTIVE RESIDENTS

Homes/Apartments for Rent By: _____ **Phone:** _____

Address: _____ Directions: _____

Size/optional features: _____

Number of bedrooms: _____ Date available: _____ Max. # of people for this home: _____

Garage: _____ Basement: _____ Fenced yard: _____

Schools: _____

Off-street parking: _____ Washer/dryer hook-up: _____ Pets allowed: _____

Rent per month _____ Biweekly _____ Per week _____ Deposit: _____ Lease term: _____

Other information: _____

Website address: _____

Address: _____ Directions: _____

Size/optional features: _____

Number of bedrooms: _____ Date available: _____ Max. # of people for this home: _____

Garage: _____ Basement: _____ Fenced yard: _____

Schools: _____

Off-street parking: _____ Washer/dryer hook-up: _____ Pets allowed: _____

Rent per month _____ Biweekly _____ Per week _____ Deposit: _____ Lease term: _____

Other information: _____

Website address: _____

Address: _____ Directions: _____

Size/optional features: _____

Number of bedrooms: _____ Date available: _____ Max. # of people for this home: _____

Garage: _____ Basement: _____ Fenced yard: _____

Schools: _____

Off-street parking: _____ Washer/dryer hook-up: _____ Pets allowed: _____

Rent per month _____ Biweekly _____ Per week _____ Deposit: _____ Lease term: _____

Other information: _____

Website address: _____

Additional Notes:
All homes are clean, well-kept, and include _____.
We do not always include appliances as part of the rental package. Let us know if they are needed.
All utilities and yard upkeep are the residents' responsibility unless otherwise indicated.
No pets are allowed, of any size or age, unless otherwise indicated.
We do check credit and references before move-in, which usually takes _____ working day(s).
Please drive by any home that interests you, then give us a call at _____ and we can make
arrangements to show you a home. Please do not knock on the door of any home listed.
We will be glad to show the home to you. Ask about our guarantee that you will like our home!

PHONE QUALIFYING WORKSHEET / SCRIPT

I'll be glad to assist you. My name is _____. I am one of the rental managers. To see if we can meet your needs, may I start by first asking you a few questions? Is that okay?

Name: _____ Date: _____

Home #: _____ Work #: _____ Cell #: _____

Where do you live now? _____How long have you lived there? _____

Are you unhappy there? Why are you moving?_____

How's the management there? Did you experience any problems with that property?

_____

How much rent are you paying now? _____

What is the price range you are looking to spend? _____

How many people will be living in your next home? _____

Is there a particular feature or amenity you want to have in your next home?

_____

How many pets? (what kind)_____

How soon do you need a place? _____

Can you tell me a little bit about where you work?

Where?_____ How long? _____

Approximate income (monthly/weekly) _____ Any other income? _____

We obtain a credit report for all applicants. Anything we should know before we run your credit report?

_____

Have you seen the home or apartment on our website? Our website address is _____

Will you be able to attend our next rental showing scheduled for _____?

Be sure and remind me to tell you about the move-in gift we give to all new residents. And please call me 30 minutes to 1 hour prior to coming, to confirm that you are still able to come. Thanks!

PHONE SUMMARY/QUICK SURVEY - Date _____

RESIDENT PROSPECT:

Name _____ Phone _____

Alternate Phone _____ Email Address _____

How did you learn about us? (Check one)

☐ Sign   ☐ Newspaper   ☐ Flyer/Letter   ☐ Internet   ☐ Referral   ☐ Other

     Name of Paper or Referrer, Flyer Location, or Website _____

     Other _____

Size of unit desired   ☐ 1 Bedroom   ☐ 2 Bedroom   ☐ 3 Bedrooms   # of Pets _____

     Move-in Date Desired _____ Number of Occupants _____

     Location or Area Desired _____

     Special or Extra Amenity/Feature Desired _____

What factor is most important to you?

☐ Location   ☐ Price   ☐ Size   ☐ Move Date   ☐ Amenity   ☐ Other

     Other factor explained _____

Why are you moving? _____

What feature do you like best about your current home? _____

What feature do you like least about your current home? _____

RESIDENT PROSPECT:

Name _____ Phone _____

Alternate Phone _____ Email Address _____

How did you learn about us? (Check one)

☐ Sign   ☐ Newspaper   ☐ Flyer/Letter   ☐ Internet   ☐ Referral   ☐ Other

     Name of Paper or Referrer, Flyer Location, or Website _____

     Other _____

Size of unit desired   ☐ 1 Bedroom   ☐ 2 Bedroom   ☐ 3 Bedrooms   # of Pets _____

     Move-in Date Desired _____ Number of Occupants _____

     Location or Area Desired _____

     Special or Extra Amenity/Feature Desired _____

What factor is most important to you?

☐ Location   ☐ Price   ☐ Size   ☐ Move Date   ☐ Amenity   ☐ Other

     Other factor explained _____

Why are you moving? _____

What feature do you like best about your current home? _____

What feature do you like least about your current home? _____

OPEN HOUSE APPOINTMENT SCHEDULE - GROUP SHOWING

1st Group Showing Time   Week: _____ Day: _____ Time: _____

Address: _____

Suggested questions to ask each caller:

      a. What size of home or apartment are you looking for?

      b. How much are you looking to spend on your next home?

      c. How soon are you looking to move?

      d. What is the reason you are moving?

      e. Will you please call 30 minutes to an hour ahead of time to confirm you're still coming?

1. Name: _____ Phone: _____

    Notes: _____

2 Name: _____ Phone: _____

    Notes: _____

3. Name: _____ Phone: _____

    Notes: _____

4. Name: _____ Phone: _____

    Notes: _____

Alternate Group Showing Time Week: _____ Day: _____ Time: _____

1. Name: _____ Phone: _____

    Notes: _____

2 Name: _____ Phone: _____

    Notes: _____

3. Name: _____ Phone: _____

    Notes: _____

4. Name: _____ Phone: _____

    Notes: _____

HOUSE FOR RENT
(Descriptive handout to give to prospective residents)

Address: _____

City:_____State:_____ZIP:_____

Subdivision: _____

School district: _____

Elementary: _____

Private elementary: _____

Middle/high school: _____

Private middle/high school: _____

Home includes: _____ Bedrooms _____

_____ Baths _____

Living room:_____

Dining room/den/other: (circle)_____

Family/additional room with: _____

Type of heat: _____

Appliances: _____

Additional/optional features: _____

_____

Parking/garage/storage: _____

Yard/lot: _____

All of this for only $ _____ per month/biweekly plus $ _____ deposit.

Call: _____ Date house available: _____

MOST POPULAR UPGRADES TO OFFER ALL NEW RESIDENTS

Dear Future Resident:

Thank you for coming out to view our property. We are glad that you are considering renting this property as your new home. We want to make you aware the home or apartment you have come to see, while it offers many nice features, is our "standard home" rental package. With other homes and apartments we rent, many of the residents have liked that we also offer additional upgrades and extras as part of a "deluxe rental home" package.

From surveys with our current residents, we have determined what upgrades are liked the most. The following are the three to five most popular upgrades that we now make available for all new residents:

- ◆ _____
- ◆ _____
- ◆ _____
- ◆ _____
- ◆ _____

As you can see, we offer more than just a typical standard home. Our goal is to offer you more in your home than you can find anywhere else, and customize it to meet your particular needs and interest. We can include all three to five popular upgrades in your home for an additional $_____ per month. If that is more than you would like to spend, we can offer you a "customized rental" package with one or two favorite items of your choice for a lower price of about $_____ per month. Would that work for you? If so, which one or two items would you like included as part of a custom home package? _____

Sincerely,

Owner/Manager

UTILITY EXPENSES

To help you make an informed decision when selecting the next home that would be best for you and your family, we have provided the following utility information. Below you will see approximate dollar amounts of how much previous residents have spent monthly toward utility expenses. (This is based on information provided by the residents or utility companies.) Of course, the amount of utility bills may vary because each family's usage may vary and utility companies may raise prices. We provide these approximate expense ranges because many other residents have found this type of information very helpful in selecting their residence and for budget planning. We want to offer you all the information you need to determine if our property will be your next home. Let us know if there is any other information we can provide, because we believe that once you've learned all you can about what we have to offer, you will want to rent our home. In fact, we offer a guarantee, see below.

Utility expenses the resident are responsible for, and approximate expenses of previous residents.

Utility   **Expense range**

_____   _____

_____   _____

_____   _____

Comment from previous resident regarding a utility expense:

_____

_____

_____

If you move into our home, and after 25 days, you do not think you made the right home selection, we will let you move without having to stay the rest of the rental term, and we will return your full security deposit (assuming no property damage). How's that for a guarantee?

30-DAY GUARANTEE

Move into one of our rentals and we guarantee that if, for any reason, you are not satisfied and decide to move within the first 30 days after your lease begins, we will refund your security deposit (as long as there has been no damage).

We will tear up your lease and you will not be obligated to pay any more rent. We are confident, however, that your rental will meet your needs.

New Resident: _____

Approved by: _____

Address: _____

Move-in Date: _____

FOLLOW-UP TO INQUIRY

Dear _____,

It was a pleasure meeting you at our rental home, and I am pleased that you are considering making it your new home. We have sent you some information about the home, which we discussed, as well as additional information to help you make your decision about whether this would be an ideal place for you and your family.

As a reminder, our home can offer you all of the following features:

_____

_____

_____

We are also located in a convenient location near the following:

_____

_____.

The best thing we will be able to offer you based on your indication of importance.

_____

_____

I hope this information is of help to you. And we look forward to discussing our home with you if you wish to ask any additional questions. As a special offer to you, we provide the following as a move-in gift for all new residents:

_____

We can't hold our property for you unless we hear from you soon.

Thank you again for your interest in our home. Please call us at: _____.

I look forward to hearing from you soon.

Sincerely,

Owner/Manager

RENTAL APPLICATION/FUTURE HOMEBUYER
(Application Fee $_____ - Per Adult)

Each adult (18 or older) must fill out a separate application. Today's date: _____

Occupancy date desired: _____Rental price range: _____ Type/size desired: _____

Rental address desired or shown: _____

How did you hear about this home or apartment? _____

APPLICANT'S PERSONAL INFORMATION

Last name: _____First: _____ Middle: _____

Birth date: _____ Driver's license/ID number/state: _____

Social Security #: _____ Phone:_____

Alternative phone: _____ Email address: _____

Any other names you've used in the past: _____

Additional Occupants (List every occupant's name, birth date, and their relationship to applicant.

How long do you plan on living in the next rental home that meets your needs? _____

Would you like to receive a rental gift on your anniversary dates as part of a 3-Star Resident Program?_____

Preferred Rental Type Desired? Standard ___ Custom ___ **Preferred Rental Due Date?** Monthly ___ Other___

Would you like to by a home within the next 2-3 years? _____ If so, what size/type? _____

Are you able to handle all the minor maintenance and upkeep in the property? Yes _____No _____

Do you already own any appliances (if so, which ones)? _____

Do you do have any of these skills? ☐ Electrical ☐ Painting ☐ Plumbing: ☐ Roofing ☐ Heating ☐ Other_____

Do you have renter's insurance? ___ Any liquid-filled-furniture? ___ Have you ever broken a lease? ___

Ever refused to pay for any reason? ___ Ever been evicted or asked to leave? ___ Ever filed for bankruptcy? ___

Ever been convicted of a crime? ___ Do you give us permission to do a criminal background check? ___

Currently have any utilities in your name? ___ Currently have phone service in your name? ___

Is there anything to prevent you from placing utilities in your name? ___ Do any occupants smoke? ___

RESIDENCE HISTORY

Present address: _____

Dates lived at this address: _____ Monthly rent: _____

Name of present landlord: _____Phone_____

Address of present landlord: _____

Reason for moving: _____ Is your rent current? _____

Number of late payments at this address:_____ Security deposit currently held by landlord: _____

Have you had any reoccurring problems with your current home or landlord?_____

Previous address: _____

Previous landlord: _____ Previous landlord's phone: _____

Dates at this address: _____ Reason for moving: _____ Monthly rent:_____

Was your full security deposit returned? _____ # of late payments: _____ Monthly rent:_____

Bonus Note: We provide cash/free property upgrade to residents who refer a friend or coworker to us and they move into one of our places. List the name and phone of anyone you know who may need a home or apartment.

_____ Phone_____

INCOME/EMPLOYMENT HISTORY

Applicant's current employment status: Full-time:_____ Part-time (less than 32 hrs.): _____ Student: _____
Retired: _____ Self-employed: _____ Unemployed: _____ Other:_____

Applicant employed by: _____ Supervisor's name: _____
Phone_____ Average weekly hours: _____ How long at that place of employment? _____
Address: _____ City: _____State: _____Zip: _____
Position: _____ Monthly/Biweekly/Weekly (Circle one) Income:$ _____
Phone_____ Average weekly hours: _____ How long at that place of employment? _____

Also employed by: _____ Supervisor's name: _____
Address: _____ City: _____State: _____Zip: _____
Position: _____ Monthly/Biweekly/Weekly (Circle one) Income:$ _____

Emergency Contact: In the event of some emergency that would prevent you from paying rent when due, is there a relative, person, or agency that could assist you with rent payments?
Emergency contact: _____Relationship _____ Phone _____
Address: _____ City: _____State: _____Zip: _____

Additional Income: (verifiable sources of income that you would like considered, please list income and source).
Additional source: _____Amount: $_____
Contact person:_____ Phone:_____
How long have you been receiving this income? _____ How long do you expect income to continue? _____

CREDIT HISTORY/ASSETS/LOANS

Number of vehicles: _____ Any business vehicles, RV, campers, boats or motorcycles? _____
Vehicle 1 (make/model/color): _____ Vehicle 2_____
Please note, only cars on application are authorized to be on premises. Do you have a car payment? $_____
List any other current monthly expenses and approximate amount: _____
Name of bank and branch: _____ Phone: _____
Do you have a checking acct? _____ Savings acct?_____ Credit card/Type?_____
Part of our verification process is to request a credit report which is provided by:_____
Is there anything negative we may find when we run a credit or criminal background check?_____

PERSONAL/PROFESSIONAL REFERENCES

Name of doctor or health care provider:_____Attorney_____
Name of nearest living relative:_____ Relationship _____ Phone_____
Address: _____ City: _____State: _____Zip: _____

Thank you for completing an application to rent from us. A fee of $ _____ is charged to all applicants for the purpose of verifying information furnished. This fee is refundable/nonrefundable. By signing below, applicant represents all information is true, complete, and authorizes annual contact/verification of information, references, and credit for continual tenancy or for collection purposes should it become necessary. If any information is found to be false, the application will be rejected and will be sufficient reason for immediate eviction and loss of deposit.

Applicant's signature:_____ Date: _____

APPLICATION ADDENDUM—ACCEPTANCE OF TERMS

Dear Rental Applicant:

We take pride in our rental homes. We offer guarantees in regard to your satisfaction and our maintenance responsibilities. And we actively seek only qualified residents to reside in our homes.

We screen our applicants carefully, and we completely verify all information provided to us on the rental application. We run a credit report on every applicant, we verify employment, and we check previous rental history.

The screening and verification process is used for every applicant the same way—fairly and consistently. We also work to observe the fair housing laws. An applicant who passes the screening criteria is offered a rental when one is still available. An applicant who does not satisfy the screening criteria is not accepted as a resident.

By making an application for one of our rentals, you acknowledge that these verifications will be done and give us permission to do them. Please completely fill in the rental application. If you do not provide us with complete information, we will not be able to process the application. We will do our best to process your application quickly, normally within a 72-hour period. If you have not heard back from us by then, feel free to contact us. Please read and sign below acknowledging acceptance of the terms of your application. Thank you for making an application for one of our rentals and we hope you will become a long-term resident with us.

1. I have double-checked the information I have provided on the rental application and agree that it is true and complete.

2. I understand that an annual update of the information on this application shall be requested. I agree to provide updated information and notify landlord or management of any changes (e.g., employment, phone number, bank, car, emergency contact).

3. My credit report/history is good. If not, I have attached a separate page to explain any credit problems.

4. I understand and agree that this application is subject to approval, based on the information on my application. If any of the information I have given turns out to be FALSE, my application will be denied.

5. I agree to pay a $_____ nonrefundable processing fee, plus a $_____ refundable holding deposit to reserve/hold the rental for me until the move-in date, should my application be accepted. If accepted, the holding deposit will be applied toward my move-in costs, including rent and security deposit.

6. I understand and agree that this application is NOT a lease or rental agreement, and should it be accepted, I will sign the lease provided within _____ business day(s) of being accepted. Should I fail to do so, the application shall be considered withdrawn, there will be no further obligation to reserve the rental, and my holding deposit will be forfeited.

7. I hereby waive any claim for damages if my application is not accepted.

8. I understand that every good faith effort will be made to have the premises ready for occupancy as promised. However, should the premises not be available for occupancy on the date promised, I hereby waive any and all rights to seek to recover damages of any kind from the landlord or management company.

9. I hereby authorize and permit the landlord and/or management company to obtain any information necessary to verify the accuracy of any information or statements I have made in this application. I authorize and permit my credit report to be obtained and further authorize the landlord or management to make future credit inquiries in regard to continued creditworthiness and for purposes of collection of unpaid rent or damages to premises, should that become necessary.

10. I permit, upon occasion, contact with my employer to verify my employment status during my tenancy.

11. I shall not hold the landlord or management responsible for any allergic reactions to the premises, inside or outside, from me, other occupants, or guests. I shall check for allergic reactions before signing the Rental Agreement.

12. I certify that I am not manufacturing, using, storing, or selling dangerous controlled substances, and understand that I will immediately be required to vacate the premises if evidence of such is found on the premises, or if I am convicted of any crimes related to possession and/or distribution of controlled, dangerous substances.

13. I understand and agree that the monthly rent will be $_____ and that a monthly rebate/discount/late charge of $_____ will be awarded or applied if the following conditions are met/not met _____.

14. I further understand and agree that the security deposit of $_____ is required in full before move-in. I agree to pay the balance of move-in costs, including any deposits or rent totaling $_____ within _____ days of being notified of acceptance. If I am unable to or fail for whatever reason to pay the balance of the amount due at that time, the application shall be considered withdrawn, and my holding deposit will be forfeited.

Applicant's signature: _____ Date: _____

Address reserved (subject to approval of application):

_____

FUTURE HOMEBUYER QUESTIONNAIRE

If you are interested in RENTING, or in BUYING A HOME please tell us about yourself and what you desire so we may best meet your needs. Let us know as soon as possible. We buy, sell, and rent all types of properties. Thanks!

☐ I AM INTERESTED IN RENTING RIGHT NOW.

☐ I AM ALSO INTERESTED IN BUYING A HOME AFTER ONE YEAR.

☐ I'LL PROBABLY BE INTERESTED IN BUYING IN TWO TO FIVE YEARS.

Name: _____ Date _____

Address: _____

City: _____ State _____ Zip _____

Telephone #'s: Home _____ Work _____ Pager_____

　　　　　　　Cell _____ Email _____

Please tell us about the home that you would like to have - please distinguish between
WANT TO HAVE and MUST HAVE

I must have _____ / want to have _____ a garage.

I must have _____ / want to have _____ a large yard or basement or attic (circle all that apply)

I must have _____ / want to have _____ at least 1___ 2___ 3___ 4___ bedrooms.

I must have _____ / want to have _____ 1_____ 2_____ bathrooms.

I must have _____ / want to have _____ the following _____

I must have _____ / want to have _____ the following _____

In what city do you want to rent or buy? _____

In what section of the city named above do you want to rent or buy? _____

What is the earliest you may be ready to buy or move? _____

What is the maximum monthly payment that you can afford to make? _____

What amount of money can you have available for a down payment? _____

Have you been PREQUALIFIED _____ or PREAPPROVED _____ by a lender?

What is the best time for us to contact you? _____

NEW RESIDENT CHECKLIST
TO IDENTIFY FIRST QUALIFIED RESIDENT

MINIMUM CRITERIA AND CHECKLIST FOR RESIDENT SELECTION

Point System. Give a score of one point (or more when applicable) for each of the following criteria. Please note, you may designate any criteria to be worth more than one point in value as long as you are consistent in giving the same value to select criteria for all applicants. (Perhaps put an * by all those worth double points.) Add up the total points to see if the applicant reaches your minimum acceptable score.

Financial Criteria (Financial History)

_____ Minimum score on credit report of _____ . (over _____ score = 2 points)*

_____ Sufficient income—Monthly income is 3 times the rental amount. (4 times = 2 points)*

_____ Verifiable source of income or employment.

_____ Same source of income for a minimum of 1 year. (2 years = 2 points, 3 years = 3 points)*

_____ Able to pay full deposit and rent requested.

_____ Currently paying comparable amount of rent.

_____ No negative remarks on credit history.

_____ No excessive financial obligations—more than _____ percent of income.

_____ Has a checking account.

_____ Has a savings account.

_____ Able to provide _____ credit references.

_____ No late notices from current landlord.

_____ No prior evictions.

_____ Able to provide a cosigner. (2 points if cosigner owns real estate)*

Cooperation/Reliability Criteria (Headache History)

_____ On time for showing appointment.

_____ Did not use any offensive language in your presence. (if so, _____)

_____ Brought items requested to showing (e.g., identification, application fee, deposit, references).

_____ Filled out application completely and truthfully.

_____ Capable of doing minor repairs and upkeep.

_____ All prospective occupants appeared to be well behaved.

_____ Did not demonstrate any hostile, negative, or combatitive behavior.

_____ Did not have anything negative to say about current landlord or property.

Rental Stability Criteria (Stability History)

_____ Resided at current address minimum of 1 year. (2 years = 2 points, 3 years = 3 points)* (resident receives points only if they were responsible for rent payment)

_____ No community standard, health, or safety violations present upon inspection of current residence.

_____ No security deposit to be withheld because of property upkeep of current residence.

_____ No notices of any kind from current landlord regarding a rental agreement violation.

_____ No neighbor complaints of residents or pets, or police reports on disturbing the peace.

_____ Resident has current phone in his or her name by a primary local telephone service provider.

_____ Petless, or owns pet and able to provide proof of license, tags, shots, references, insurance, neutered, declawed.

_____ Good report from the landlord prior to the current landlord.

_____ No criminal history.

Additional Criteria

_____ Able to verify all above criteria.

_____ Move-in date within an acceptable time period _____.

_____ Personal appearance and automobile appearance is neat and clean.

_____ Able to have rent payments paid directly from checking account, employer, or income provider.*

_____ Able to pay additional deposit (not above maximum permitted by law).*

_____ _____

_____ _____

_____ _____

_____ **Applicant's Total Score—(A total score of _____ points is acceptable)**

If score is between _____ and _____ points, resident may still qualify if he or she meets the following conditions:

_____

Date of application: _____

Above criteria verified by: _____   Date verified_____

Action taken: _____

Applicant notified of acceptance or denial: _____

Date applicant notified: _____   By what method: _____

Any other follow-up actions taken: _____

NONACCEPTANCE CHECKLIST FOR NEW RESIDENTS

The following criteria may be used to help with screening applicants. Unlike the more comprehensive New Resident Checklist (where you see if applicant attains a certain score), using this checklist, if an applicant matches up with any ONE of the following criteria (unless there are other compensating factors) this criteria alone would be a reason for nonacceptance of his or her rental application.

☐ Applicant's total gross household income is less than _____ times the monthly rent payment.

☐ Applicant has been evicted _____ times from another property and still owes money to former landlord(s) and has not made satisfactory arrangements for payments.

☐ Applicant has been convicted of a violent felony, or a drug-related felony.

☐ Applicant provided income or rental history information on the application that could not be verified.

☐ Applicant provided information that was verified to be false and the correct information would not have qualified the applicant to be accepted.

☐ Applicant demonstrated an abusive or offensive behavior or language at any point in the application process toward owner, management, residents, or any others.

☐ Applicant has had his current main source of income for less than _____ months (this does not refer to employees transferring from out of town but working for same employer).

☐ Applicant has resided in _____ or more properties during the last _____ months.

☐ Applicant has more than _____ judgments/collection item in the last _____ months.

☐ Applicant has a pet and you have a "no pets" policy. (Service animals are not considered in the same category as pets and are exempt from this criteria.)

Name of person who applied: _____

Did the individual submit a written application? _____ Date application was submitted?_____

How was the above criteria verified regarding this applicant? _____

PET APPLICATION/REGISTRATION FORM

Pet owners must complete a Pet Application and Registration form before occupying the apartment. If the pet is either a dog or a cat, a current photograph should be attached.

Permissible Pets:

1. **Dogs** Number allowed: _____ Weight limit: _____ Restrictions: _____
2. **Cats** Number allowed: _____ Restrictions: _____
3. **Rabbits** Number allowed: _____ 4. **Birds** Number allowed: _____ Type: _____
5. **Fish** Tank capacity: _____ 6. **Caged Animals** Number allowed: _____ Type: _____
7. Other: _____

Name of pet owner: _____

Rental address: _____

City:_____ State:_____ Zip_____

Home telephone: _____ Work telephone: _____

Pet Information

Please list all pets separately:

Pet's name	Type/Breed	Age	License or ID#

Pet References:

Veterinarian:_____ Phone: _____

Address: _____

City:_____ State:_____ Zip_____

Your Previous Residence:

Landlord/manager (circle one): _____ Phone: _____

Address: _____

City:_____ State:_____ Zip_____

Insurance:

Agency:_____ Phone: _____

Address: _____

City:_____ State:_____ Zip_____

Pet's Emergency Caretaker:

Name:_____ Phone: _____

Address: _____

City:_____ State:_____ Zip_____

I have read and understand the house rules pertaining to pets, and I and members of my household promise to fully comply.

Signature of pet owner: _____ Date: _____

Approved by: _____

NEW PET CHECKLIST
(To Help Identify Qualified Applicants with a Dog)

Point System. The applicant may meet your minimum criteria for renting a home. However, if you accept residents with a dog, use this checklist to determine if the "dog" qualifies. Give a score of one point for each of the following criteria. It is okay to designate any criteria to be worth more than one point, if you deem certain criteria more important than others as long as you are consistent in giving the same value to select criteria for all applicants. Add up the total points to see if the dog reaches your minimum acceptable score. **Note:** If the dog does not qualify and the owner says that they will get rid of the dog so that they can still rent the home, that is NOT a good indicator of a responsible resident. **It should also be noted** that "service animals" are not legally considered as "pets" and are exempt from the following criteria.

CRITERIA: Point 1 point (or more) in front of each of the following criteria which the dog meets.

_____ Applicant willing and able to pay additional $_____ deposit.

_____ Applicant willing and able to pay additional $_____ monthly rent.

-------- Applicant will obtain renter's insurance with liability coverage for the dog.

_____ Dog is at least 12 months of age or older.

_____ Dog was given a satisfactory reference from previous landlord.

_____ Applicant is able to provide a veterinary reference for her dog.

_____ Dog has received veterinary care in the past 12 months.

_____ Dog is NOT one of the following breeds, (fully or partially), Pit bull, Terriers, Rottweiler, German Shepherd, Husky-Alaskan malamute, Doberman Pincher, Chow Chow, Great Dane, Saint Bernard, Akita, Mastiff, or Wolf hybrids.

_____ Applicant does not try to misrepresent the breed of the dog.

_____ Applicant does not claim that dog will never go into the house.

_____ Dog is able to demonstrate during interview that it is well behaved and has good manners.

_____ Dog (or applicant) does not growl nor stare during the interview nor demonstrate any sign of aggressive behavior.

_____ Dog (and applicant) appears clean and well groomed

_____ Dog is wearing clothing made specifically for dogs.

_____ Applicant is able to easily control the pet during the entire showing and application process.

_____ Dog has no history of complaints from previous neighbors (regarding noise or behavior).

_____ Dog has no history of attacks or biting of humans or other animals.

_____ Applicant has proof that dog has had current rabies vaccination.

_____ Applicant has proof that dog has been neutered.

_____ Applicant does not allow dog to roam free at any time during the showing without a leash.

_____ **Dog's Total Score – (A total score of _____ points is acceptable)**

Applicant's name _____ **Date Applied_____ Phone**_____

CONSENT TO PERFORM CREDIT, BACKGROUND, AND REFERENCE CHECKS

I, _____, (rental applicant), authorize and permit

_____, (rental owner/manager) to perform background checks

and obtain information about me from credit reporting sources, current and previous landlords, personal and professional references, employers, banks, and law enforcement agencies.

I also authorize and give permission for all parties listed to disclose any information requested about me to the rental owner or manager stated above.

I further authorize and permit the rental owner or manager to obtain updated information annually and on future occasions for rental renewal consideration and for collection purposes should that be deemed necessary.

Thanks to all parties for your cooperation with this matter.

Rental Applicant (signature): _____

Date: _____   Phone: _____

Social Security Number: _____

LAW ENFORCEMENT REPORT WAIVER

By signing this authorization, I state that I have never been convicted of a felony. I further authorize the city police department(s) of _____ and the sheriff's department(s) of _____ counties to give to the company _____ or its representative(s) _____ any information that it might request to determine my fitness as a prospective client.

I also understand that any false information I may have given, written or oral, will be sufficient cause for rejection of services from the above named company.

In many cases prospective clients are requested to take this form directly to the local police department. If this is the case, when you present this at the police department, you must show your ID, preferably with your picture on it. Each adult applicant must fill out a separate form. If you live out in the country, this form must go to the sheriff's department.

Name: _____
       (full first name)   (middle name)   (last name)

Other Names: _____
          (maiden name or other married names)

Social Security Number: _____

Address: _____

City:_____ State:_____ Zip:_____

Birth Date: _____ Signature: _____

EMPLOYMENT VERIFICATION

From: _____ , prospective resident

Re: _____ , address

Date: _____

To: _____ , employer

_____

_____

I authorize you to give the requested information below to my prospective landlord:

_____

_____

_____

Signed: _____

Date: _____

==

Dear Sir or Madam:

_____ has applied to rent one of our rentals and has given your name as his or her employer.

To verify the information he or she has given to us on the rental application, can you please supply us with the needed information below? I have enclosed a self-addressed envelope for your convenience.

Thank you for your cooperation.

Sincerely,

Rental Manager

==

Job title of applicant: _____

Full-time position (yes or no): _____ Permanent (yes or no): _____

Income: _____ Weekly/Biweekly/Monthly: _____ Hourly wage: $_____

Pleased with job performance? Yes ____ No ____ Likelihood of continuing: Good, Fair, or Poor?

Name of person providing this information: _____

Title:_____ Phone: _____

PHONE QUESTIONS TO ASK FORMER LANDLORD(S)

One of your current or former residents has applied to rent a property that I manage. The resident has given me your name and permission to ask if you could please verify a few quick things regarding his rental with you. This would be a big help to him or her. May I?

1. Can you verify that if the resident is or was paying you $_____ per month in rent? Please note: Ask the former landlord to verify an amount that is actually different (by $50 or $100) than the amount stated by the applicant on the rental application. The purpose of this initial question is to see very quickly if you are dealing with a landlord who will be honest with you and who is not just trying to get rid of a resident. If the landlord does not correct you about the amount of rent paid, you know that you either have a landlord willing to lie to you or a friend just pretending to be the landlord. No need to ask further questions. Just simply say, "Thank you; you've been very helpful."

2. How many weeks advance notice has the resident given you that he or she is moving?

3. Is the resident currently up to date with his or her payments?

4. Has the resident been late once or more than once during the last 12 months?

5. Has the resident ever been late more than 30 days?

6. How many months/years did the resident reside in your property?

7. Is the resident vacating early, before the full term or end of his agreement?

8. Did you receive any complaints of any kind from neighbors regarding the resident?

9. How many people occupied the residence?

10. Were there any noise or nuisance complaints?

11. Were there any police calls at the residence that you were aware of?

12. How much notice did the resident give you that he or she was moving? Or did the residents give proper notice to vacate?

13. How many pets did the resident have on the premises? Had the animal(s) lived there with your permission?

14. Were there any complaints from the neighbors regarding pets or animals?

15. Have you had to give a notice to the resident for any reason during the last 12 months because of a rental violation? If so, what rental violation was the notice for?

16. Was the resident asked to move because of nonpayment or for breaking one of the lease terms? Or is he or she moving voluntarily?

17. Did or will you have to withhold any deposit to cover any unpaid rent or damages?

18. Did or will you have to repaint or clean the carpets after the resident vacates?

Thank you very much for your assistance.

Please note that these were all objective questions, wherein the answers could be easily documented. Do not put other landlords in a position where you are seeking subjective answers that cannot be easily documented or defended (e.g., what kind of residents were they? Or was he or she a good resident?).

LANDLORD VERIFICATION

From: _____ , prospective resident

Re: _____ , address

Date: _____

To: _____ , current/former landlord

_____

_____

I authorize you to give the requested information below to my prospective landlord:

_____

_____

_____

Signed: _____

Date: _____

Dear Sir or Madam:

_____ has applied to rent one of our rentals and has given your name as present or former landlord.

To verify the information he or she has given to us on the rental application, can you please supply us with the needed information below? I have enclosed a self-addressed envelope for your convenience.

Thank you for your cooperation.

Sincerely,

Rental Manager

==

The applicant rented from you from when to when? _____

Rent amount: $_____ Always pay on time? _____

Payment record: Excellent: _____ Fair: _____ Poor: _____

Did or will he/she receive full security deposit back? _____

If not, why not? _____

Did applicant break any rental violations or do damage? _____

Did you ever have to place notice to fill out court summons? _____

Evicted? (Why?) _____

_____

_____

_____

CREDIT REFERENCE VERIFICATION

From: _____ , prospective resident

Re: _____ , address

Date: _____

To: _____ , credit reference

_____

_____

I authorize you to give the requested information below to my prospective landlord:

_____

_____

_____

Signed: _____

Date: _____

===

Dear Sir or Madam:

_____ has applied to rent one of our rentals and has given your name as credit reference.

To verify the information he or she has given to us on the rental application, can you please supply us with the needed information below? I have enclosed a self-addressed envelope for your convenience.

Thank you for your cooperation.

Sincerely,

Rental Manager

===

Amount the applicant owes you: _____

Monthly payments: _____ Since: Month: _____ Year: _____

Approximately how many more payments is the applicant responsible for? _____

Is payment currently up to date? _____

Has applicant ever been late? _____ Approximately how many times? _____

About how many times has applicant been more than 30 days late? _____

Payment record: Excellent: _____ Fair: _____ Poor: _____

Name of person providing above information: _____

Title: _____ Date: _____

BANK REFERENCE VERIFICATION

Have rental applicants sign this form to permit their banks to provide you with information needed to process their application.

From: _____   To (name of bank): _____

_____   Branch: _____

_____   Address: _____

City: _____ State: _____ ZIP: _____

Re: Rental Applicant: _____

I authorize you to give the requested information below to the following rental owner/company: _____

_____

I also authorize for automatic bank drafts from my bank account so that I do not have to worry about mailing a rent check each month, or the possibility of mailing the rent late and having to pay late charges.

Signature: _____   Date: _____

Dear Sir or Madam:

Your immediate reply is requested. One of your bank customers, _____, has made an application with us for a rental home and has given your bank as a reference.

To assist us in processing the person's rental application, can you please supply us with the information requested below? The applicant has given authorization so that this information may be released. I have enclosed a self-addressed stamped envelope for your convenience or you may fax it to the following number _____.

Your reply is appreciated and will be held in strict confidence. If you need to contact me by phone, my number is

_____.

Thank you for your cooperation.

Rental Owner/Manager

_____

Rental applicant: _____ Social Security #: _____

Checking account #: _____ Date opened: _____

Average balance: _____ Would a check in the amount of $ _____ clear at this time?

Yes _____ No _____ (This is the amount of monthly rent and/or deposit.)

Savings account #: _____ Date opened: _____

Average balance: _____ Is this a joint account? _____

Does applicant currently have a loan through your bank? _____ If so, date loan created? _____

Loan #: _____ Monthly payment amount? _____

Current loan balance? _____ Payments current? _____ If not, how late? _____

This information provided by: _____

Bank title: _____ Date completed: _____

VERIFICATION AND AUTHORIZATION
FOR TRANSFER OF SECURITY DEPOSIT

To (Current Landlord/Manager of Applicant): _____

From (Possible Future Landlord of Applicant): _____

Dear Landlord or Manager:

The following applicant, _____ , has applied for rental at one of our homes or apartments. The applicant gives permission, with a signature below, for you to verify the amount of security deposit now being held on the applicant's behalf. The applicant also authorizes and gives permission to have the security deposit transferred directly from you to us, upon completion of the terms of your rental agreement. Your agreement to transfer the deposit is part of the terms under which we will accept the applicant. Therefore, we need to verify that this transfer of the security deposit is acceptable and agreeable with you. Please complete the items below and return this form by mail directly to us, at the following address _____ , so that we may complete the application process for the applicant.

We thank you very much for your cooperation and will notify you if the applicant is accepted and inform you of how and where the deposit is to be transferred.

===

Amount of deposit now being held by current landlord? $ _____

In which bank are the funds presently held? _____

Is there any reason (unpaid rent or damages) that you know of now that would prevent the full or partial security deposit to not be available for transfer to us at the end of the rental term? _____
Will you be able to transfer the security deposit within two weeks after the end of the applicants rent term with you? _____ If not, how long do you anticipate it will take to transfer and mail the funds directly to us? _____

Signature of current landlord/manager: _____ Date: _____

===

I have applied to rent a dwelling from the following prospective landlord: _____
_____ . I authorize and give permission for my current landlord/manager to verify the amount of the security deposit presently being held on my behalf and to supply the prospective landlord with the information requested above. I also authorize the transfer of my full security deposit directly to the prospective landlord upon completion of my current rental term. I further understand that if the full deposit is not transferred, for whatever reason, my application with the prospective landlord may be denied.

Applicant's signature: _____ Date: _____

COSIGNER AGREEMENT

This agreement is between _____ resident(s), _____, owner(s) and _____, cosigner(s).

This agreement is entered into on the following date: _____ , and forms part of the rental agreement between resident and owner listed above for the leased premises at the following address: _____.

The cosigner has completed a separate rental application for the purpose of permitting the owner to check the cosigner's creditworthiness, including running a credit report.

Though the cosigner has no intention of occupying the leased premises, which would/wouldn't be a violation of the rental agreement, the cosigner agrees to be liable (if resident does not pay in a timely manner) for any of the resident's financial obligations of the rental agreement. Those obligations include, but are not limited to: unpaid rent, property damage, cleaning and repair charges, and legal fees that exceed the resident's security deposit.

Though the owner has no legal obligation to report to the cosigner any nonpayment of financial obligation by the resident, both the resident and the cosigner understand that the owner reserves the right to send notices to the cosigner of resident's failure to meet any financial obligations of the rental agreement. Prompt payment by the cosigner who receives notice of pending legal action may help to avoid additional legal or court costs.

If any legal proceedings arise out of the rental agreement, the prevailing party shall recover reasonable attorney fees, court costs, and reasonable fees necessary to collect a judgment. Hopefully with the assistance of the cosigner, these added expenses will not be necessary.

Resident's signature_____ Date _____

Cosigner's signature_____ Date _____

Owner's signature_____ Date _____

APPROVAL OF RENTAL APPLICATION

DATE: _____

FROM: _____

       _____

       _____

       _____

Dear _____ :

Your rental application has been approved for _____

with occupancy to begin _____ .

Please come to _____ on/by_____ or set up an

appointment within _____ hours to sign the lease and to pay the balance of the required deposits and/or rent

as follows. Failure to pay the balance due and sign the lease will cause forfeiture of rent/deposit paid to date.

Balance due is as follows:

First month's rent: _____

Additional rent: _____

Deposit: _____

Additional deposit: _____

Fee(s) or other: _____

        Total   _____

Paid to date: _____

Balance due: _____

Sincerely,

Rental Manager

Phone: _____

TRANSFER UTILITIES FORM

To Applicant/Resident:

Your rental application has been accepted. However, before you can take possession of the home or apartment, this form must be completed within _____ days and signed by representatives of each utility company that will provide utility service to you. These are services that, according to the rental agreement, you, as a resident, will be responsible for. You must apply in person at each utility company and make the necessary arrangements. Your signature gives permission for the owner/manager to verify the following information provided by the utility company.

Resident's signature: _____

To Utility Companies:

We have accepted the following applicant(s): _____
for residency at: _____ .
Property is owned or managed by: _____ .

It is important that the utility be put into the resident's name as soon as possible to provide correct billing and payments. The above applicant/resident gives permission for the information below to be provided to the owner/manager to complete the rental application process. Thank you for your assistance.

Gas company: _____

Utility to be turned on/transferred to applicant/resident on following date:

_____

Name on account: _____ Amount of deposit required: $ _____

Account number: _____

Utility co. representative/date: _____

Electric power company: _____

Utility to be turned on/transferred to applicant/resident on following date: _____

Name on account: _____ Amount of deposit required: $ _____

Account number: _____

Utility co. representative/date: _____

Water department: _____

Utility to be turned on/transferred to applicant/resident on following date: _____

Name on account: _____ Amount of deposit required: $ _____

Account number: _____

Utility co. representative/date: _____

HOLDING FEE RECEIPT

Move-in Date: _____

Applicant's name: _____ Phone: _____

Current address: _____

The applicant agrees to rent housing accommodations located at: _____
on a _____ month-to-month basis or _____ for a period of _____ months.
The applicant also posts a holding fee for the accommodations in the amount of $ _____. This holding
fee shall be applied toward the tenant's _____ security deposit or _____ rent when the
rental agreement is signed.

In the event the application for residency is not approved or accepted, or if the residence is not ready for occupancy,
the fee will be returned to the applicant. If the applicant fails to sign the rental agreement, fails to provide additional
funds required for occupancy, or does not take occupancy on the scheduled move-in date, $ _____ of
this holding fee will not be refunded to the applicant and will be retained by the owner/manager.

By signing below, applicant acknowledges receipt of a copy of this notice.

Date _____ Monies received $ _____ By cash _____ By check # _____

SCREENING DISCLOSURE

1. **Disclosure.** The owner intends to investigate the information that you have set forth on your application. This
   may include obtaining a credit report or other report from a credit bureau or a tenant screening service con-
   firming information that you have set forth in your application. The landlord may also contact prior landlords,
   employers, financial institutions, and personal references.

2. **Screening Fees.** Before the owner will conduct this review of your application, you must pay a tenant screening
   fee. The owner/manager charges a fee of $_____. The owner/manager acknowledges receipt
   of this fee. This fee represents payment for costs incurred by the landlord to screen your application. The owner's
   costs may include costs incurred for a credit report or other screening report, long-distance phone calls, and for
   time spent calling landlords, employers, financial institutions, and personal references.

3. **Applicant's Rights.** You have a right to dispute the accuracy of the information provided by the tenant screening service, credit bureau, or the entities listed on your application who will be contacted for information about
   you. However, the landlord is forbidden by law from giving you certain information about your credit report, and
   this may be obtained from the credit bureau or tenant screening agency named below.

4. **Tenant Screening Service.** The tenant screening service or credit bureau used by owner, if any, is:

   Name: _____ Address: _____

   City, State, ZIP: _____

5. **Copy Received.** By signing below, applicant acknowledges receipt of a copy of this notice.

   Applicant's Signature _____ Date _____

   Applicant's Signature _____ Date _____

   Manager/Owner's Signature _____ Date _____

PRIORITY WAITING LIST REQUEST

DATE OF THIS AGREEMENT _____

I have completed a rental application and request to be placed on the priority waiting list of rentals owned or managed

by _____.

I was referred to your rental by _____.

In consideration for being placed on the waiting list, I agree to pay a $_____ fee. I understand that his fee will

be applied toward the rent or to total move-in costs. This fee is also to hold an upcoming rental at the following address

or one of the following addresses: _____

or _____

Or to hold the next rental available that matches the housing needs listed below:

Within 10 miles from: _____

Number of bedrooms: _____

Number of bathrooms: _____

Appliances needed: _____

Rental price range: _____

Additional need(s): _____

I agree to move into the rental address above or another available rental that matches my housing needs and pay required move-in costs, within 30 days after offered to me. I understand that if I fail to pay total move-in costs or fail to move into the rental offered within specified time period (for whatever reason), the waiting list fee will be forfeited. However, if the owner/manager is unable to provide the rental listed above or another rental matching my requested needs within 90 days of the date of this agreement, my waiting list fee will be refunded in full.

Future Resident's Signature _____ Date _____

Future Resident's Signature _____ Date _____

Owner/Manager's Signature _____ Date _____

REASON FOR NONACCEPTANCE
(Return of Fee/Deposit if Applicable)

Date: _____

From: _____

_____

_____

Dear: _____:

This letter is to inform you that your application for residency at the following address:

_____, has not been approved.

If applicable, enclosed is the amount of $ _____, which constitutes the return of your

_____, less the nonrefundable processing fee of $ _____.

We thank you for your interest in the residence, and we invite you to call us in the future if we can be of any other assistance to you or if you would like to find out more about other rentals we have available now or in the future. If we have any others available now, they are listed below along with a brief description.

_____

_____

_____

_____

If you wish to view or discuss any of these rentals, please contact us at _____.

Best of success in finding a residence for you and your family.

Rental Manager

P.S. If you would like to know the reason your application was not accepted at this time, send us your request with a self-addressed stamp envelope. I'll be glad to send that information to you.

REASON FOR NONACCEPTANCE

FROM: _____

_____

_____

Date: _____

Dear: _____

_____

_____

Your request for tenancy has been denied for the reason(s) indicated below:

_____	Application incomplete	_____	Unable to verify employment
_____	Insufficient credit references	_____	Temporary or irregular employment
_____	Unable to verify credit references	_____	Length of employment
_____	No credit file	_____	Insufficient income
_____	Insufficient credit line	_____	Unable to verify income
_____	Delinquent credit obligations	_____	Bankruptcy
_____	Profit and loss account(s)	_____	Previous eviction(s)
_____	Excessive obligations	_____	Garnishment, foreclosure, or repossession
_____	We don't offer rentals on the terms you have requested.	_____	Too short a period of residence
_____	Other _____	_____	Because of negative information received from third party listed below.

Disclosure of Use of Information Obtained from Outside Source
(If you were turned down because of information provided by a third party, that party or agency is listed below.)

Information was obtained from: _____

_____

_____

_____

Under the Fair Credit Reporting Act, you have the right to make a written request, within 60 days of receipt of this notice, for disclosure of the nature of the adverse information. The Federal Equal Credit Opportunity Act prohibits creditors from discriminating against credit applicants on the basis of race, color, religion, national origin, sex, marital status, age (provided the applicant has the capacity to enter into a binding contract), because all or part of the applicant's income derives from any public assistance program, or because the applicant has in good faith exercised any right under the Consumer Credit Protection Act. The federal agency that administers compliance with this law concerning creditors is the Federal Trade Commission, Equal Credit Opportunity, Washington, DC 20580.

DENIAL BASED ON CREDIT REPORT

FROM: _____

_____

_____

Date: _____

Dear: _____

_____

_____

This notice is to inform you that your request for tenancy has been denied because of the item checked below:

_____ Insufficient information on the credit report provided by the following:

_____

The above includes the name and telephone number of a consumer credit reporting agency providing the credit report (includes a toll-free number if this is a national credit reporting agency).

_____ Negative information on the credit report provided by the following:

_____

The above includes the name and telephone number of a consumer credit reporting agency providing the credit report (includes a toll-free number if this is a national credit reporting agency).

The consumer credit reporting agency above did not make the decision not to rent to you and cannot explain why your tenancy was denied. The agency only provided information about your credit history.

This notice is provided to meet the requirements of the Federal Fair Credit Reporting Act. You have the right under this Act to obtain a free copy of your credit report from the consumer credit reporting agency named above, if you request it within 60 days of this notice. You also have the right to dispute the accuracy or completeness of your credit report and add your own "consumer statement" (up to 100 words) to the report. For more information, contact the above-named consumer credit reporting agency.

Owner/Manager's Signature: _____ Date: _____

PART TWO

Leasing Forms and Addendums

Forms to Create Win-Win Relationships That Maximize Your Profits

STANDARD, CUSTOMIZED, OR DELUXE RENTAL PACKAGES

Do a survey (see the Announcement and Upgrade Survey) of your current residents and discover what amenities or upgrades they like and appreciate or would be willing to pay extra for if you made them available as part of the rental home package. This strategy will increase your cash flow and upgrade the quality of your residents and your properties. I should warn you that once this revelation really hits you, it can totally change the way you rent your properties. If you plan on continuing to rent properties successfully in this century, read this tip once a month, until numerous light bulbs begin exploding in your head. This section will open your eyes to landlording in the future.

■ *Tip Number* **11**

Offer more than four walls and a floor.

Start asking all prospective and renewing residents if they would prefer your standard, customized, or deluxe rental package. The standard package is what most landlords now offer—you know, clean walls, running water, working toilet, and a heat source. No extras, no frills.

More and more apartment communities are offering additional housing extras, features, amenities, services, and guarantees that make many other landlords end up with only mediocre residents and wonder why. Smart landlords and apartment owners are now promoting the fact that they can provide housing consumers some of the extras, amenities, and features at a price far lower than the cost of ownership, and the arrangement to start is easy. This is pretty appealing to renters who want immediate gratification of living luxuries.

This brings me back to the idea of always asking prospective and renewing residents if they would prefer the standard, customized, or deluxe rental package. Please grasp the beauty of this question. Even without saying what the various packages may include, I have already gotten residents thinking, *Wow, this guy has more than the average landlord.* In fact, offering the different options is far more important and profitable than if you simply included a few extras as part of your normal rental. By "packaging" my rental with the special "Custom Home" name, I add value to whatever I include, even if it's only a used refrigerator tied with a ribbon. Never again simply give items to your residents, or throw in rental items, as part of your standard rental. Include anything extra as a bonus in one of your rental packages (e.g., ceiling fan, mini-blinds, curtains, choice of wall color, refrigerator, microwave, washer-dryer hook up, maintenance guarantee, reduced rate at nearby gym).

Let's make sure you see how the strategy of offering three rental packages works. The first package option, the standard rental package, only includes what you must provide by law (four lead-free walls, running water, working toilet, etc.). The deluxe package includes three to five rental extras, services, or guarantees that are offered from $100 to $200 more than the standard rental. The cost to provide these extras will range from 25 to 50 percent of the added annual cash flow. The customized package allows the resident to select one or two of the extras he or she most desires from the extras included in the deluxe package. Residents pay only $25 to $50 above the standard rental rate for the customized package.

Begin offering the three different rental packages, starting first with the deluxe package, even though you will discover that very few, if any, residents will select the deluxe package. By offering this higher-priced alternative first, you whet the appetite of many residents who then will want the customized package, instead of the standard, no extras option. This means your cash flow will receive a boost of $25 to $50 per month per rental. This packaging strategy will work with all type rentals. Only the extras may vary.

THE RENTAL AGREEMENT

■ *Tip Number* **12**

Incorporate money-making concepts into your rental agreements.

"So how do I put your money-making management concepts into my rental agreement?" That's what smart landlords ask after hearing me, at a seminar, share some of the innovative concepts that have revolutionized the way thousands of landlords manage their properties. I'm glad many of you don't stop at just hearing the concepts, because it's not enough to just get excited about a concept. Your objective when attending a seminar or reading a newsletter should always be to learn how you can implement strategies into your business immediately and practically.

If you are not a subscriber to my newsletter, you may not be familiar with many of the classic concepts which help thousands of rental owners monthly increase their net rental income. This book introduces classic concepts such as:

1. Offer more than four walls and a floor
2. 3-Star loyalty programs
3. Biweekly payday rent payment plan
4. Future homebuyers program
5. Rental property maintenance guarantee or we pay you

These are just five out of dozens of the most popular concepts that can totally change the way you work with rental residents. The many money-making management concepts, discussed in complete detail, will soon be available in a new book, *Landlord to Landlord,* a companion guide to this book. I also encourage you to take advantage of the free six-month introductory newsletter offer at the back of this book so that you can learn many more management ideas that will help you be or stay successful as a rental owner.

Because your agreement is the key contractual document that you and your resident will refer to as the foundation for your relationship, *it is vital that the money-making management concepts be fully interwoven into your rental agreement.*

In the sample rental agreement included in this section of the book, we have included clauses that incorporate these money-making concepts. Use this agreement as a starting point for developing your own agreement or as a cross-reference. You may wish to select certain clauses and include or add them to your existing agreement. While I have attempted to include clauses to strengthen your agreement, ones that should not conflict with local or state laws, laws are continually changing, so I recommended that you have an attorney review any clauses you believe will make your lease stronger before adding them to your agreement.

If you are a member of a local real estate association, it is also suggested that you consider using the rental agreement or lease provided by the association, which has probably been reviewed by an attorney familiar with state laws. If you are not a member of a local association, another option for obtaining, comparing, and reviewing a state-specific, attorney-reviewed lease agreement is also available online at *www.mrlandlord.com/legalforms*.

THE AGREEMENT SIGNING SESSION

Before Meeting the New Resident Use a Rent-Up Checklist before the agreement signing to ensure that you have all the required paperwork on hand, and to ensure that everything needed for move-in has been completed. The sample Rent-Up Checklist in the forms in this section can be used with new or renewing residents. Feel free to alter it to suit your needs.

■ *Tip Number* **13**

Get all the paperwork complete before move-in.

Once all of the necessary paperwork has been prepared, including agreements, condition checklist, addendums, disclosures, and receipts, look at the Rent-Up Checklist and neatly cross off any items that do not apply to brand-new residents. Verify that you have all the needed documents.

Go through the documents and sign or initial everything as needed. This will save time later. Taking time to prepare for the agreement signing will allow that session to go smoothly and help to eliminate confusion.

During the Signing Session Hand a copy of the rental agreement to each resident, pointing out any provisions or programs that you want to stress, such as due dates, late fees, holding residents accountable, and the future homebuyers program (more on the last two issues later).

■ *Tip Number* **14**

Provide residents with a set of House Rules.

To keep the rental agreement or lease from being excessively long and overwhelming, you may want to address some of the rules pertaining to resident conduct and property upkeep in a separate House Rules document. It's usually easier to add to or modify House Rules than it is to change terms of a lease prior to the end of the rental term. House Rules may address issues such as lawn care, decorations, trash removal, temperature setting, pest control, window covering, unauthorized cooking, or vehicle maintenance, etc. A sample set of House Rules is provided. All issues regarding property upkeep, which are important to you, are better addressed upfront and in writing, rather than incorrectly assuming that residents will perform a certain way. Without clear communication of the rules, you will always find yourself notifying residents after problems arise, that they are not abiding by rules you thought or merely assumed should have been followed. Don't make assumptions when it comes to how you think residents will take care of your property.

Also inform residents that you will do the property condition checklist with them. Now wait while the residents read the rental agreements addendums and disclosures. Keep quiet, except for answering questions.

After the residents have read all documents, collect them. Hand over one document at a time, starting with the main rental agreement. Ask residents to sign and initial the agreement where needed. Remember, you signed them in advance. As the first resident finishes with each document, he or she should hand it to the other for a signature. Collect all of the signed copies of the agreement and inspect them to be sure everyone has signed or initialed everywhere that you did. Do not hand the resident copies at this point. Set aside the agreement and repeat the process with each additional document. When everything has been signed, set all documents into a folder that you possess.

PROPERTY CONDITION CHECKLIST

■ *Tip Number* **15**

Always confirm in writing the condition of property before move-in.

The Property Condition Checklist (PCC) may be worth thousands of dollars to you when a resident vacates the property. If there is costly damage (e.g., stains in the carpet or marks on the wall), who is to say that the property was not like that when the resident moved in. You do not want to go before a judge and merely have the argument boil down to your word versus the resident's. In most cases, you will lose out.

In addition, the PCC reminds residents at move-out what type of condition the property should be returned to in order to get back their full deposit. Give the resident a copy of the original PCC two weeks prior to move-out to encourage them to do what is necessary to return the property to the same condition and, most importantly, to avoid arguments about whether certain property damages occurred after the resident moved in and should be rightfully deducted from the deposit. Do not simply give the checklist to the resident on move-in day and say, "Take up to a week or so to mark down anything wrong you see in the property." That approach is asking for trouble and will result in the resident looking for things wrong with the property. If he or she finds even the smallest problems, this starts off the relationship on a negative note. Instead, I suggest that the owner or manager and the resident do a walk-through of the property together, with the landlord highlighting positive features, simply asking for confirmation in each room that all is satisfactory, marking them so on the checklist, and completing the form together. At the end of the walk-through, have the resident sign the form and give a copy to the resident.

If your inspection reveals an item that is not satisfactory, have the resident sign a maintenance request form. That shows the resident how requests are handled, gets the item into your maintenance schedule, and gives you permission to enter the rental, which is now officially occupied.

Some landlords also take pictures of the various rooms of the rental at this point (with the resident in the picture) to include in their files. Have the resident initial each item on your Rent-Up Checklist indicating that each item has been completed. If the item says that the resident has received a particular document, provide the document at that time, including a receipt. You conclude by filing the completed Rent-Up Checklist along with your copies of all documents. You now congratulate new residents and present them with their new custom home. Another idea is to give the residents all the documents as part of a New Home Manual (see the Receipt of New Home Manual form).

STORAGE SPACE LEASES

■ *Tip Number* **16**

Lease storage space separately.

Have you tried adding a storage facility/shed to your property (if building codes permit) or offering the existing detached garage as an optional item available for additional rent (separate from the regular rental agreement)? If so you may want to use a separate agreement (see the Garage/Storage Rental form). Because the financial risk is less for both parties, a lease of storage space facilities can be a lot simpler than for a residence. Some states even offer landlords special liens or quick eviction procedures. Owners of such units should check local laws.

INTRODUCE THE NEIGHBORHOOD

■ *Tip Number* **17**

Connect your residents to the neighborhood.

Get your residents connected to the neighborhood by raising awareness to residents of what is available nearby. Provide residents with the Welcome to the Neighborhood! letter. Believe it or not, if landlords were asked by new residents where a good restaurant for a certain type of food was, or where someone can rent a video or buy coffee, most would not have an answer. Your rental(s) may be in a great neighborhood, but if your new residents do not get connected, why should they stay around? Regularly update the information to help keep residents current.

Solicit current resident volunteers to complete this Welcome to the Neighborhood! letter, especially get restaurant testimonials. They add more spice to your recommendations. Do it as part of your annual year-end resident survey. You can also get valuable feedback from exit surveys (see the Resident Exit Survey form in Part Five). Remember to give Welcome to the Neighborhood! to prospects and include it in their move-in packet. Be sure to include phone numbers of neighborhood hot spots.

LEAD DISCLOSURES

Federal law requires landlords to make disclosures about the presence of lead-based paint and lead-based paint hazards for target housing. Target housing includes residential properties built before 1978. If your rental properties were built after 1978, no disclosure is necessary (unless you have knowledge that lead-based paint exists on the property). Under the lead disclosure law, you are required to give your residents a copy of a pamphlet from the U.S. Environmental Protection Agency titled "Protect Your Family from Lead in Your Home" and have them sign a disclosure form when a new lease is entered into (whether it is written or oral).

■ *Tip Number* **18**

Give disclosures for some properties as required by law.

In addition, you are also required to give them the same EPA pamphlet and have them sign a disclosure seven days prior to doing any repair or renovation work in a pre-1978 building that will disturb more than two square feet where lead-based paint may be. A copy of the pamphlet and disclosure forms are included in this book.

You may make copies of the pamphlet and forms and provide your residents with a copy. When copying the pamphlet, the *entire* pamphlet must be copied and given. Also include the following specified disclosure language in your leases: "The leased premises were built before 1978 and/or known lead-based paint and/or lead-based hazards exist on the premises. See the attached Lead-Based Paint Addendum."

Do not omit these provisions. The civil penalty at the time of this book's printing is up to $10,000 for each violation. Knowing and willfully violating this law is punishable by up to one year of imprisonment.

PET POLICIES

Owners who allow pets should tell pet-owning residents exactly what's expected of them. A pet agreement laying out rules and regulations in advance heads off misunderstandings and disputes with pet owners, but only if the agreement is clear and well written (see the sample Pet Addendum form). The first thing a pet agreement should do is explain what a *pet* is and which pets are acceptable. This may seem like an obvious point; unfortunately some owners forget to do it. General agreements are hard to enforce. The definition of the word *pet* is by no means cut and dry. To a resident it might

mean any kind of domestic creature. To a landlord it might mean a dog or cat only.

■ *Tip Number* **19**

"Interview" the pet and clearly specify what is allowed.

A pet agreement that doesn't say which creatures it covers will be hard to enforce. It opens a loophole for residents who own snakes, lizards, birds, and even fish. Residents may claim that your rules don't apply to them because they don't own a dog or cat.

RENTAL DUE DATES

Pay very close attention, because I am getting ready to share with you the precise wording or dialogue to say to new residents that can immediately add $1,000 or more (per rental) to your annual rental income for 25 to 50 percent of all your rentals. Do I have your attention? Good. Let's build your cash flow. Here's another money making management principle: *Simply give people what they want!*

The reason for this is simple. I have found it extremely profitable to give residents what they want, including their choice of a rent due date. I would much rather give residents the option of paying me at a time they consider more convenient, especially if they are willing to pay me additional rent for the privilege to do so. I'm not suggesting that you allow residents to pay any time of the month they please. If you did, you would be collecting rents all month long. I'm suggesting offering two payment options: biweekly or monthly.

■ *Tip Number* **20**

Offer residents more than one rent-due-date option.

Here's another secret most landlords have not discovered: Some residents prefer to pay biweekly instead of monthly. Talking with aggressive-minded landlords using this tactic, 10 to 20 percent of residents prefer to pay biweekly, an option for *good* residents, not as a last resort for problem residents. Of course, for the privilege of paying rent biweekly, you add 10 percent (or whatever works for you and your residents) to the normal monthly rent.

I'm sure you see the advantage of offering the biweekly payment option—more cash flow! Let's take the example of receiving $275 every two weeks instead of $500 monthly. You now receive $550 every four weeks!

That's an extra $50 monthly, $600 extra per year. In addition, you receive 26 biweekly payments during the course of a 52-week year, the equivalent of 13 months of rent. You receive an extra month of payments or $550 by year's end on top of the other $600 in extra monthly rent. In this real-life example, this strategy has increased your cash flow by $1,150. Over a thousand dollars! All you do is ask your resident if he or she prefers to pay biweekly or monthly (and yes, you will have a little extra bookkeeping).

Here's how the idea is presented to the resident. "If rent is paid biweekly, it would be due every other Friday (or Monday) by 5:00 PM. For the privilege of paying biweekly instead of monthly you pay an additional biweekly amount. For example, instead of $500 once a month, you pay $275 every two weeks, which includes an added $25 every two weeks for the convenience and privilege of paying biweekly. Some of our residents prefer paying biweekly because they can more easily budget their rental payment from their paychecks. So, Mrs. New Resident, I need to know which rental payment plan and due date you want included in your lease. Would you prefer to pay the old-fashioned way—once a month—or would you prefer and find it more convenient to pay every two weeks to coincide with your paycheck?"

Please note that by modifying the lease in this way you are creating a biweekly agreement not a monthly agreement. When a payment is made, you are not accepting a partial monthly payment. Rent is considered paid in full and, if a biweekly payment is not made, you can immediately start eviction proceedings just as you do when someone defaults on a monthly payment. Likewise, if you charge a late fee when a monthly payment is missed, a late charge can be assessed each time a biweekly payment is missed. Anytime you modify your rental agreement, it's a good idea to discuss it with your local attorney to make sure you are properly wording your agreement and not violating any local or state rental statutes.

Send a letter to all your current residents informing them that you now offer two rent payment options (see the Payday Payment Plan form). If they choose the biweekly plan, with their permission, the rental agreement can be immediately modified. You do not have to wait until the lease runs out. Every year, at the time of the anniversary date, remind residents of your two payment plans and again offer the option.

In case you are wondering, "What if they figure out that they are paying too much?" remember that your objective is to meet the needs of your resident. In fact, when you first offer the payment options, it's important for you to assure the resident that you always want to make available the payment plan that is best for the resident. So, you say to the resident, "If at anytime in the future, you prefer to switch from one payment plan to another, you always have the option. We only ask that you are up to date with your payments and that you give management at least a 4-week or a 30-day advance notice." With that said, residents should be much more open to considering your offer. You will find that it is highly unlikely that residents will want to switch from paying say $330 every two weeks to $600 a month. And on the rare occasion they desire to go back to the old-fashioned, once-a-month plan, do not become greedy—let them. Remember, you are still getting the amount you wanted. Just not getting the extra—for the time being. However, you will discover that it is much more likely that the reverse situation occurs. When money starts to get kind of tight, as it often does for many residents, you will find that some residents will ask if they can switch from the $600-a-month plan to the payday plan of $330 every two weeks.

Mr. Landlord Challenge Start asking all residents which payment plan they prefer: monthly or biweekly (payday plan). What do you have to lose by simply asking?

AUTOMATIC RENT PAYMENT PLANS

Whether you are collecting rent every month or every two weeks, are you still collecting the money the old-fashioned way? The future is now . . . Eliminate late payments! I challenge you to *stop* collecting rents the old-fashioned way—residents mailing you the payment or, even worse, you collecting the rent in person. Instead, start telling all new residents (and old) that they never have to worry about late fees again. Because, you now offer the option of paying rent automatically each month worry free!

Find out from residents, when they apply for your property, which checking account they will be using during the term of the rental, and request their permission to draft that account on agreed-upon date(s) each month. *Let residents know that this procedure is one of your standard methods of rent collection.* Other collection methods you may consider offering are automatic payroll deduction or automatic debit from their check or credit card. Most residents will select the automatic check draft or deposit option.

■ *Tip Number* 21

Change your standard collection method.

It's important that you present the automatic draft or deposit selection on your rental application as a normal or standard collection method with advantages to the resident. The more you treat this as a standard collection method, the more your residents will embrace the idea of convenience. Residents will not have to waste time each month writing out checks and rushing to get them delivered in time to avoid a late fee. In fact, the resident will not have to worry about late fees at all. In addition, the resident may qualify for a special year-end bonus or rebate for timely payments throughout the year (this is a nice way of selling the idea).

Some rental owners require residents whose payments are made by third parties to utilize the auto-draft program. Parents of college-age students like the convenience of this type of arrangement because they don't have to physically put money in a student's bank account each month. Stories have been told that students getting "housing" money from mom and dad party all weekend and then don't have money for rent. This can now be avoided, plus parents don't have to mail a check each month. If you have residents who attend private colleges or universities, you should immediately switch from old-fashioned forms of collection to auto-pay plans.

Obviously, you can offer the automatic payment plan to current residents (see the Automatic Rent Authorization form). You simply must get written permission from your residents to use an automatic payment plan. Automatic payment plans are the way of the future for rent collection. Other industries, such as health clubs and insurance, have used this method of payment collection for decades. You

are now encouraged to make your life easier while you get your rents on time, every time.

After sharing the above cash flow idea at seminars, I get calls from excited subscribers who run into a stumbling block implementing the idea. They say, "Jeffrey, my bank says they can't set me up for automatic drafts. I'm not a company, and I don't have a storefront. I'm not a merchant, blah, blah, blah. . . . And, they want to charge me hundreds of dollars." Or landlords discover they may need a computer and training.

There are several nationwide companies that specialize in working with rental owners across the country by helping them receive automatic payment plans, automatic paper drafts, and direct deposits from the residents' checking accounts into the landlords'. Check out MrLandlord.com for contact information on such companies.

RESIDENT ORIENTATION/TRAINING

■ *Tip Number* 22

Provide a New Home Manual at move-in.

With the agreement and all the recommended forms, addendums, and information, one "Mr. Landlord" subscriber provides or presents all this information in a novel manner. He provides each resident with a New Home Manual, which is a loose-leaf notebook divided into sections containing information related to the specific property the resident is renting.

I'd suggest something as simple as a Welcome Folder (two pocket, three-prong folder found in office supply stores) that can contain many of the recommended forms suggested in this book, divided into sections such as:

- Agreements and addendums
- Home and neighborhood information
- Maintenance and care of the property

Individual forms may possibly include:

- Copy of the Rental Agreement or Lease
- House Rules
- Security Deposit addendum
- EPA pamphlet and disclosure form
- Property Condition Checklist
- Invitation for worry-free payments
- Welcome to the Neighborhood

- Move-in information
- Utilities (local companies, cut-off locations)
- Emergency contacts and procedures
- Renter's insurance information

When providing the Welcome Folder to the residents at move-in, the landlord also gives them a Receipt of Welcome Folder form, which must be returned. This form confirms that they have received their folder, that they have read the contents, and that they understand there is a $25 fee for not returning the folder or notebook when they move out. This eliminates potential problems such as, "I didn't know I was supposed to disconnect the hoses when the temperature drops below freezing," or "I didn't know I shouldn't use abrasive cleaners on the tub." They have signed a form indicating that they have read all this information in the folder. Providing a New Welcome Resident Folder, perhaps with a move-in gift certificate enclosed, is a "professional" and positive way to start off the relationship with your residents.

ADDENDUMS

■ *Tip Number* **23**

Use additional forms for major rental concerns.

For certain rental concerns, a single clause in the rental agreement does not come close to adequately addressing the issue. The more cooperation a landlord wants from a resident, the more clearly his or her expectations must be communicated. Quite frankly, much landlord-tenant conflict arises because of a lack of mutual understanding. This section of the book includes a series of addendums that you will not need to use with every resident. However, when you do need to address a particular major rental issue with one or more residents, these specialized addendums and agreements will make sure you fully cover the issue for greater mutual understanding. Major rental issues that sometimes need to be addressed in detail include roommates, pets, waterbeds, garages, parking, crime, lead-based paint, and military personnel. Use the addendums included in this book to stay in control of every management concern.

WELCOME FOLDER FOR NEW RESIDENTS

Welcome to Your New Home!
Enclosed You Will Find the Following Documents.
Please Keep These Important Documents in a Safe Place.

☐ Move–in Gift Certificate

☐ Lease / Rental Agreement

☐ House Rules

☐ Addendum _____

☐ Addendum _____

☐ Disclosure _____

☐ _____

☐ _____

☐ _____

STANDARD RENTAL AGREEMENT

1. PARTIES: This agreement is entered into on this date _____, between the following parties,
RESIDENT(S): _____ and **OWNER / MANAGEMENT**:
_____. Resident agrees to rent from the owner, subject to the terms and conditions of
this agreement, the **RENTAL ADDRESS:** _____.

2. MOVE-IN COSTS AMOUNT

		CHARGE / DESCRIPTION
Rent	$ _____	Monthly or biweekly rent (circle one)
Security deposit	$ _____	Refundable deposit per agreement
Key deposit	$ _____	Refundable deposit per agreement
Additional deposit	$ _____	See attached addendum
Other	$ _____	
Total due	$ _____	

3. STANDARD/CUSTOM HOME:
The Resident(s) agree to rent from the Owner(s) the premises located at the above address and the home includes the
following furnishings, amenities, and upgrades:_____
_____

4. RENTAL TERM—3-STAR RESIDENT: The rental term will begin on _____ and continue for either _____a) one
year period and ending _____, or ____ b) month-to-month basis. (Management checks the appropriate
term). If on a month-to-month basis, either party may terminate the tenancy by giving the other party ____ days written notice. With either term, we welcome you as part of our Resident 3-Star Program. Unless notice is given otherwise, we, the management, look forward to serving your housing and related needs for at least the next ___ year(s).

5. RENT DUE DATE AND PAYMENT OPTIONS: Resident has the option to pay rent either monthly, the amount of
$ _____ payable in advance on or before the first day of each month, or if Resident prefers and considers it more
convenient, Resident may pay rent biweekly (every two weeks to coincide with paychecks), the "payday" rent plan
amount of $ _____ payable in advance on or before _____ of every other week. Resident chooses to use
the a) Monthly Plan or b) Payday Plan (circle one).

6. STANDARD WORRY-FREE PAYMENT METHODS: Residents may select one of the following Standard "Worry-Free"
payment methods for paying rent during the rental term, so they don't have to worry about late charges every
month. Residents agree by signing this agreement to give permission and authorization to arrange for rent collec-
tion by the method selected and debit appropriate account(s).
Preferred Method of Payment Selected:
_____ Electronic debit from checking/savings account on following days/dates each month:_____
_____ Debit card or credit card debit from following account:_____
_____ Payroll deduction sent directly from employer biweekly or monthly.
Payment made by one of the worry-free methods is entitled to a discounted rent. For payments made by check or
money order, pay the normal rental rate. Make checks payable to:_____ and deliver
to_____.

7. DISCOUNTED RENT: Based on the payment plan selected, the normal rent rate is $_____every due date.
For rent paid using one of the worry-free methods of payment, and received on or BEFORE the due date, Residents
will be entitled to pay the discounted rent of $_____ (where state law permits).

8. LATE PAYMENT CHARGE: Rent payments are due by the_____. Resident agrees that if rent is not received
(not just mailed) by the due date, Resident shall pay a late charge of either a) $_____ or b) _____% of the month's
rent (circle one). Be advised that any payments not paid in full or lost in the mail will be treated as late or unpaid until
actually received by Management. Any dishonored check shall be treated as unpaid rent, and be subject to a returned check fee of $_____, and must be made good by cash, money order, or certified check within 24 hours
of notification. After the _____ time a Resident's check is returned, Resident must thereafter secure a cashier's
check or money order for rent for a minimum of _____ months before being permitted again to pay by check.
The late payment or a returned check may cause owner or management to incur costs and expenses, the exact
amounts of which are difficult and impractical to determine, so both parties agree that these charges represent a fair
and reasonable estimate of the costs Owner/Management may incur.

9. **ADMINISTRATIVE FEE:** Should the owner or management have to request an unlawful detainer or other court action for unpaid rent or other violation of this agreement, an administrative service fee of $_____ will be charged to the resident. Unlawful detainers and/or other court actions are requested if payment is not received by the ___ of the month. If court actions are handled by an attorney, legal fees may be due in place of or in addition to the administrative fee. If management has to pursue court action more than once during the tenancy, this is grounds for terminating the agreement.

10. **ALLOCATION OF MONEY RECEIVED:** Any money received from the resident shall first be applied to: 1) any past due charges or fees, 2) any damages that have been repaired but still owed by resident, 3) any unpaid utility charges that the resident is responsible for. Any remaining money received will then be applied toward rent due.

11. **OCCUPANTS:** No more than_____ occupants shall occupy the premises, and only the following listed residents:
_____

12. **ADDITIONAL RESIDENTS:** Persons other than those specifically listed on the Rental Agreement shall be strictly prohibited from staying in the rental unit for more than 7 consecutive days, or a total of 20 days in any 12-month period. For purposes of this section, "staying in the rental unit" shall include, but not be limited to, long-term or regular house guest, live-in babysitters, and visiting relatives. Resident shall notify the Management in writing any time the Resident expects any guest will be staying in excess of the time limits in this paragraph. Additional residents cannot occupy the premises without first being approved by Management and are subject to full screening procedures. If additional residents are accepted, this is also subject to additional rent and security deposit being required. Unauthorized residents are a violation of this agreement and are grounds for termination.

13. **ASSIGNMENT and SUBLETTING:** Resident agrees not to transfer, sublet, or relet any part of the premises or assign this Agreement without prior consent of the Owner or Management.

14. **UTILITIES:** Resident(s) is/are responsible for all utility charges, except for the following, which will be paid by Owner:_____. Resident further agrees to make all utility payments, which he/she is responsible for, during the term of this tenancy and will be considered in breach of this Agreement, if service is suspended for nonpayment and will be held liable for any resulting added charges and damages. Past-due utility bills may be paid by the owner, and the resident will be charged that past-due amount as additional rent.

15. **NOTICES AND SERVICE:** Any notice is deemed served on the day on which it is mailed by first-class mail to the Resident, and/or attached in a secure manner to the main entrance of the portion of the premises of which Resident has possession. All notices to Resident shall be served at Resident's premises. The name and address authorized to accept legal service for the owner is: _____.

16. **REMEDIES/ATTORNEY'S FEES:** If civil action is instituted in connection with this Agreement, the prevailing party shall be entitled to recover court costs and any reasonable attorney's fees.

17. **ABANDONMENT:** Any goods, vehicles, or other property left on the premise after termination of the tenancy by any means shall be considered abandoned and disposed of as provided by statute.

18. **INSURANCE:** Resident acknowledges that the owner's insurance policy does NOT cover Resident's liability to claims because of Resident's actions or negligence or loss or damage to Resident's personal possessions due to fire, theft, rain, smoke, wind, flood, water, pipe leaks, or acts of others. Nor will owner or management be held liable for such losses. It's therefore a) recommended or b) required (circle one) that residents retain insurance coverage for fire, extended coverage, and liability to cover accidental injury and damage or loss of personal property due to fire, theft, smoke, rain, flood, wind, or Resident's actions or negligence. Residents understand those who do not maintain a current renter's insurance policy not only lack protection for their personal belongings, the residents may also be responsible to others for the full cost of any injury, loss, or damage to the property caused by your actions or the actions of your occupants or guests. If renter's insurance is required, residents' agree to show evidence of policy within a month from the date of this agreement

19. **COMPLIANCE WITH THE LAW:** Residents shall not violate any applicable local, state, or federal law or regulation in or about the premises, including the use, possession, or sale of illegal drugs.

20. **NONWAIVER:** Should the Owner or Manager accept any partial or late payments, this in no way constitutes a waiver of rights, nor affects any notice of eviction proceedings previously given. Waiver by either party of strict performance of any provision of this agreement shall not be a waiver of or prejudice that party's right to require strict performance of the same provision in the future or any other provision.

21. **PETS** Resident or guest shall not maintain any pets upon the premises, without prior written consent of Management. No animal, bird, or fish of any kind will be kept on the premises, even temporarily, except properly trained dogs/animals needed by blind, deaf, disabled, or other prescribed needs and only under the following circumstances _____ _____. If a pet is accepted (again not referring to trained animals needed for assistance), this is subject to payment of a higher monthly rent and additional deposit. Please refer to Pet Addendum (if applicable).

22. **EXTENDED ABSENCE:** Resident will notify Management in advance if Resident will be away from the premises for ___ or more consecutive days. During such absence, Management may enter the premises to inspect property's condition.

23. **DISCLOSURES:** Resident acknowledges that Owner/Management has made the following disclosures: _____ Disclosure of information on Lead-Based Paint and/or Lease-Based Paint Hazards (if applicable) _____ Other Disclosure: _____

24. **USE OF PREMISES:** The premises shall be used as their personal residence. They further agree not to use the premises for any business or commercial use of any kind without first obtaining written permission from management.

25. **ALTERATIONS:** Resident shall not make alterations (including painting, nail holes, contact, or wallpaper) to the premises without Management's prior written consent. All curtains, mini-blinds, fixtures, shelves, and carpet present in the premises before move-in must remain when resident vacates. In addition, locks may not be changed or added without Owner's or Management's prior written permission.

26. **IMPROVEMENTS:** All improvements built, constructed, or placed on or around the House by Resident (with prior written approval of owner/management), shall, unless otherwise provided by written agreement, remain with the property.

27. **LOCKOUTS:** If Resident is locked out of the premises, there is a charge of $_____ to open the premises between the hours of _____ during the week. There is a charge of $ _____ for opening the premises outside of those hours and on weekends or holidays. Additional charges apply if a key is lost and locks must be changed.

28. **PLUMBING:** Expense or damage caused by stoppage of waste pipes or overflow of bathtubs, toilets, or wash-basins caused by Resident's conduct shall be Resident's responsibility.

29. **VEHICLES:** Only the following authorized vehicles may be parked on the premises: _____ _____. All vehicles kept on the premises must be operational and have current registration, tags, decals, and license required by local and state laws and parked in authorized areas. Any vehicle not meeting these requirements or unauthorized vehicles will be removed at Resident's expense after being given 72-hour notification.

30. **REPAIR/REPORTING:** Resident shall promptly notify Owner/Management immediately in writing of all equipment malfunctions, failure to supply service, or repairs needed to any defective or dangerous conditions on the premises. Resident will be held responsible if any damages occur to any equipment or part of the premises and that damage is a result of the resident's neglect to promptly notify management of a malfunction or defective condition. Resident shall not tamper with or repair heating/AC or any equipment on the premises without first obtaining written consent of owner.

31. **APPLIANCES:** Unless otherwise stated as part of the custom rental package, appliances that are located on the premises are there solely at the convenience of the Owner, who assumes no responsibility for their operation. While on the premises, Residents are free to use them; however, Residents do so at their own risk. In the event appliances fail to function, Owner is not liable for repair or damages. If Residents wish, at any time, they may request that the appliances be removed. Owner will dispose of them at his/her expense.

32. **UNAUTHORIZED WORK/LIENS:** Except with respect to activities for which Management is responsible, Resident shall pay as due all claims for work done on and for services rendered or material furnished to the premises, and shall keep the premises free from any liens caused by Resident's failure to meet Resident's obligations.

33. **DAMAGE/DESTRUCTION:** If the premises are severely damaged or destroyed by fire or other casualty, either party may terminate the lease. If the damage was caused by Resident's action or neglect, resident will be held liable for damages.

34. SECURITY DEPOSIT: Management may withhold part or all of the deposit, once all occupants move out, to cover items beyond normal wear and tear, such as: a) cleaning charges (including carpet) if not done or arranged by Resident, b) damages to the property, and c), unpaid rent and any other unpaid charges/fees that the Resident was responsible for. It is agreed that all dirt, holes, tears, burns, and stains of any size or amount in the carpets, walls, and/or on any other part of the premises do not constitute reasonable wear and tear. Security deposit may not at any time during the tenancy be applied to any rent due by the Resident, or any other charges, and may not be used for last month's rent. Any deposit that the Resident is entitled to, along with a written accounting of the disbursement of the deposit, will be returned to the Resident within ___ days after all occupants have completely moved and possession given back to Management. For such purposes, the Resident is asked to provide a forwarding address to Management. If what the Resident owes, including costs to repair damages, exceeds the amount of the deposit originally given, Resident shall be responsible for all such excess costs.

35. OWNER'S/MANAGER'S RIGHT TO ACCESS: Owner/Manager shall have the right to enter the premises in order to inspect the premises, make necessary or agreed repairs or improvements, supply necessary or agreed services, or show the premises to prospective residents, purchasers, or contractors. Except in case of emergency, agreement to the contrary by Resident, or unless it is impractical to do so, Owner/Manager shall give Resident at least 24 hours notice of Manager's intent to enter, and may enter only at reasonable times. Owner/Manager shall also have the right to enter the premises when it appears Resident has abandoned or surrendered the premises, or during any absence of Resident in excess of 7 days. Resident shall not unreasonably withhold consent for Owner/Manager to enter the premises.

36. RESIDENT'S TERMINATION NOTICE: Resident may not terminate this Rental Agreement without giving _____ days written notice if this is a month-to-month tenancy. Failure of Resident to provide appropriate written notice to terminate a month-to-month tenancy will result in a Resident's continuing obligation under this Agreement for up to 30 days.

37. JOINT LIABILITY: Each Resident signing this agreement is jointly and severally liable for all terms of this agreement.

38. POSSESSION: If Owner/Management is unable to deliver possession of the residence to Residents on the agreed date, for any reason, the Resident and/or Management may immediately cancel and terminate this agreement upon written notice to the other party, whereupon neither party shall have liability to the other, and any sums paid under this Agreement shall be refunded in full. If neither party cancels, this Agreement shall be prorated and begin on the date of actual possession.

39. SATISFACTORY INSPECTION: Resident has personally Inspected the premises, and finds it satisfactory at the time of execution of this agreement, except for anything to be noted on the Property Condition Checklist. No promises have been made to Resident except as contained in this Agreement, and there are no other provisions, other than any listed below.

_____

40. VALIDITY OF EACH PART: If any portion of this Agreement is held to be invalid, its validity will not affect the enforceability of any other provision.

41. KEYS AND ADDENDUMS: Resident acknowledges receipt of the following: (_____) Keys for_____ _____, House Rules (circle if applicable) and Other Addendum(s)_____
_____
.

42. GROUNDS FOR TERMINATION: The failure of Resident or guests to comply with any term of this Agreement is grounds for termination with appropriate notice and procedure as required by law. Residents also acknowledge that any separate addendum(s) are made part of this agreement and a violation of any of the rules is a breach of this agreement.

43. READ THIS ENTIRE AGREEMENT: Resident(s) has read, understands, and accepts all the stipulations contained in this Rental Agreement, agrees to comply with its terms, and has received a copy thereof.

Resident's Signature: _____ Date: _____

Resident's Signature: _____ Date: _____

Owner/Manager's Signature: _____ Date: _____

RENTAL AGREEMENT
(3-Star Addendum)

This addendum is part of the rental agreement entered into on this date _____, between the following parties,
RESIDENT(S): _____ and **OWNER / MANAGEMENT:**_____
RENTAL ADDRESS: _____

1. **3-STAR RESIDENT BENEFITS:** As part of our 3–Star Program, which rewards long-term residents, during the next _____ year(s), you will receive the following benefits as a resident in good-rental-standing. On your first, second, and third anniversary dates, you will receive a choice of property upgrades. Examples of property upgrades may include: _____.
In addition (if applicable), as part of the 3-Star Program, the following upgrade (in the Custom Home rental package): _____, will become your property after the _____ year of your rental term. Since this item will become your property, you the resident are responsible for maintenance and/or repair of the item(s). In addition, Management requires that an additional Upgrade deposit of $_____ be held for the first six months of this term. This deposit is completely refundable at the time of the first six-month home inspection, upon satisfactory inspection of the item.

2. **FREE UPGRADE REFERRAL:** The Owner/Management agrees to offer a free property upgrade once a year to any 3-Star Resident who recommends and refers just one qualified prospective resident to one of our rentals.

3. **MAJOR MAINTENANCE GUARANTEE**: 3-Star Residents understand and agree that the following major repairs are the responsibility of the Owners and Managers:

   1. _____

   2. _____

   3. _____

   The Owners/Managers agree to guarantee that these major repairs will be fixed within 72 hours after notification of the problem to Owner/Manager. Resident understands that if a major repair is not corrected within 72 hours after notification, Resident will receive FREE RENT on a prorated basis starting the fourth day after the day of notification until the problem is corrected. Residents further understand and agree that the 72-hour clock does not start ticking until after the Owner has been directly notified of the problem and provides confirmation of that acknowledgment to Resident. The maintenance guarantee will not be honored if the maintenance problem was caused by the Resident's negligence, abuse, or fault. Resident also agrees that in order for the Owner to honor the guarantee, the Owner or Manager must be given access into the building, with the Resident's permission, to correct the problem. Free rent will be awarded in the form of cash rebate following the next on-time rent received.

4. **FINANCIAL HARDSHIP ASSISTANCE:** Because unforeseen circumstances may occur during the rental term which may create difficulty for Resident to make timely rent payment, Resident agrees to work with Owner/Management and permit direct contact from Owner/Management with the following individuals, companies, or organizations for assistance in past-due rental payments. Please provide names and phone numbers of individuals who may be able to provide assistance for payment of rent should you need temporary financial assistance.

Emergency Contact_____ Phone_____

Parent or Cosigner _____ Phone: _____

Agency_____ Phone: _____

5. FUTURE HOMEBUYER: As part of the 3-Star Resident Program, Residents are offered the opportunity to work with Management toward obtaining a home in the future. When a resident has resided in the property for a minimum of _____ months, and ready to purchase a home from the Owner/Management or a broker or builder in our 3-Star network, money will be given toward the purchase price at closing on your behalf. The amount of money that will be given at closing is based on your performance during the time you reside at the property.

Each time a 3-Star Resident makes on-time payment, that adds $_____ to the amount that will be given at closing on your behalf. During your tenancy, the total accumulated amount to be given at closing will be referred to as the Future Homebuyers Account, which can only be used solely for the purchase of a house and is credited or paid out at time of real estate closing. The house the Resident may purchase and apply the Future Homebuyers Account towards can be selected from either the same residence in this agreement or a selected house owned or managed by the Owner or Management or a house from one of the builders or brokers who work in association with us.

Please note that the money total that will be given increases each month with every on-time payment received by the following due date _____. If, however, payment is received late, the total money accrued into the Homebuyers Account up to that point becomes null and void. The total starts again to accumulate with the next on-time rental payment. Residents further understand and agree that they are responsible for the following Property Upkeep requirements:

1. Responsible for handling all normal upkeep and minor repairs. (Owner is still responsible for all major repairs, unless of course repairs were caused by the residents or due to their negligence).

2. Responsible to pass semiannual property inspections.
   By meeting those two Upkeep requirements, Residents will receive an additional $ _____ every 6 months (following each inspection) added toward their Future Homebuyers Account. Two property inspections are conducted yearly with a checklist provided to Residents in advance of inspections. Failure to handle minor upkeep or failure to pass a property inspection nullifies the total amount up to that point that will be given to the Residents at closing.

6. BUILD YOUR CREDIT REPUTATION: A review of each Resident's performance is performed every six months and Owner will provide Residents with a copy of a GOOD performance report when so earned. Good reports are earned by Residents who pay on time and follow ALL terms of the Rental Agreement. Residents can then give copies of their report to future landlords, loan officers, banks, and mortgage companies. These reports may be beneficial in helping you rent or buy a car or house in the future. Building your credit reputation may also help Residents participating in the Future Homebuyers Program. Please note: A poor payment performance and or violations of the rental agreement are also kept on file and made available to future landlords, banks, lenders, and any other creditors who inquire, that residents may want to do business with in the future when seeking to buy a car, insurance, home, or other large purchase. Any debts left owing by Residents are also reported directly to all three major credit bureaus so that the debt will appear on your credit report. Therefore, it is important that Residents understand that the credit they establish during this tenancy (good or bad) can follow them for many years. Because of such importance of performances reported or filed, Resident will always be notified before a nonpayment, rental violation, or debt is reported and/or filed, thereby giving the Resident an opportunity to immediately correct any poor performance before such action occurs.

7. OTHER PROVISION:_____

_____

_____

Resident's Signature: _____ Date: _____

Resident's Signature: _____ Date: _____

Owner/Manager's Signature: _____ Date: _____

HOUSE RULES ADDENDUM–A

This addendum is part of the rental agreement entered into on this date _____, between the following parties, **RESIDENT(S):** _____ and **OWNER / MANAGEMENT:**_____, for the premises located at the following address:

_____.

The policies and rules contained herein may be modified and new policies and rules adopted by Owner or Management, and shall become effective on the date indicated on the addendum, or thirty days after delivery of a copy of the amendment, or amended rules, to Resident, whichever is later.

1. **ACTIONS OF GUESTS:** Residents are totally responsible for the actions of their guest(s), friend(s), family member(s), other occupant(s), and anyone who visits and enters their residence.

2. **REFERRALS:** The Owner/Management agrees to offer a free property upgrade once a year to any 3-Star Resident who recommends and refers just one qualified prospective resident to one of our rentals.

3. **ADDITIONAL APPLIANCES**: No air conditioners, washing machine, clothes dryer, or any other appliances can be installed without permission of Management. Additional monthly charge may apply.

4. **FINANCIAL HARDSHIP ASSISTANCE:** Because unforeseen circumstances may occur during the rental term which may create difficulty for Resident to make timely rent payment, Resident agrees to work with Owner/Management and permit direct contact from Owner/Management with the following individuals, companies, or organizations for assistance in past-due rental payments. Please provide names and phone numbers of individuals who may be able to provide assistance for payment of rent should you need temporary financial assistance.

   Emergency Contact_____ Phone_____

   Parent or Cosigner_____ Phone: _____

   Agency_____ Phone: _____

5. **CANDLES & COMBUSTIBLE SUBSTANCES:** The Resident is prohibited from using candles or kerosene lamps without permission, and Residents are prohibited from using or keeping in their homes, garages, or storage spaces any gasoline, explosives, inflammable, or combustible materials.

6. **CARPETS CLEANED:** Resident agrees to have carpets cleaned at the end of the rental relationship.

7. **CARWASHING:** Absolutely forbidden - $25.00 fine if violated. Repairing cars should not be done on the premises. Broken-down cars cannot be parked in the parking areas. If you have any kind of an oil leak, please repair immediately. It is very difficult to remove the grease from the concrete, plus individuals walk in the spills and spread oil everywhere.

8. **COMMON GROUNDS:** In multi-units, personal items, with the exception of one or two plants are not to be left outside the apartments. It makes the apartment complex look unattractive and it is a fire code violation.

9. **DECORATIONS:** Decorations shall be installed in such a way as not to damage substantially the walls, floors, and carpets. No decorations shall be installed on or from the ceilings, doors, windows, their frames, or any existing cabinetry.

10. **ELECTRICAL OVERLOAD:** If the resident overloads an electrical circuit or blows a fuse, the resident will be charged to have problem corrected.

11. **EXTENDED ABSENCE:** Resident shall notify Management of any extended absences (more than __ days) from the premises. During extended absences by Resident, Owner or Management will provide access to no other persons, unless expressly requested to do so by Resident in writing. Management reserves the right to arrange for reasonable or emergency inspection during an extended absence.

12. **FIRE EMERGENCY PROCEDURES:**
    a. If you hear a smoke alarm and/or see smoke or fire, call 911.
    b Direct any family members in the dwelling to exit.
    c Stay near the floor if you must evacuate through a smoke-filled corridor. Smoke rises, so the clearest air will be at floor level. Breathe sparingly and move quickly as possible toward the nearest exit.
    d. Leave the fire area, closing all doors behind you, but do not lock them.
    e. Never go back into a burning building to save pets or personal possessions – no matter how valuable they are to you.

13. **GARBAGE DISPOSAL:** Residents will not use the kitchen sink or toilet for garbage or waste. Garbage and rubbish and recyclable materials shall be disposed of in containers designated for that purpose. Large boxes and containers shall be broken down so as not to consume too much space in the garbage containers.

14. **HAZARDOUS DISPOSAL:** No hazardous substances may be disposed of in the garbage containers, but must be disposed of as required by applicable health and safety regulations and codes.

15. **ILLEGAL DRUGS:** No illegal drugs of any kind are permitted on the premises, whether stored, used, or sold.

16. **LANGUAGE AND LOITERING:** No profane language, loitering, and loud music from car audio systems which interferes with the quiet enjoyment of neighbors is permitted outside the rental. In addition, playing, skateboarding, roller skating, or bicycle riding on the sidewalks, driveway, parking areas, steps, or in common areas in such a way that causes damage to others personal property or blocks passage or free use of occupants or neighbors is prohibited. Residents are responsible for asking all occupants, guests, and visitors to the premises to abide by this policy, and Residents will be held liable for the actions of anyone coming to or from home or apartment, and subject to eviction for repeat violations of this policy.

17. **LIQUID-FILLED FURNISHINGS:** No liquid-filled furniture or receptacle containing more than ____ gallons of liquid is permitted without prior written consent and meeting the requirements of the Owner/Management. Resident also agrees to carry insurance deemed appropriate by Owner/Management to cover possible losses that may be caused by such items.

18. **LOCKS:** Residents will not change or install additional locks to the doors or windows or any of the common areas. With regard to broken or uncooperative locks, Resident shall immediately notify Owner/Management if any door or window lock in the home becomes unserviceable.

19. **NOISE/CONDUCT:** Resident, family, and guests shall not make or allow loud or unreasonable noise or sounds. Resident and/or guests shall not disturb other Residents' peaceful enjoyment of the premises. Resident shall refrain from playing any musical instrument, radio, music system, entertainment system, or television set at a volume that can be heard outside the home and that causes disturbance to other residents. Loud noise or disorderly conduct will result in a notice to vacate the premises and termination of agreement. In addition, Residents are responsible for all actions and damages caused by Resident's guests.

20. **OFF LIMITS:** Residents shall not go upon the roof of the house or apartment building. Residents shall not enter any area clearly designated as being closed to Residents and others.

21. **OUTDOOR TOYS:** No bicycles, play equipment, toys, skateboards, or other personal belongings shall be left outside of the premises when not in immediate use.

22. **PARKING:** No unauthorized vehicle may be parked on the premises. No disabled or unregistered vehicles or vehicles with expired registration shall be parked on the premises. Vehicles must be parked only on paved or designated areas. Resident further understands that no repairing, servicing, or painting of the vehicle is permitted on the premises. Resident also agrees never to park or store a recreational vehicle, motor home, or trailer of any type. Such vehicles will be towed to a storage yard at the car owner's expense.

23. **PEST CONTROL:** The home got treated for pests before you moved in. Resident acknowledges that the rental is free of pests at beginning of the occupancy and agrees that Resident is responsible for keeping the premises clean and free of pests and will pay for pest control service if desired or needed.

24. **PETS/STRAYS:** Any animal discovered on or around the property will be considered a stray. All strays will be reported to the proper authorities and removed at the Resident's expense.

25. **PICTURE HANGINGS:** No room should have more than 3-4 wall hangings. Excessive displaying of objects on the walls damages the walls. Do not hang anything on walls with wallpaper – use only small nails with metal bracket. This size generally doesn't leave a hole. If you have a large object that you would like to hang, contact Management for instructions.

26. **PLUMBING:** Residents shall be responsible for keeping the kitchen and bathroom drains free of things that may tend to cause clogging. Grease and objects other than toilet paper will stop up the plumbing. Drain stoppages are your responsibility. It costs a minimum of $_____ to unplug a drain. If you do not let grease, food, hair, or other objects go down the drains, you should never have a problem.

27. **POLICE REQUESTED:** If police are called to the home or apartment on more than one occasion for a Resident-related problem or disturbance, this Agreement is subject to termination.

28. **REPAIR NOTIFICATION:** Resident shall notify Owner or Management of any necessary repairs to the premises or emergency situations as soon after the discovery thereof as possible. For example, notify Management if flooding from plumbing break, no heat in the winter, damage caused by wind, storm or fire, sewer backup, roof leak, gas leak, or electrical failure. Residents will be held responsible for any damages if damage was the result of Resident neglecting to promptly report needed repairs.

29. **SATELLITE DISH/CABLE TV:** Resident shall not attach, install, or have installed by anyone else an antenna, satellite dish, cable TV, or computer-related wiring or any other equipment to the dwelling exterior without the Owner's or Management's written permission.

30. **SIGNS:** No signs, notices, or visual displays of any kind are to be posted on doors or exterior walls.

31. **SNOW/ICE:** Resident agrees to keep walkways clear from snow and ice. Should the landlord have to hire someone to remove snow or ice left unattended, the Resident will be charged for the service.

32. **SMOKE DETECTORS:** For Resident safety, Resident agrees to periodically check to make sure the smoke detector battery is working. It is your responsibility to replace the battery or notify Owner or Management that the smoke detector is not working.

33. **SMOKING:** Yes, smoking is permitted or _ No, smoking is not permitted in residence (Check one).

34. **TEMPERATURE:** During the heating season, Residents agree to maintain the heat in their home at a minimum temperature, (no less than ___ degrees) sufficient to protect the pipes and water facilities from damage by freezing. If Residents are negligent in this regard, they are responsible for repair.

35. **TRASH REMOVAL:** Resident shall maintain the home (inside and out) free of accumulations of trash and garbage at all times and agree to dispose of trash in appropriate receptacles for collection. Resident is responsible for hauling away anything too large for normal collection. Management will hire someone, at Resident's expense, to pick up trash or debris if left neglected for more than one week.

36. UNAUTHORIZED COOKING: Resident shall not use barbecues, grills (gas or charcoal), or other outdoor cooking equipment indoors. They are not to be used outside without permission nor used in such a way as to create a fire hazard or substantial risk of damage to the rental or common areas.

37. VEHICLE MAINTENANCE: No car washing, changing of oil or other vehicle fluids, installation of oil or other vehicle fluids, or vehicle repairs of any kind or description shall be conducted on the premises, parking areas, or driveways.

38. WATER LEAKS: Please report all water leaks IMMEDIATELY. A small leak can cause high water damage and sewage bills. Check your commode for continuous cutting on and off.

39. WINDOW COVERINGS: Window coverings shall be restricted to those provided by Owner or Management already existing in the home at the time of move-in or those approved by Management. Under no circumstances shall sheets, clothing, flags, aluminum or any metal foil, newspapers, or any other such items be used as a window covering. No other items shall be hung from, or out of windows.

40. WINDOWS CLOSED: In the event of inclement weather (rain, snow, sleet, hail, or high winds), Residents are required to close all windows. Damage to the window treatments, property interior, or floor coverings resulting from the violation of this rule will be charged to the Resident.

41. WINDOWS: The Resident is responsible for payment of any window that is broken, regardless of cause, during the rental term, and the glass must be replaced with that of equal or better quality.

42. YARD/GROUNDS: Resident shall properly care for and mow the grass and adequately water the lawn, shrubbery, and grounds and remove weeds. If yard is not properly maintained, Management reserves the right to hire someone to mow or care for yard and charge the expense to Resident as additional rent, after first advising Resident that they have 72 hours to handle the responsibility. In regard to yard upkeep, Management is only responsible for _____.

43. _____

_____

_____

_____

_____

RECEIPT OF COPY ACKNOWLEDGED: Residents hereby acknowledge that they have read these Rules and Policies and understand that this addendum is incorporated into and made part of the lease. Residents understand it, agree to it, and have been given a copy.

Resident's Signature: _____ Date: _____

Resident's Signature: _____ Date: _____

Owner/Manager's Signature: _____ Date: _____

HOUSE RULES ADDENDUM–B

This addendum is part of the rental agreement entered into on this date _____, between the following parties, **RESIDENT(S):** _____ and **OWNER / MANAGEMENT:**_____, for the premises located at the following address:

_____.

The policies and rules contained herein may be modified and new policies and rules adopted by Owner or Management, and shall become effective on the date indicated on the addendum, or thirty days after delivery of a copy of the amendment, or amended rules, to Resident, whichever is later.

1. _____
_____
_____
_____
_____

2. _____
_____
_____
_____
_____

3. _____
_____
_____
_____
_____

4. _____
_____
_____
_____
_____

5. _____
_____
_____
_____
_____

RECEIPT OF COPY ACKNOWLEDGED: Residents hereby acknowledge that they have read these Rules and Policies and understand that this addendum is incorporated into and made part of the lease. Residents understand it, agree to it, and have been given a copy.

Resident's Signature: _____ Date: _____

Resident's Signature: _____ Date: _____

Owner/Manager's Signature: _____ Date: _____

SECURITY DEPOSIT ADDENDUM

This Agreement is between _____,Resident(s), who has given $_____ dollars as a Security Deposit to _____, Owner/Management, (other party of this agreement) for the property located at _____. The Owner/Management will hold this security deposit during the period the Resident occupies the dwelling unit under the terms of the Rental Agreement/Lease dated _____ between the same two parties.

The Security Deposit (plus accrued interest, if applicable) will be returned to the Resident within _____ days after the Resident has vacated the premises if all of the following conditions are met:

1. Resident stayed the full length of the rental term, and the lease term has expired.

2. Resident gave proper notice to terminate the agreement.

3. All keys returned to Management.

4. All monies due Owner/Management by Resident have been paid.

5. Residence is clean and free of all items, trash, and debris, including the carpets professionally cleaned. (If carpet has not been cleaned by approved company, there will be a $___ charge.)

6. No damages to the property and property left in its original condition, except for normal wear and tear. Please note that any dirt, holes, tears, burns, and stains of any size or amounts on the carpet, walls, or any part of the premises, are NOT considered normal wear and tear.

7. Management is in receipt of copy of paid final bills of the following utilities that the Resident was responsible for _____.

Resident understands that the Security Deposit may not apply to any of the rent payment or any other charges during the term of the rental agreement and that under no circumstances can the security deposit be used to cover all or part of last month's rent.

Resident understands that the Security Deposit will not be returned in full if Resident leaves before the lease time is completed.

Resident understands that the Security Deposit may be applied by Management to satisfy all or part of Resident's obligations and doing so shall not prevent Management from claiming damages in excess of the deposit and that excess money owed may be reported to the major credit bureaus.

Resident understands that the Owner/Management will provide the Resident with a written itemized list of all charges against the Security Deposit and after deducting the amount used as reimbursement for charges, Management shall refund the full balance due to the Resident.

Resident understands that in order for the Owner/Management to return the Security Deposit to the Resident after vacating the premises, the Resident must provide the Management with a forwarding address where Resident can be reached and where he or she will receive mail.

Signed/Resident: _____ Date: _____

Signed/Landlord/Manager: _____ Date: _____

Owner/Manager's Signature: _____ Date: _____

RECEIPT FOR FIRST MONTH'S RENT AND SECURITY DEPOSIT

Date: _____

To: _____

_____

_____

Re: Receipt for rent, fees, and/or deposits.

On the above date, _____, owner/management has received

from_____, resident(s), the following:

Total $_____

Rent $ _____   Of that total, this amount is being applied to first month's rent.

Deposit $ _____   From the balance of the money received, the resident is paying this amount
toward the security deposit to be held by Owner/Management.

Other $_____   If applicable the remainder of the money received will be used toward

_____.

The next payment amount that will be due from the resident will be $_____

and it will be for _____.

Management looks forward to a long and mutually beneficial relationship with the resident as we aim to meet all your current and future housing needs. Once we have assisted you in all that we can and the relationship concludes, the resident shall provide owner/management with a forwarding address so that all or part of the deposit, which the resident is entitled to, can be returned to him or her.

Payment Received by: _____

Management contact information _____

ROOMMATE SECURITY DEPOSIT ADDENDUM

The following is an addendum to the security deposit regarding the following rental address,

_____ ,

and the terms outlined below are agreed to by the following residents (roommates):

_____ .

The security deposit is a deposit to secure the terms and conditions of the rental agreement and stays with the owner of the rental unit until the last roommate of those listed above vacates the rental. All roommates agree to give a forwarding address to the owner or manager before vacating the premises. If one or more roommates moves out prior to the others, it has been agreed among all parties that the balance of the security deposit (after the final accounting of any debts or charges owed) will be refunded and or divided according to the marked instructions below after the last roommate vacates. Please note: If additional roommates are added to the rental agreement, and who contribute to the security deposit, it is understood that all parties (both old and new) must agree to the originally marked instructions below regarding disbursement of any deposit due at the termination of the tenancy. However, any disbursement of deposits will not apply to any roommate who did not contribute monies to the deposit.

(   ) The final accounting and itemization of security deposit, including any refund due, will be equally divided between or among all roommates, whether or not they were the last ones residing at the premises at the conclusion of the tenancy.

(   ) The final accounting and itemization of security deposit, including any refund due, will be given to the last roommate still residing in the premises at the termination of this tenancy. In the event there is more than one roommate residing at termination of tenancy, then any refund due shall be equally divided between or among those remaining individuals.

(   ) A copy of the final accounting and itemization of security deposit, including any refund due, should be sent directly to the individual(s) who paid the deposit (and based on the proportions paid) regardless of who is residing in the premises at the time the termination of this tenancy. Therefore if two people each contributed 50 percent of the total deposit paid, then only those two people will receive 50 percent of the deposit due, even if one is no longer living in the premises and others later moved in and stayed until the tenancy ended.

The undersigned residents (roommates) acknowledge that they have read and understood this Roommate Security Deposit Addendum. And they further agree that the security deposit stays with the owner until the tenancy is terminated and all rents, debts, charges, and damages have been paid.

Signatures:

Resident: _____   Date: _____

Resident: _____   Date: _____

Resident: _____   Date: _____

Resident: _____   Date: _____

Owner/Manager: _____   Date: _____

PROPERTY CONDITION CHECKLIST

Dear _____

Address _____

Welcome to your new residence. We thank you for choosing to rent from us. Please check off each of the following areas of the rental unit to confirm with us that each area is in satisfactory condition prior to your moving in. Any additional notes to this list must be submitted to the management within three days of the date of this checklist. Thank you for your cooperation. (For large homes, attach a second page to this checklist.)

	Satisfactory				Satisfactory	
	Yes	No			Yes	No
Entrance door	_____	_____	Bedroom #1		_____	_____
knocker/bell	_____	_____	ceiling		_____	_____
peephole	_____	_____	walls		_____	_____
deadbolt lock	_____	_____	floors		_____	_____
Living room	_____	_____	windows		_____	_____
ceiling	_____	_____	screen		_____	_____
walls	_____	_____	elec. fixtures		_____	_____
floors	_____	_____	Bedroom #2			
windows	_____	_____	ceiling		_____	_____
screen	_____	_____	walls		_____	_____
elec. fixtures	_____	_____	floors		_____	_____
Din Rm or Bedroom #3			windows		_____	_____
ceiling	_____	_____	screen		_____	_____
walls	_____	_____	elec. fixtures		_____	_____
floors	_____	_____	Bathroom			
windows	_____	_____	ceiling		_____	_____
screen	_____	_____	walls		_____	_____
elec. fixtures	_____	_____	floors		_____	_____
Kitchen	_____	_____	windows		_____	_____
stove	_____	_____	screen		_____	_____
refrigerator	_____	_____	elec. fixtures		_____	_____
cabinets	_____	_____	medicine cab.		_____	_____
sink	_____	_____	mirror		_____	_____
counter tops	_____	_____	toilet		_____	_____
ceiling	_____	_____	tub		_____	_____
walls	_____	_____	sink		_____	_____
floors	_____	_____	shower		_____	_____
windows	_____	_____	General			
screen	_____	_____	porch/balcony		_____	_____
elec. fixtures	_____	_____	heating system		_____	_____
General	_____	_____	water heater		_____	_____
back door	_____	_____	front yard		_____	_____
mail box	_____	_____	back yard		_____	_____
garage/driveway	_____	_____				

Special Remarks (cleaning or repairs needed) _____

_____

We hereby acknowledge that we have inspected the above-mentioned rental unit and have found everything to be in satisfactory condition except as stated otherwise. We understand that we are liable for any new damages that may occur during our occupancy.

Resident(s) Signature _____ Date _____

Owner/Manager Signature _____ Date _____

RECEIPT FOR KEYS

Resident(s): _____

Address: _____

City: _____State_____Zip_____

Resident has received the following number of keys:

Entrance door keys: _____

Other keys: _____ for the following: _____

Resident acknowledges receipt of the keys referred to above for the premises indicated. Resident has also given a key deposit of $ _____. Loss of any keys should be reported immediately to the manager. It is understood that the resident will not add any additional locks or make any lock changes or additional keys without the landlord's specific written permission. It is further understood that if the resident is permitted to rekey or adds/changes the locks, a set of new keys will immediately be given to the management. In case of an emergency, it is essential that management have access if there is a substantial safety risk to residents and to the property. At the end of the rental relationship, and once keys are all returned, the key deposit will be returned within _____ days, as long as:

a) the locks are in working order and have not been damaged, changed, or replaced, and
b) all of the resident's financial obligations to the owner and responsibilities for returning the premises
    to the management have been satisfied, according to the terms of the rental agreement.

If you lose, damage, or lock yourself out of the premises, management will be able to provide you access, and a fee will be charged for this service.

For access, due to lockouts, between 9:00 a.m. and 5:00 p.m. the service fee is $_____.

For access, due to lockouts, between 5:00 p.m. and 9:00 a.m. the service fee is $_____.

When a key is lost, a new lock replacement is required. After the lock is replaced, a new key is issued. Lock replacements are done between 9:00 a.m. and 5:00 p.m. and the service fee is _____ payable in advance or at time of service.

Signed/Resident: _____ Date: _____

Signed/Landlord/Manager: _____ Date: _____

Owner/Manager's Signature: _____ Date: _____

NOTICE OF ACCOUNTABILITY
(Given to new residents—Please read this carefully)

Name: _____   Date _____

Address: _____   RE: Lease dated _____

City, State, Zip _____

Dear Resident(s):

As our resident, it is important you know that our company works with one or more nationwide credit reporting agencies. The functions of these agencies are to track and maintain credit records on residents, including information of your credit history and pay performance as a resident. This information is then made available to future landlords, property managers, lenders, creditors, and employers as they request it.

The management of this property is our business. We will treat you in a professional, business-like manner, and we expect to be treated the same in return. It is our policy to hold all of our residents accountable for their actions—whether favorable or unfavorable. Your reputation as a resident and as a creditworthy individual is on the line. The payment reputation you establish here will remain on your records for many years to come.

Every business, company, or person who reviews your record in the future will have access to payment records you establish with us. We do a semi-annual review of your payment record and give you a copy of all satisfactory reviews of your payment records. A good payment record should prove helpful to you. You can use any satisfactory payment reviews we provide to give to future landlords, banks, loan agencies, etc. If, on the other hand, you give us cause to report unfavorable information about you to credit reporting agencies, that will also be available to employers, banks, home mortgage companies, insurance companies, and other creditors with whom you wish to do business and who request a report. An adverse credit and rental history report can make it very difficult for you in the future to:

- Get the job you want
- Rent an apartment of your choice
- Get a car, student, or medical emergency loan
- Buy life insurance or medical insurance for you or your family
- Obtain any gasoline credit cards or department store charge accounts

Remember that a favorable record is a vital key to your future. You can use your time as a rental resident to build a good payment history and build your credit.

Signature of Landlord/Manager: _____

Date notice was delivered: _____   Delivered by whom: _____

Method of delivery (check appropriate):   Hand delivered to resident: _____   Sent by certified mail: _____

Signature of Resident: _____   Date: _____

Signature of Resident: _____   Date: _____

PS: In the event there is ever a dispute over the accuracy of information reported by a credit reporting agency, there are certain procedures that you may follow, including the right to be given the name and phone number of the agency reporting any information you dispute. The landlord reserves the right to regularly and routinely furnish information to credit reporting agencies about the performance of lease obligations by residents. Such information may be reported at any time, and may include both favorable and unfavorable information regarding the resident's compliance with the lease, rules, and financial obligations. Please note, however, that a resident will always be given a 72-hour warning notice to correct or remedy a payment or lease violation before any information is reported to a credit reporting agency.

MOVE-IN INFORMATION FOR NEW RESIDENTS

New Property Address: _____

Property Manager: _____

Office Hours: _____ Phone Number: _____

Management's Email Address: _____

Send Rent Payments to: _____

Utilities

Electric: _____

Gas company: _____

Water company: _____

Telephone company: _____

Other: _____

City Services

Police: _____

Fire: _____

Post office: _____

Transportation: _____

Trash pickup: _____

School Information

Elementary: _____

Junior high/middle: _____

High: _____

Day care: _____

Other: _____

Recommended Services

Bank: _____

Renter's insurance: _____

Lawn care: _____

Pest control: _____

Other: _____

Your water shut-off is located: _____

Your electrical shut-off is located: _____

Your gas shut-off is located: _____

Other important items and their locations: _____

_____

_____

_____

WELCOME TO THE NEIGHBORHOOD!
This neighborhood has it all.

We have asked other residents what they like about this neighborhood. Below is what they like!

Restaurant (most popular) _____

Restaurant (second most popular) _____

Restaurant (third most popular) _____

Pizza _____

Burgers _____

Chicken _____

Bakery/donut shop _____

Coffee shop _____

Health food store _____

Bank _____

Post office _____

Gym/health spa _____

Movie theater _____

Recreational center _____

Supermarket _____

Hardware store _____

Drug store _____

Dress shop _____

Shoe store _____

Shopping mall or plaza _____

Hair salon _____

Barber shop _____

Auto repair _____

Medical emergency _____

Office supply _____

Dry cleaners _____

Video store _____

Library _____

Park _____

Pet doctor _____

ANNOUNCEMENT AND UPGRADE SURVEY TO CURRENT RESIDENTS
Rental "Extras" Now Available

Date: _____

Resident: _____

Address: _____

_____

_____

Dear _____:

Good news for the new year! We have discovered that many residents would like to have an upgrade or "extra" added to their rentals. Some are so excited about having upgrades that they prefer to sign up for a rental package that includes one or more extras. As you may know, we conduct regular surveys of our 3-Star Residents to make sure we are meeting ALL of your housing related needs. We offer far more than four walls and a floor in our homes and apartments. We have therefore made special arrangements to make available to residents any of the following items or services and let you design or customize a rental package for your home to your needs.

Please indicate on this survey or contact us within the next three days if you would like one of the upgrades listed below added to your custom home for a small monthly rent increase, or if you would like a deluxe rental package with three or more extras. We provide the following items at a rate better than any rental company can offer. Let us know if you find a better rate than we can offer. We will provide upgrades on a first request, first-served basis, so call quickly if there is one or more upgrades you really want soon. In addition, select upgrades can or will become yours to keep after residing a specified number of months.

____ Computer		____ Internet access	
____ Ceiling fan		____ Mini satellite dish or cable TV	
____ Additional door lock		____ Garage/extra storage	
____ Water filter system		____ Membership at local gym	
____ Closet organizers		____ Weekly house cleaning	
____ TV or surround sound		____ Phone answering service	
____ Microwave oven		____ Lawn service	
____ Choice of wall color		____ Grocery home delivery	
____ Extra phone jack or fax		____ Flood lights front/side	
____ Washer and/or dryer		____ Alarm monitoring service	
____ Screen door or added AC		____ Renter's insurance	
____ Other _____		____ Other _____	

____ Check here if you wish to have one or more of the upgrades or services added to your custom rental home package and would like owner/management to get back with you as soon as possible.

Call us at _____ Or return to _____

Resident _____ Phone_____ Date _____

ATTENTION ALL RESIDENTS

NEW RENT PAYMENT OPTION!
Direct Deposit Rent Every Month
Setup Is Fast, Easy, & Secure.
And It's FREE!

BENEFITS INCLUDE:

- **Pay rent on time** – Your rent will always be on time whether you're on vacation or traveling for business. No more late fees or lost checks in the mail!

- **Forget about the paper** – Once setup, you don't have to write any more checks, buy stamps, mail your rent, or rush somewhere to make your payment.

- **Guaranteed security** – Automatic payments are secure. The process is similar to direct deposits for payroll. With your authorization, your rent is electronically transferred every month when rent is due.

- **Build your credit** – Your automatic time payments can be reported to credit bureaus to help you build your credit.

Enrollment is easy. Just fill out an authorization form that we can provide for you and you provide a voided check. That's it!

Make Your Life Easier and Never Worry about Late Charges Again!

CALL US TODAY TO SIGN UP! _____

INVITATION TO ALL RESIDENTS FOR WORRY FREE PAYMENTS
To insure you receive monthly rent discount or never have to pay a late charge!

Dear New or Renewing Resident:

We look forward to serving you and your family during the upcoming years as you reside in your (new) home. We will do our part to provide excellent housing for you, and we know that you will make your monthly rental payments on time as well. As outlined in your rental agreement, under our company's special rent discount program, you receive a discount for making your rental payments by the first of each month. To help guarantee that you receive this discount every month, we invite you to take part in our special payment program, which is explained below.

Our special rent payment program is called Auto Rent Service—our automatic debit program. With Auto Rent Service, you will enjoy the convenience of electronic payments. Each month, with your permission, the funds necessary to pay your rental payment are transferred automatically from your savings or checking account, saving you the time and inconvenience of preparing and mailing a check, and ensuring that you pay only the discounted rent amount. This will help to make paying rent easy and painless. You won't have to worry again about forgetting to mail your check or paying a late charge for late rent!

Simply complete the Auto Rent Authorization Agreement below. If you elect to have your checking account debited, we will need a voided check. If instead you will have your savings account debited, we will need a savings deposit slip with your account number. It's as simple as that, and you won't have to worry about your rent being paid on time (just be sure to keep enough money in the bank to cover the payment). Your monthly payments will be credited on the first of every month (or the day we both agree to).

Verification of your Auto Rent transaction can be made by referring to your monthly bank statement. If you decide to change banks while you are renting from us, the Auto Rent plan can be easily transferred to your new account. Give us at least two weeks, advance notice that you will be changing banks.

During the years you rent from us, Auto Rent Service will save you time and postage, alleviate worry, and ensure that payments are made on time and you pay only the discounted rental amount, which will save you $ _____ each year. Plus you will not have to pay any additional late charges. Of course, when you decide to change residences, this Auto Rent plan will immediately stop.

Auto Rent Service Authorization Agreement

_____ Yes, I want to ensure that I pay only the discounted rental amount each month of only $ _____ instead of the normal monthly rental amount of $ _____ . If my present rental agreement does not include rent discount provision, I understand that the Auto Rent Service will help to ensure that I never have to pay a late charge. I give authorization to _____, owner of my residence, to debit $_____ monthly from my _____ checking account _____ savings account. My checking or savings account number is: _____. Name of bank: _____

Bank address: _____ . Attached is a copy of a voided check or deposit slip with this form. I give authority for banks handling my checking or savings account to honor electronic transfers or preauthorized checks drawn by _____ until further notice is given. I further understand when I give 30 days advance notice and move from my present residence, this Auto Rent Service will immediately be canceled.

Resident's signature: _____ Date: _____

PAYDAY PAYMENT PLAN IS NOW AVAILABLE
Announcement to Current Residents

Phone: _____   Best time to call: _____

Date: _____

Resident: _____

Address: _____

_____

_____

Dear _____ :

Good news! This letter is to inform you of a new program we have begun, that gives you, the resident, the option of changing your rent payment plan. We have discovered from a top management consultant that many residents prefer to pay rent other than by the old-fashioned, once-a-month method.

Because most residents are paid every two weeks, some residents like the convenience of paying rent biweekly at the same time they receive their paycheck. Therefore the name—Payday Payment Plan. In this way, you can budget your money better by making smaller rent payments every two weeks, instead of one big monthly payment due on the first.

This letter is sent to give you the opportunity to pay your rent in smaller biweekly payments. If you select this payday payment plan option, your rent payment would be due the same day every other week, in your case every other _____ . Having payments due on _____ gives you time to receive your paycheck on _____ and mail, deliver, or deposit the required rent to us by the _____ due date, before any additional late charges would be due. Your rent would be in equal payment amounts. For the convenience and privilege of paying biweekly instead of once a month, the amount of each biweekly payday payment would be $ _____ , which includes $ _____ more every two weeks than you would pay if you were paying by the once-a-month method.

The payday or biweekly payment plan is an option most landlords do not offer because of the extra administrative work. However, because many residents now find it more convenient to make smaller biweekly payments, we are glad to offer you the option. If at any time you wish to switch back to your previous payment plan, simply give us a 30-day advance notice. Please contact us within the next three days if you prefer to pay biweekly using the Payday Payment Plan. Our phone number is _____ .

Sincerely,

Owner/Manager

RENTER'S INSURANCE

From: _____

Date: _____

To: _____

Dear _____:

We want to make sure your family's belongings are protected against fire or theft during the time you are residing in our property. Please be advised, therefore, the insurance we carry for our building covers only the building itself against fire. Our insurance does not cover your property in the event of fire or burglary. If your child breaks a neighbor's window or your guest is accidentally injured because of a hazard you allowed to be left on your property, there is a lot you can lose by not having renter's insurance.

Many tenants are unaware rental policies by the owner of the property do not protect them or their personal belongings against such calamities. To fully protect yourself, it is suggested that you get a renter's insurance policy, which most insurance companies provide. Your most likely loss would come from theft, vandalism, or fire. How much is your entertainment system worth? What about your jewelry or other valuable possessions? In the event of a fire, do you know that all your furniture, clothing, and other possessions probably add up to tens of thousands of dollars? Many rental residents have learned through a tragedy they lost everything because they did not buy renter's insurance.

Here's the good news. If you are already carrying auto insurance, adding renter's insurance through the same company may cost you very little more. Most insurance companies offer a multipolicy discount if you add renter's insurance to your current policy. This will save you some money.

We can recommend a company providing renter's insurance at a reasonable rate. We can even allow you to pay your renter's insurance in installment payments with your next three rent payments. Let us know if you wish this option for obtaining renter's insurance. Whatever you do, don't put your family's personal property at risk. Renter's insurance is something you do not want to be without. It's well worth it.

All you need to do is contact us or an insurance agent today (e.g., the one you bought auto insurance from). If you are not currently working with an insurance agent, below is the name and phone number of an insurance agent who should be able to assist you.

_____

Be sure to tell him or her you were referred by:

_____.

During the year, we may have representatives from the insurance company that has coverage on the building you are living in visit the dwelling for an inspection and take pictures of the property's condition.

We always ask the insurance company to give us advance notice so we may inform you ahead of time. We would appreciate your cooperation when we call on you.

Sincerely,

Rental Manager

ADD ANOTHER INSURED PARTY ON POLICY

(Note: If one of your residents has renter's insurance, request that you are named as an additional insured party on the insurance policy. Here is an example of a letter you might write to the company that insures the property.)

From: _____

Date: _____

To: _____

_____

_____

RE: Policy Number _____

Policy Name _____

Resident _____

Property Address _____

City _____ State _____ Zip _____

Dear Sirs:

You are hereby notified that the owner of the property located at the above address has an interest in the property.

Please add the below-named individual or company as an additional insured to the above described policy and as a loss payee.

Should there be a lapse of insurance due to nonpayment of the premium, please notify the owner at the address below.

Sincerely,

Signed:

Information regarding owner to be added as an additional insured party (beneficiary)

Owner's Name: _____

Mailing Address: _____

City _____ State _____ ZIP _____

Telephone: _____

APPROVAL OF ADDITIONAL RESIDENT/ROOMMATE

From: _____

Date: _____

To: _____

_____

_____

Dear _____ :

As the current resident and occupant of the premises, you had asked for permission to add another resident and/or roommate to the rental agreement now on file between you and owners of the property where you are currently residing. This letter is to advise you that the rental application of _____ has been accepted and approved.

Before this new resident can move in, both you and he/she must sign a new updated rental agreement. In addition, below is a breakdown of any additional monies that must be collected as well:

$ _____ Rent for the following period _____ .

$ _____ Additional security deposit required.

$ _____ Additional fees or charges for _____ .

$ _____ Total due BEFORE move-in of additional resident/roommate.

An additional deposit of $ _____ and the following rent $ _____ and fees $ _____

Please understand that you, as the current resident, will become jointly and severally liable for all current and future payments required of the new resident and for his or her performance of all other terms of the rental agreement. Please contact us as soon as possible so that we can arrange to meet with both you and the new resident to sign the new rental agreement, collect all monies due, and give keys and all necessary items and documents needed for move-in. We can be reached at _____ during our regular business hours _____ .

Thank you for your continual cooperation.

Rental Manager

PET ADDENDUM

Owner: _____

Resident(s): _____

Address: _____

City: _____ State: _____ Zip: _____

Description of pet(s):   (picture of pet must accompany this addendum)

Type_____ Size _____ Weight _____ Color _____ Name_____

Type_____ Size _____ Weight _____ Color _____ Name_____

Other than any pet listed above and approved by the owner, no other animals of any kind are permitted on the rental premises (even on a short-term or temporary basis), including dogs, cats, birds, fish, reptiles, or any other animals. The Owner grants to Resident permission to keep the aforementioned pet in the premises subject to the following terms and conditions, and this becomes part of the rental agreement.

Additional Deposit $ _____ Additional Monthly Rent $ _____ Other Fee _____

1. It is mutually agreed between the parties that Resident may keep the pet described above.
2. The additional deposit listed above may only be used after Resident has vacated to apply, if necessary, toward carpet replacement, cleaning, spraying of the rental, repair of damages, or delinquent rent. This deposit, or portion thereof, will be returned within _____ days once any damages are assessed and it is proven that the pet has vacated the premises.
3. Resident agrees to purchase special liability insurance, with a minimal amount of $ _____ liability coverage, that would cover injuries or damage that may be caused by the pet. Resident also agrees to list Owner as an "additional insured" on the policy.
4. Resident agrees that this agreement is only for the specific pets described above and agrees to not harbor, substitute, or "pet-sit" any other pet and remove any of the pet's offspring within 30 days of birth. Any animal found on the premises other than the pet specified above will be considered a stray and removed at Resident's expense.
5. Resident agrees to have an identification tag on pet whenever it is outside the premises.
6. The pet shall be on a leash (maximum length of _____ feet) or otherwise under Resident's control, and not left unattended, when it is outside Resident's unit.
7. Please note that the pet(s) is (are) not permitted in the following restricted areas:
   _____.
8. Resident agrees to immediately clean up after the pet, both inside and outside the premises and to dispose of any pet waste promptly and properly.
9. Resident agrees not to leave food or water for the pet outside the premises, where it may attract other animals.
10. Resident agrees to abide by all local, city, or state ordinances, licensing, and health requirements regarding pets, including vaccinations and other listed concerns _____.
11. The pet shall not cause any sort of nuisance or disturbance to neighbors. Noise, day or night, must not disturb others. Resident agrees to do whatever is necessary to keep the pet from making noise that would cause an annoyance to others and take steps to immediately remedy complaints by neighbors or other residents made to the Owner or Manager.
12. Resident agrees to immediately pay for any damage, loss, or expense caused by the pet. Any payment not made for such damage or expense will be considered as additional rent due.
13. Failure to comply with the terms of this addendum shall give Owner the right to revoke permission to keep the pet, and is also grounds for immediate termination of the rental agreement, and Resident shall be liable for any damages caused by the pet and the deposit shall be applied to said damages.

Resident(s) Signature:_____ Date: _____

Owner/Manager Signature: _____ Date: _____

OPTION TO LIMIT FUTURE RENT INCREASES

This agreement is between _____ , Resident(s), and _____ Owner(s), regarding rental premises located at _____ . The Resident wishes to have the option to renew the rental agreement, upon its expiration, with a cap or limit to the amount of future rent increase the landlord can request. The resident agrees to pay a nonrefundable option fee of $ _____ . This option entitles Resident to the right to renew or extend the rental agreement at stated location for an additional _____ period once the initial rental/lease agreement expires. The initial rental/lease agreement between the two parties begins _____ and ends _____ . This option also limits any future rent increases to NO MORE THAN _____ percent or to no more than the dollar amount of $ _____ . This option to renew and limit rent increase is guaranteed, as long as the terms of the rental agreement are fully complied with.

Landlord Agrees To:

1. Give Resident the option to renew/extend rental lease for a another term of _____ beginning on expiration of original term for period stated above.

2. Limit any future rent increase to no more than _____ percent or no more than the following dollar amount $ _____.

3. Refund to Resident _____ percent of option consideration given, after resident has completed _____ years of the rental term, if there were no rental violations during those years.

   Landlord may choose to allow this option to be used more than once, following each renewal period. If so, please indicate here how many times the option may be exercised, along with any special provisions or required consideration. _____

Resident Understands and Agrees:

1. To notify the Owner at least _____ days/months before expiration of the original term, if Resident plans to exercise his or her option.

2. That notification must be in writing and delivered to Owner/Agent at the following address:

   _____.

3. That failure to properly exercise this option will cause the lease to expire and the option consideration to be forfeited.

4. That should Resident violate any of the terms stated in the rental/lease agreement, that shall be immediate cause for termination and forfeiture of option consideration.

I acknowledge that I have read and understand this agreement and have been given a copy on this date. _____.

Resident Signature:_____ Date: _____

Resident Signature:_____ Date: _____

Owner/Manager Signature: _____ Date: _____

GARAGE/STORAGE RENTAL AGREEMENT

The following tenant, _____ , agrees to rent garage/shed located at _____ , from _____ owner(s). The term of this agreement is month to month with a minimum term of _____ months starting and continuing until terminated by either party as provided in this agreement. If tenant vacates prior to the minimum term for any reason, tenant agrees to be responsible for payment of a rerental fee of $ _____ that will be due to cover the cost of obtaining a new tenant.

The discount rental rate is $ _____ per month when paid by the _____ of the month, which is the rent due date. The normal rent if paid after the _____ day of the month is $ _____ . In the event the rent is received more than _____ days after the rent due date, there is an additional late fee. The late fee is either a flat amount of $ _____ or a per-day late fee assessed of $ _____ per day.

A security deposit of $ _____ is also required. This deposit is refundable to the tenant at the end of the rental agreement, as long as the garage/shed is returned in the same condition it was given and the tenant is not in default. Either party must give the other a written notice at least 30 days prior to the end of any rental month, if either desires to end the agreement.

Tenant agrees to the following terms:

1. In the event a check bounces, a fee of $ _____ shall be due immediately.
2. Tenant agrees to provide his or her own lock or security measures. Owner is not responsible for any security.
3. Tenant agrees to carry insurance on belongings in the garage. Owner is not liable for any loss or damage to items stored in the garage or storage facility.
4. Tenant shall not store any hazardous, explosive, inflammable, illegal, or combustible materials in the facility.
5. Tenant shall not keep any pets or animals in the facility.
6. Tenant is responsible for keeping facility and surrounding area clean and free from oil and grease.
7. Owner has the right to enter the storage space for periodic inspections.
8. Tenant shall make no alterations to the storage space without written consent of the owner.
9. Owner is not responsible for snow removal.
10. Tenant agrees not to disturb or create conflict with tenants or neighbors who may be living on or near the premises adjacent to the facility. Loud noises are not permitted in and around the premises.
11. No doorways or walkways are to be blocked at any time, and no unmovable items may be left outside of the facility or on the common driveway or parking areas. No car parts to be stored outside of the garage.
12. Any items left outside, including a nonoperative vehicle, will be removed at the tenant's expense, if left unattended for more than three days. No car repair or painting is permitted on the premises.
13. No business of any kind is to be operated on the premises without written permission of the owner. Tenant shall not assign or sublet the storage space.
14. Unless otherwise agreed in writing, tenant is responsible for upkeep and minor repairs of the facility.
15. In the event the premises are damaged by fire or other casualty, and rendered unusable, either party may cancel this agreement.
16. In the event the tenant fails to pay rent due under this agreement, or in any other way breaches this agreement, this agreement is terminated and if state law permits the landlord may deny the tenant access to the facility and remove any property (at the tenant's expense) belonging to the tenant. In addition, for any unpaid rent or damages, landlord shall have the right to sell the property at public or private sale to recoup any losses.

I acknowledge that I have read and understand this agreement and have been given a copy on this date. _____ .

Tenant(s) Signature:_____ Date: _____

Owner/Manager Signature: _____ Date: _____

NONAPPARENT DISCLOSURE

Address: _____

City: _____ State: _____ Zip: _____

Dear _____,

This notice is to inform you that the property you are applying for at the above address has a unique set of conditions related to it that are not readily apparent. These conditions, in no way, take away from the safety of the building, but at times could require either adjustments on your part or a reduction in the enjoyment of the dwelling.

The following conditions may exist during your tenancy:

_____

_____

_____

Though this may seem very minor, we feel it is our responsibility to notify you of everything related to the rental dwelling so you will be fully informed in making a decision about your next residence. So often landlords will hide conditions from you until after you sign the lease and move in. We do all we can to be straightforward with you and we expect the same in return. That is the best way to have a good business relationship.

Sincerely,

Rental Manager

PARKING AGREEMENT

Date: _____

Car Description: Make: _____

Model: _____

Year: _____ Color: _____

Plate #: _____

License #: _____

State issued: _____

Parking Address: _____

Rental Period From: _____ To: _____

Rate per Month or Biweekly (circle one): _____

****

A month's rent, a month's security, and the last month's rent was received. A penalty of _____ per month will apply for each payment received after the first of each month. Rent is due on the _____ of the preceding month. If the tenant breaks the lease at any time before the lease expires, the two-month security will be forfeited. The tenant must notify the landlord in writing 90 days before lease expires of the intention to vacate or renew lease. Failure to do so will be considered a breach of contract and results in forfeiture of all security deposits.

****

Authorization to Verify All Information

I, _____ , hereby authorize the landlord or his authorized agents to verify all the above information, including but not limited to obtaining a credit report.

I also agree to reimburse the fee to obtain a credit report on myself and/or other applicants at _____ per person.

Resident's name: _____ Date of birth: _____

Tenant's phone: Business: _____ Home: _____

Tenant's Address if different than parking address: _____

Please forward your checks to the following address before the _____ of each preceding month:

Resident's Signature: _____ Date: _____

Owner/Manager's Signature: _____ Date: _____

CRIME/DRUG FREE ADDENDUM

In consideration of the execution or renewal of a lease of the premises at the following address_____, Owner and Resident agree as follows:

1. Resident any other member of Resident's household or guest, or other person under Resident's control, shall not engage in criminal activity, including drug-related criminal activity, on or near the said premises. "Drug-related activity" means the illegal manufacture, sale, distribution, use, or possession with the intent to manufacture, sell, distribute, or use a controlled substance.

2. Resident, any member of Resident's household or a guest, or other person under Resident's control, shall not engage in any act intended to facilitate criminal activity, including drug-related criminal activity on or near the said premises.

3. Resident or members of the household will not permit the dwelling unit to be used for or to facilitate criminal activity, including drug-related criminal activity, regardless of whether the individual engaging in such activity is a member of the household or a guest.

4. Resident, any member of Resident's household or a guest, or another person under Resident's control, shall not engage in the unlawful manufacturing, selling, using, storing, keeping, or giving of a controlled substance at any location, whether on or near the dwelling unit, premises, or otherwise.

5. Resident, any member of Resident's household, or a guest or another person under Resident's control, shall not engage in any illegal activity, including prostitution, criminal street gang activity, threatening or intimidating, battery, including but not limited to the unlawful discharge of firearms on or near the dwelling unit premises, or any breach of the lease agreement that jeopardizes the health, safety, and welfare of the landlord, his agent, or other tenants, or involving imminent or actual serious property damage.

6. **Violation of the above provisions shall be a material and irreparable violation of the lease and good cause for termination of tenancy**. A single violation of any provision of the added addendum shall be deemed a serious violation and a material and irreparable noncompliance. It is understood that a single violation shall be good cause for immediate termination of the lease. Unless otherwise provided by law, proof of violation shall not require criminal conviction, but shall be by a preponderance of the evidence.

7. In case of conflict between provisions of this addendum and other provisions of the lease, the provisions of the addendum shall govern.

8. This LEASE ADDENDUM is incorporated into the lease executed or renewed this day between Owner and Resident(s).

Resident's Signature: _____   Date: _____

Resident's Signature: _____   Date: _____

Owner/Manager's Signature: _____   Date: _____

SMOKE FREE ADDENDUM

Date:_____

To:_____

Re:_____

City_____ State _____Zip _____

Due to the increased possibility of smoke-related damage to the property, beyond normal wear and tear due to smoking, and the increased risk of fire, **smoking is prohibited in and around any area of the home or apartment** located at the above address. This "no smoking" policy applies to all residents and guests.

For clarity of this agreement, the term **No Smoking** means not inhaling, exhaling, burning, nor carrying any lighted cigar, cigarette, or other tobacco product (or any other "lighted" item or substance) in any manner or in any form.

Resident acknowledges that this no smoking policy and Smoke Free Addendum is made part of the lease or month-to-month agreement and agrees that he or she will not smoke in any room or area of the property, nor around the outer perimeter of the premises. In addition, Resident further understands that he or she will be responsible for enforcing this policy with all relatives and guests who visit the premises. If Resident fails to abide by this policy, he or she understands that Resident's tenancy may be subject to immediate termination.

Receipt of Copy Acknowledged: Residents hereby acknowledge that they have read and understand that this addendum is incorporated into and made part of the lease.

Residents understand it, agree to it, and have been given a copy.

Resident's Signature: _____ Date: _____

Resident's Signature: _____ Date: _____

Owner/Manager's Signature: _____ Date: _____

OIL AGREEMENT

Address: _____

City:_____ State: _____ Zip: _____

This agreement is between _____,Resident, and

_____ Owner/Management, regarding the oil tank located at the above stated

address. Both parties agree that the oil tank was measured on the following date, _____, prior to or

within three days after resident took occupancy of dwelling. The measurement indicated that the approximate

amount of oil in the tank was _____ gallons. The measurement also represents that the amount of oil in the

tank was approximately _____/_____ full. Resident understands Resident is responsible for refilling the tank and

agrees not to let the level of oil drop below _____ gallons or _____/_____ full at any time. If Resident fails to keep

oil level above this amount or level and as a result damage occurs, Resident understands he or she will be obligated

to immediately pay for damages and repair.

At the end of the rental term, Resident agrees to leave a minimum of_____ gallons of oil in the tank, or must be

filled (at resident's expense) to at least the same level as original measurements. A second measurement will be taken

within three days of Resident vacating and before the security deposit is returned. Resident is to pay for any shortage

of the minimum oil requirement.

Date of oil initial tank measurement: _____ By: _____

Resident's Signature: _____ Date: _____

Resident's Signature: _____ Date: _____

Owner/Manager's Signature: _____ Date: _____

WATERBED AGREEMENT

The following Resident(s), _____ , wishes to have a waterbed at the following address: _____ . This addendum becomes part of the Rental Agreement dated _____ between stated Resident and _____ , Owner. Because this agrment specifically prohibits keeping waterbeds without Owner's permission, Residents agree to the following terms and conditions in exchange for permission to have waterbed on premises:

1. **Additional Deposit.** In consideration of the additional risks involved in waterbed installation, Resident agrees to pay additional deposit of $ _____ . At the end of the rental term, Owner will inspect the property for any damages that were caused by the waterbed and deduct from said deposit any monies needed for repairing and or cleaning of floors or floor covering and any other related waterbed damages. Resident agrees to pay promptly for any damages exceeding the amount of the deposit on hand.

2. **Waterbed Specifications.** Resident agrees to keep one waterbed approved by Owners for the dwelling. The waterbed shall consist of a mattress with the following minimum specifications: _____ _____ , which meets the Waterbed Manufacturers' Association standards.

3. **Installation.** Resident agrees to allow Owner to inspect the waterbed installation at any and all reasonable times, and Resident agrees to remedy any problems or potential problems immediately. Money will not be deducted from deposit, but instead be paid by Resident. Any money due related to waterbed damages or problems will be immediately considered as additional rent due and grounds for termination of the rental agreement if not paid.

4. **Location.** Resident agrees to consult with the Owner about the location of the waterbed. Resident agrees to hire qualified professionals to install and dismantle the bed according to the manufacturer's specifications and further agree not to relocate it without the Owner's consent.

5. **Insurance.** Resident agrees to furnish Owner with a copy of a valid certificate of waterbed liability insurance policy for at least $100,000 covering the waterbed installation. Resident also agrees to keep the insurance policy in force at all times and to renew the policy as necessary for continuous coverage and provide a copy of the renewal policy to Owner.

6. **Breach of the Agreement.** Resident agrees to not damage the waterbed or allow a guest to do the same and agrees to become personally liable for any and all damages should damage occur. Resident agrees to pay immediately for any damage caused by the waterbed and, in addition, will add $ _____ to the security deposit, any of which may be used for cleaning, repairs, or delinquent rent when Residents vacate. This added deposit, or what remains of it when waterbed damages have been assessed, will be returned to Resident within _____ days after Resident vacates the property. Failure to comply with any of the terms of this agreement allows Owner to exercise the right to revoke this permission to keep a waterbed, should Resident break this agreement

Resident's Signature: _____ Date: _____

Resident's Signature: _____ Date: _____

Owner/Manager's Signature: _____ Date: _____

MOLD ADDENDUM

Date:_____

To:_____

_____

_____

The presence of mold can create health ailments and/or hazards for you or other occupants or guests visiting the leased premises. We therefore request that residents be responsible for preventing mold growth in your property, and not create or ignore conditions that can lead to mold growth. This can be done in several ways as outlined below. Resident agrees to be responsible for the following terms in regard to maintenance of their leased premises and mold prevention. This addendum becomes part of, or is incorporated into, the rental agreement. Failure to comply with any of the items listed is a violation of the rental agreement, grounds for eviction, and the resident may be held liable for any damages resulting from your failure to comply. Thank you for your cooperation.

1. Resident is responsible to report (in writing) any water or plumbing problems to the owner or manager.

2. Resident is responsible to remove any excess or accumulation of moisture (which mold needs to grow). This responsibility includes not allowing any standing water to remain present in the interior of the premises. Also to report any standing water in common areas (if applicable).

3. Because mold also needs a food source to grow, the resident is responsible for keeping his or her property clean (especially kitchen area) and free of food sources which may allow mold to grow.

4. Resident is responsible for keeping the humidity and climate in the leased premises at reasonable levels. In addition, resident is responsible to report the malfunction of any heating, air-conditioning, or ventilation system that can affect the humidity or climate levels.

5. Resident is responsible to regularly allow air to circulate within the home by regularly opening windows and using bathroom or ceiling fans where available.

6. Resident is responsible for removal of mold growth on the property.

7. Resident is responsible for reporting, in writing, any mold growth on the premises that they are not able to clean or remove. The owner or manager reserves the right and the option to hire someone to remove mold growth and to bill the resident for the expense.

8. Resident understands that, other than emergency situations, the owner or manger may not enter your home without your express permission, and therefore relies upon occupants to keep the interior of the property clean and free of mold or notify management of any problems.

Resident has read, understands, and agrees to all terms in this agreement.

Resident's Signature: _____ Date: _____

Resident's Signature: _____ Date: _____

Owner/Manager's Signature: _____ Date: _____

WATER SOFTENER ADDENDUM

This agreement is entered into this _____ day of _____ between Owner/Management _____, and Residents _____ as an addendum and made part of the lease/agreement for the property you are renting, located at _____.

We are pleased to inform you that the property is equipped with a water softener, which you will be able to benefit from. It is located in the _____. We do, however, need you to be responsible for monitoring its operation and its proper upkeep. It is therefore agreed that residents will check the level of salt in the softener tank at least every _____ months to be sure that the tank is at least half filled with salt. It is also agreed that residents will keep the tank adequately filled with salt at all times at the residents' expense. Residents understand that the tank will be filled to the top with salt at the start of lease, or as of this date _____, of which the owner/resident shall furnish this.

If the water softener is found less than half filled with salt during quarterly inspections, residents understand that they will be billed for every bag of salt that management has to bring and pour to bring the level back up to half full, and they will be billed a service fee. Residents understand that it is in both the residents' and owner's best interest to have the water softener doing its job of softening the water through the house at all times. It extends the life of the pipes and creates fewer plumbing problems in general. It also minimizes cleaning in the home as there is no mineral deposit build-up. Residents agree to immediately notify owner/management by telephone should water softener appear to be malfunctioning.

Resident's Signature: _____ Date: _____

Resident's Signature: _____ Date: _____

Owner/Manager's Signature: _____ Date: _____

SWIMMING POOL/HOT TUB/SPA ADDENDUM

This addendum becomes part of the rental agreement for the property known as/located at:
_____, between the Owner/Management_____
and Resident(s)_____.

Resident___ Landlord/Manager ___ will arrange for pool opening and closing, including bearing the costs of any related service and all chemicals and supplies needed. If arranged by resident, service must be performed by a landlord-approved vendor and proof of receipt is required upon completion of service.

Resident agrees not to open pool prior to the following date, _____ and agrees to close the pool by or before _____.

Resident agrees to be responsible for normal maintenance on the pool/tub/spa, to include the purchase of chemicals, supplies, and other equipment necessary for normal use. This includes obtaining, at the resident's expense, testing and periodically checking water for proper balance and maintaining appropriate water quality and chemical balance/levels. The owner/management assumes no responsibility for improper concentrations or use of pool/tub/spa chemicals.

Resident is required to maintain renter's liability insurance for the entire term of the lease with a minimum coverage of _____ and agrees to name the landlord (and management company, if applicable) as an additional insured party.

Resident agrees to use ordinary and reasonable care and caution in the use of the pool/tub/spa equipment and agrees to maintain all utilities and services necessary for normal maintenance of the pool.

Resident is responsible to immediately notify and report any problems or functional discrepancy with the pool/tub/spa to owner or management.

It is agreed that all minor repairs and upkeep to the pool/tub/spa shall be the responsibility of the resident. All major repairs shall be the responsibility of the landlord, except when such repairs are due to negligence, nonreporting of problems, misuse or any damage to the pool and/or hot tub caused by the resident or resident's guests, including but not limited to: broken glass, sharp objects or other items introduced into the pool, contamination of the water, damage to the filter or other related equipment. In such cases, repairs will result in charges to the resident, who will bear any and all costs for correction of any cosmetic or functional discrepancies.

If pool is equipped with a heating system of some kind, please note that this is not guaranteed to sustain any constant temperature due to uncontrollable circumstances of nature including but not limited to weather, fungus or algae caused by varying temperatures, or excessive use or contamination of the water by residents or guests and the owners or management are not responsible for compensation of lost use.

Resident agrees to be responsible for the security of the pool/tub/spa and the safety of their guests. Access to the pool/tub/spa is under the control of the resident and access shall be limited through the use of locks, covers, and other appropriate/necessary means as required by local jurisdictions when not in use. All access to pool/tub/spa area shall be secured when resident intends to be away for more than 24 hours.

Resident agrees to properly store, maintain, and protect any pool cover or other equipment provided, and agrees to be responsible for upkeep and return in the same condition at end of the rental term.

The landlord/management (or a representative) reserves the right to have access to the property (with proper notice) to monitor the condition and upkeep of the pool/tub/spa.

I have read, understand, and agree to the terms of this agreement.   Date:_____

Resident's Signature: _____   Resident's Signature _____

Owner/Manager's Signature: _____   Date: _____

MILITARY ADDENDUM

We recognize the tremendous contributions given by those who serve in our armed forces. We realize that military orders may require military personnel and/or their family to move, and we are glad to work with all rental residents who are active in the military, should that become necessary. According to the Soldiers and Sailor's Civil Right Act of 1940, residents who are currently active in military service or who enter military service after signing a rental agreement or lease have a federally legislated right to be able to terminate their agreement provided certain conditions are met. Management requires that steps are taken as outlined below and that the resident agrees to the following terms:

1. Residents must mail written notice of their intent to terminate their tenancy for verifiable military reasons to the landlord or manager.

2. The termination notice must give the exact date of when resident plans to move out.

3. Once a notice of intent to move is mailed or delivered, the tenancy will terminate 30 days after the next rent due date. This means that if the next rent due date is March 1st, and the resident mails a notice on February 25, the tenancy will terminate on April 1st (30 days after March 1st).

4. Mail any notice or communication to the landlord or manager at the following address:

   _____ .

5. The owner may show the premises to any prospective resident any time during the following hours: _____ . If the resident can't be reached after the owner or manager has made a good-faith effort to do so, owner or manager may enter and show the rental.

6. Promptly return the keys to the owner and completely move and vacate the premises on or before the date stated in your termination notice.

7. Leave the rental in a clean condition and free of any and all damages.

8. Provide a forwarding address to the owner prior to vacating the rental, so that the security deposit can be returned, provided that the resident has complied with the above terms, that there are no unpaid outstanding charges of any kind due from the resident, and that there are no damages to the property.

Resident's Signature: _____ Date: _____

Owner/Manager's Signature: _____ Date: _____

LEASE ADDENDUM
RESIDENT GRIEVANCE AND APPEAL PROCEDURE

Do You Have a Complaint?
You have the right to file a GRIEVANCE and to APPEAL almost any adverse action we take against you. The purpose of this grievance and appeal procedure is to make sure all of our residents are treated fairly, while at the same time allowing us to maintain and safeguard our home and apartments.

When Can You File a Grievance?
You can file a grievance if we fail to act in accordance with your lease, or local housing regulations, and, as a result, you don't get all the benefits you are entitled to. This might include:

1. A refusal or failure to make repairs
2. A disputed bill for damages we feel you, your family, or your visitors caused
3. A false report that you are in violation of your lease
4. Failure to compensate you for harm or damages done to you

The grievance procedure DOES NOT apply to:

1. Eviction notices (However you can contest these in court and may wish to talk to an attorney before moving.)
2. Disputes between tenants

How Does the Grievance Procedure Begin?
It begins when you present your complaint to the owner or manager. This must be done within 10 days after your complaint arose or you received notice from us that you feel is in error. Please put your complaint in writing and keep a copy of it. We will meet with you within five working days of your request to try to work things out. In almost all cases we should be able to resolve your concern.

What if I Still Disagree with the Decision?
You can ask for a hearing before a neutral mediation panel. This must be done in writing, no more than 10 days after you get the summary of our meeting. You should state why you are asking for a hearing and what you want done. The hearing officer or panel will meet with all of us and has the power to reverse our decision. We will send you a written summary of our meeting no later than 10 days after we meet.

Who Will Choose the Hearing Officer or Panel?
Two options: The first option is we use a third-party mediation service helpful in deciding disputes with landlords and residents. The following company provides service _____. Or we can select a mediation panel more informally. Each of us select a person to serve on a panel, and the two selected then choose a third and all three hear the case. The mediation panel must be willing to listen to both sides and cannot be paid. They must also write down their decision and the reasons for their decision. If we can't agree on an informal panel, the mediation service will be used.

What Are My Rights at the Hearing?
1. You have the right to examine all relevant documents, records, and regulations BEFORE the hearing.
2. You have the right to present evidence at the hearing and to question all available witnesses, if applicable.

When Will I Get a Decision?
You will receive a written decision within 10 days after the hearing. It must set out the reasons for the decision and be based solely on the facts presented at the hearing. This decision is binding unless the local housing office determines it is contrary to their regulations. If the decision is found in favor of the resident, the resident will be entitled to full reimbursement for any expenses or damages incurred, plus up to three months' worth of rent, depending on the seriousness of the situation.

What If I Still Do Not Agree with the Decision?
At this point you may then wish to talk to an attorney, after first going through the above steps. However, management will do everything it can to treat all residents fairly so this final step will not be necessary.

Thank you for your cooperation in helping us to resolve this matter to your satisfaction.

Rental Manager

DISCLOSURE OF INFORMATION OF LEAD-BASED PAINT OR LEAD-BASED PAINT HAZARDS

As appropriate, this disclosure is provided to:

_____ A current tenant.

_____ An applicant prior to signing a rental agreement.

Lead Warning Statement

Housing built prior to 1978 ***may*** contain lead-based paint. Lead from paint, paint chips, and dust can pose health hazards if not managed properly. Lead exposure is especially harmful to young children and pregnant women. Before renting pre-1978 housing, landlords must disclose the presence of known lead-based paint and/or lead-based paint hazards in the dwelling. Tenants must also receive a federally approved pamphlet on lead poisoning prevention.

1. **Lessor's Disclosure**—initial (a), (1) or (2); and initial (b), (1) or (2)
   (a) Presence of lead-based paint and/or lead-based paint hazards. (initial one)
   _____ (1) Known lead-based paint and/or lead-based paint hazards are present in the housing.
   Explain: _____
   _____ (2) Lessor has no knowledge of lead-based paint and/or lead-based paint hazards in the housing.
   (b) Records and reports available to the tenant. (initial one)
   _____ (1) Lessor has provided the tenant with all available records and reports pertaining to lead-based paint and/or lead-based paint hazard in the housing. (list below):
   _____
   _____ (2) Lessor has no knowledge of lead-based paint and/or lead-based paint hazards in the housing.

2. **Lessee's Acknowledgement**—initial
   _____ (c) Lessee has received copies of all information above; AND
   _____ (d) Lessee has received the pamphlet "Protect Your Family from Lead in the Home."

3. **Agent's Acknowledgement** (initial)
   _____ (e) Agent has informed the lessor of the lessor's obligation under 42 U.S.C. 4582(d) and is aware of his/her responsibility to ensure compliance.

4. **Certification of Accuracy**
   The following parties have reviewed the information above and certify, to the best of their knowledge, the information they have provided is true and correct.

Lessee	Date	Lessee	Date
Lessor	Date	Lessor	Date
Agent	Date	Agent	Date

Protect Your Family From Lead In Your Home

 EPA United States Environmental Protection Agency

United States Consumer Product Safety Commission

 United States Department of Housing and Urban Development

Are You Planning To Buy, Rent, or Renovate a Home Built Before 1978?

Many houses and apartments built before 1978 have paint that contains high levels of lead (called lead-based paint). Lead from paint, chips, and dust can pose serious health hazards if not taken care of properly.

OWNERS, BUYERS, and RENTERS are encouraged to check for lead (see page 6) before renting, buying or renovating pre-1978 housing.

Federal law requires that individuals receive certain information before renting, buying, or renovating pre-1978 housing:

LANDLORDS have to disclose known information on lead-based paint and lead-based paint hazards before leases take effect. Leases must include a disclosure about lead-based paint.

SELLERS have to disclose known information on lead-based paint and lead-based paint hazards before selling a house. Sales contracts must include a disclosure about lead-based paint. Buyers have up to 10 days to check for lead.

RENOVATORS disturbing more than 2 square feet of painted surfaces have to give you this pamphlet before starting work.

IMPORTANT!

Lead From Paint, Dust, and Soil Can Be Dangerous If Not Managed Properly

FACT: Lead exposure can harm young children and babies even before they are born.

FACT: Even children who seem healthy can have high levels of lead in their bodies.

FACT: People can get lead in their bodies by breathing or swallowing lead dust, or by eating soil or paint chips containing lead.

FACT: People have many options for reducing lead hazards. In most cases, lead-based paint that is in good condition is not a hazard.

FACT: Removing lead-based paint improperly can increase the danger to your family.

If you think your home might have lead hazards, read this pamphlet to learn some simple steps to protect your family.

1

Lead Gets in the Body in Many Ways

Childhood lead poisoning remains a major environmental health problem in the U.S.

Even children who appear healthy can have dangerous levels of lead in their bodies.

People can get lead in their body if they:

◆ Breathe in lead dust (especially during renovations that disturb painted surfaces).

◆ Put their hands or other objects covered with lead dust in their mouths.

◆ Eat paint chips or soil that contains lead.

Lead is even more dangerous to children under the age of 6:

◆ At this age children's brains and nervous systems are more sensitive to the damaging effects of lead.

◆ Children's growing bodies absorb more lead.

◆ Babies and young children often put their hands and other objects in their mouths. These objects can have lead dust on them.

Lead is also dangerous to women of childbearing age:

◆ Women with a high lead level in their system prior to pregnancy would expose a fetus to lead through the placenta during fetal development.

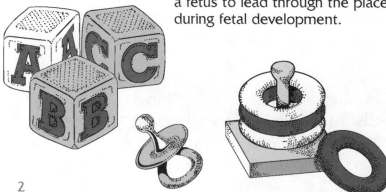

2

Lead's Effects

It is important to know that even exposure to low levels of lead can severely harm children.

In children, lead can cause:

◆ Nervous system and kidney damage.

◆ Learning disabilities, attention deficit disorder, and decreased intelligence.

◆ Speech, language, and behavior problems.

◆ Poor muscle coordination.

◆ Decreased muscle and bone growth.

◆ Hearing damage.

While low-lead exposure is most common, exposure to high levels of lead can have devastating effects on children, including seizures, unconsciousness, and, in some cases, death.

Although children are especially susceptible to lead exposure, lead can be dangerous for adults too.

In adults, lead can cause:

◆ Increased chance of illness during pregnancy.

◆ Harm to a fetus, including brain damage or death.

◆ Fertility problems (in men and women).

◆ High blood pressure.

◆ Digestive problems.

◆ Nerve disorders.

◆ Memory and concentration problems.

◆ Muscle and joint pain.

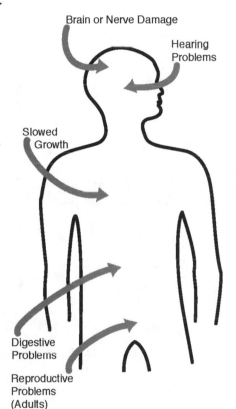

Brain or Nerve Damage

Hearing Problems

Slowed Growth

Digestive Problems

Reproductive Problems (Adults)

Lead affects the body in many ways.

3

Where Lead-Based Paint Is Found

In general, the older your home, the more likely it has lead-based paint.

Many homes built before 1978 have lead-based paint. The federal government banned lead-based paint from housing in 1978. Some states stopped its use even earlier. Lead can be found:

◆ In homes in the city, country, or suburbs.

◆ In apartments, single-family homes, and both private and public housing.

◆ Inside and outside of the house.

◆ In soil around a home. (Soil can pick up lead from exterior paint or other sources such as past use of leaded gas in cars.)

Checking Your Family for Lead

Get your children and home tested if you think your home has high levels of lead.

To reduce your child's exposure to lead, get your child checked, have your home tested (especially if your home has paint in poor condition and was built before 1978), and fix any hazards you may have. Children's blood lead levels tend to increase rapidly from 6 to 12 months of age, and tend to peak at 18 to 24 months of age.

Consult your doctor for advice on testing your children. A simple blood test can detect high levels of lead. Blood tests are usually recommended for:

◆ Children at ages 1 and 2.

◆ Children or other family members who have been exposed to high levels of lead.

◆ Children who should be tested under your state or local health screening plan.

Your doctor can explain what the test results mean and if more testing will be needed.

4

Identifying Lead Hazards

Lead-based paint is usually not a hazard if it is in good condition, and it is not on an impact or friction surface, like a window. It is defined by the federal government as paint with lead levels greater than or equal to 1.0 milligram per square centimeter, or more than 0.5% by weight.

Deteriorating lead-based paint (peeling, chipping, chalking, cracking or damaged) is a hazard and needs immediate attention. It may also be a hazard when found on surfaces that children can chew or that get a lot of wear-and-tear, such as:

◆ Windows and window sills.

◆ Doors and door frames.

◆ Stairs, railings, banisters, and porches.

Lead from paint chips, which you can see, and lead dust, which you can't always see, can both be serious hazards.

Lead dust can form when lead-based paint is scraped, sanded, or heated. Dust also forms when painted surfaces bump or rub together. Lead chips and dust can get on surfaces and objects that people touch. Settled lead dust can re-enter the air when people vacuum, sweep, or walk through it. The following two federal standards have been set for lead hazards in dust:

◆ 40 micrograms per square foot ($\mu g/ft^2$) and higher for floors, including carpeted floors.

◆ 250 $\mu g/ft^2$ and higher for interior window sills.

Lead in soil can be a hazard when children play in bare soil or when people bring soil into the house on their shoes. The following two federal standards have been set for lead hazards in residential soil:

◆ 400 parts per million (ppm) and higher in play areas of bare soil.

◆ 1,200 ppm (average) and higher in bare soil in the remainder of the yard.

The only way to find out if paint, dust and soil lead hazards exist is to test for them. The next page describes the most common methods used.

5

Checking Your Home for Lead

Just knowing that a home has lead-based paint may not tell you if there is a hazard.

You can get your home tested for lead in several different ways:

◆ A paint **inspection** tells you whether your home has lead-based paint and where it is located. It won't tell you whether or not your home currently has lead hazards.

◆ A **risk assessment** tells you if your home currently has any lead hazards from lead in paint, dust, or soil. It also tells you what actions to take to address any hazards.

◆ A combination risk assessment and inspection tells you if your home has any lead hazards and if your home has any lead-based paint, and where the lead-based paint is located.

Hire a trained and certified testing professional who will use a range of reliable methods when testing your home.

◆ Visual inspection of paint condition and location.

◆ A portable x-ray fluorescence (XRF) machine.

◆ Lab tests of paint, dust, and soil samples.

There are state and federal programs in place to ensure that testing is done safely, reliably, and effectively. Contact your state or local agency (see bottom of page 11) for more information, or call **1-800-424-LEAD (5323)** for a list of contacts in your area.

Home test kits for lead are available, but may not always be accurate. Consumers should not rely on these kits before doing renovations or to assure safety.

6

What You Can Do Now To Protect Your Family

If you suspect that your house has lead hazards, you can take some immediate steps to reduce your family's risk:

◆ **If you rent, notify your landlord of peeling or chipping paint.**

◆ **Clean up paint chips immediately.**

◆ **Clean floors, window frames, window sills, and other surfaces weekly**. Use a mop or sponge with warm water and a general all-purpose cleaner or a cleaner made specifically for lead. REMEMBER: NEVER MIX AMMONIA AND BLEACH PRODUCTS TOGETHER SINCE THEY CAN FORM A DANGEROUS GAS.

◆ **Thoroughly rinse sponges and mop heads after cleaning dirty or dusty areas**.

◆ **Wash children's hands often, especially before they eat and before nap time and bed time.**

◆ **Keep play areas clean.** Wash bottles, pacifiers, toys, and stuffed animals regularly.

◆ **Keep children from chewing window sills or other painted surfaces.**

◆ **Clean or remove shoes before entering your home to avoid tracking in lead from soil.**

◆ **Make sure children eat nutritious, low-fat meals high in iron and calcium,** such as spinach and dairy products. Children with good diets absorb less lead.

7

Reducing Lead Hazards In The Home

Removing lead improperly can increase the hazard to your family by spreading even more lead dust around the house.

Always use a professional who is trained to remove lead hazards safely.

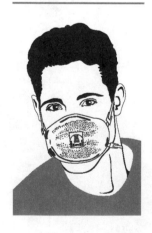

In addition to day-to-day cleaning and good nutrition:

◆ You can **temporarily** reduce lead hazards by taking actions such as repairing damaged painted surfaces and planting grass to cover soil with high lead levels. These actions (called "interim controls") are not permanent solutions and will need ongoing attention.

◆ To **permanently** remove lead hazards, you should hire a certified lead "abatement" contractor. Abatement (or permanent hazard elimination) methods include removing, sealing, or enclosing lead-based paint with special materials. Just painting over the hazard with regular paint is not permanent removal.

Always hire a person with special training for correcting lead problems—someone who knows how to do this work safely and has the proper equipment to clean up thoroughly. Certified contractors will employ qualified workers and follow strict safety rules as set by their state or by the federal government.

Once the work is completed, dust cleanup activities must be repeated until testing indicates that lead dust levels are below the following:

◆ 40 micrograms per square foot ($\mu g/ft^2$) for floors, including carpeted floors;

◆ 250 $\mu g/ft^2$ for interior windows sills; and

◆ 400 $\mu g/ft^2$ for window troughs.

Call your state or local agency (see bottom of page 11) for help in locating certified professionals in your area and to see if financial assistance is available.

8

Remodeling or Renovating a Home With Lead-Based Paint

Take precautions before your contractor or you begin remodeling or renovating anything that disturbs painted surfaces (such as scraping off paint or tearing out walls):

◆ **Have the area tested for lead-based paint.**

◆ **Do not use a belt-sander, propane torch, high temperature heat gun, dry scraper, or dry sandpaper** to remove lead-based paint. These actions create large amounts of lead dust and fumes. Lead dust can remain in your home long after the work is done.

◆ **Temporarily move your family** (especially children and pregnant women) out of the apartment or house until the work is done and the area is properly cleaned. If you can't move your family, at least completely seal off the work area.

If not conducted properly, certain types of renovations can release lead from paint and dust into the air.

◆ **Follow other safety measures to reduce lead hazards.** You can find out about other safety measures by calling 1-800-424-LEAD. Ask for the brochure "Reducing Lead Hazards When Remodeling Your Home." This brochure explains what to do before, during, and after renovations.

If you have already completed renovations or remodeling that could have released lead-based paint or dust, get your young children tested and follow the steps outlined on page 7 of this brochure.

9

Other Sources of Lead

While paint, dust, and soil are the most common sources of lead, other lead sources also exist.

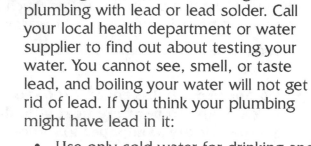

◆ **Drinking water.** Your home might have plumbing with lead or lead solder. Call your local health department or water supplier to find out about testing your water. You cannot see, smell, or taste lead, and boiling your water will not get rid of lead. If you think your plumbing might have lead in it:

- Use only cold water for drinking and cooking.

- Run water for 15 to 30 seconds before drinking it, especially if you have not used your water for a few hours.

◆ **The job.** If you work with lead, you could bring it home on your hands or clothes. Shower and change clothes before coming home. Launder your work clothes separately from the rest of your family's clothes.

◆ Old painted **toys** and **furniture.**

◆ Food and liquids stored in **lead crystal** or **lead-glazed pottery or porcelain.**

◆ **Lead smelters** or other industries that release lead into the air.

◆ **Hobbies** that use lead, such as making pottery or stained glass, or refinishing furniture.

◆ **Folk remedies** that contain lead, such as "greta" and "azarcon" used to treat an upset stomach.

10

For More Information

The National Lead Information Center

Call **1-800-424-LEAD (424-5323)** to learn how to protect children from lead poisoning and for other information on lead hazards. To access lead information via the web, visit **www.epa.gov/lead** and **www.hud.gov/offices/lead/.**

EPA's Safe Drinking Water Hotline

Call **1-800-426-4791** for information about lead in drinking water.

Consumer Product Safety Commission (CPSC) Hotline

To request information on lead in consumer products, or to report an unsafe consumer product or a product-related injury call **1-800-638-2772**, or visit CPSC's Web site at: **www.cpsc.gov.**

Health and Environmental Agencies

Some cities, states, and tribes have their own rules for lead-based paint activities. Check with your local agency to see which laws apply to you. Most agencies can also provide information on finding a lead abatement firm in your area, and on possible sources of financial aid for reducing lead hazards. Receive up-to-date address and phone information for your local contacts on the Internet at **www.epa.gov/lead** or contact the National Lead Information Center at **1-800-424-LEAD.**

For the hearing impaired, call the Federal Information Relay Service at **1-800-877-8339** to access any of the phone numbers in this brochure.

11

EPA Regional Offices

Your Regional EPA Office can provide further information regarding regulations and lead protection programs.

EPA Regional Offices

Region 1 (Connecticut, Massachusetts, Maine, New Hampshire, Rhode Island, Vermont)

> Regional Lead Contact
> U.S. EPA Region 1
> Suite 1100 (CPT)
> One Congress Street
> Boston, MA 02114-2023
> 1 (888) 372-7341

Region 2 (New Jersey, New York, Puerto Rico, Virgin Islands)

> Regional Lead Contact
> U.S. EPA Region 2
> 2890 Woodbridge Avenue
> Building 209, Mail Stop 225
> Edison, NJ 08837-3679
> (732) 321-6671

Region 3 (Delaware, Maryland, Pennsylvania, Virginia, Washington DC, West Virginia)

> Regional Lead Contact
> U.S. EPA Region 3 (3WC33)
> 1650 Arch Street
> Philadelphia, PA 19103
> (215) 814-5000

Region 4 (Alabama, Florida, Georgia, Kentucky, Mississippi, North Carolina, South Carolina, Tennessee)

> Regional Lead Contact
> U.S. EPA Region 4
> 61 Forsyth Street, SW
> Atlanta, GA 30303
> (404) 562-8998

Region 5 (Illinois, Indiana, Michigan, Minnesota, Ohio, Wisconsin)

> Regional Lead Contact
> U.S. EPA Region 5 (DT-8J)
> 77 West Jackson Boulevard
> Chicago, IL 60604-3666
> (312) 886-6003

Region 6 (Arkansas, Louisiana, New Mexico, Oklahoma, Texas)

> Regional Lead Contact
> U.S. EPA Region 6
> 1445 Ross Avenue, 12th Floor
> Dallas, TX 75202-2733
> (214) 665-7577

Region 7 (Iowa, Kansas, Missouri, Nebraska)

> Regional Lead Contact
> U.S. EPA Region 7
> (ARTD-RALI)
> 901 N. 5th Street
> Kansas City, KS 66101
> (913) 551-7020

Region 8 (Colorado, Montana, North Dakota, South Dakota, Utah, Wyoming)

> Regional Lead Contact
> U.S. EPA Region 8
> 999 18th Street, Suite 500
> Denver, CO 80202-2466
> (303) 312-6021

Region 9 (Arizona, California, Hawaii, Nevada)

> Regional Lead Contact
> U.S. Region 9
> 75 Hawthorne Street
> San Francisco, CA 94105
> (415) 947-4164

Region 10 (Alaska, Idaho, Oregon, Washington)

> Regional Lead Contact
> U.S. EPA Region 10
> Toxics Section WCM-128
> 1200 Sixth Avenue
> Seattle, WA 98101-1128
> (206) 553-1985

12

CPSC Regional Offices

Your Regional CPSC Office can provide further information regarding regulations and consumer product safety.

Eastern Regional Center
Consumer Product Safety Commission
201 Varick Street, Room 903
New York, NY 10014
(212) 620-4120

Western Regional Center
Consumer Product Safety Commission
1301 Clay Street, Suite 610-N
Oakland, CA 94612
(510) 637 4050

Central Regional Center
Consumer Product Safety Commission
230 South Dearborn Street, Room 2944
Chicago, IL 60604
(312) 353-8260

HUD Lead Office

Please contact HUD's Office of Healthy Homes and Lead Hazard Control for information on lead regulations, outreach efforts, and lead hazard control and research grant programs.

U.S. Department of Housing and Urban Development
Office of Healthy Homes and Lead Hazard Control
451 Seventh Street, SW, P-3206
Washington, DC 20410
(202) 755-1785

U.S. EPA Washington DC 20460
U.S. CPSC Washington DC 20207
U.S. HUD Washington DC 20410

EPA747-K-99-001
June 2003

13

Simple Steps To Protect Your Family From Lead Hazards

If you think your home has high levels of lead:

◆ Get your young children tested for lead, even if they seem healthy.

◆ Wash children's hands, bottles, pacifiers, and toys often.

◆ Make sure children eat healthy, low-fat foods.

◆ Get your home checked for lead hazards.

◆ Regularly clean floors, window sills, and other surfaces.

◆ Wipe soil off shoes before entering house.

◆ Talk to your landlord about fixing surfaces with peeling or chipping paint.

◆ Take precautions to avoid exposure to lead dust when remodeling or renovating (call 1-800-424-LEAD for guidelines).

◆ Don't use a belt-sander, propane torch, high temperature heat gun, scraper, or sandpaper on painted surfaces that may contain lead.

◆ Don't try to remove lead-based paint yourself.

 Recycled/Recyclable
Printed with vegetable oil based inks on recycled paper (minimum 50% postconsumer) process chlorine free.

RECEIPT OF NEW RESIDENT WELCOME FOLDER

I have received the Welcome New Resident Folder/Notebook with information regarding residence at:

_____

I understand that my New Resident Welcome Folder/Notebook includes the following:

_____ Rental Agreement

_____ Property Condition Checklist (and I have inspected rental home)

_____ House Rules

_____ Deposit Receipt/Addendum

_____ Notice of Accountability

_____ Emergency Numbers and Utilities Information

_____ Information regarding special Resident programs

_____ Maintenance/Property Upkeep Information (for example: yard upkeep, carpet cleaning, handling drain stoppages, changing air filters, maintenance guarantee, etc.)

_____ EPA Pamphlet for properties built before 1978 and the Lead Disclosure form (if applicable).

_____ Additional Addendum: _____

_____ Additional Addendum: _____

_____ Additional Addendum: _____

_____ Move-In Gift Certificate: _____

_____I have also completed the following tasks that were required before move-in:

_____ Utilities turned on _____   _____

_____ Other task _____

I also understand that the notebook should be left in the residence when I vacate, and that there is a $25 fee for not returning the notebook intact.

Date: _____

Resident Signature: _____

Resident Signature: _____

MOVE-IN CHECKLIST
(For owner/manager use)

Address: _____

City _____State _____ Zip _____

Resident: _____

Dates

Application filled out and fee collected   _____

Verification forms signed   _____

Credit check run   _____

Fee given to reserve rental   _____

Utilities turned on   _____   _____   _____

First month's rent collected (Amount?_____)   _____

Security deposit collected   (Amount?_____)   _____

Additional rent or deposit due? And, if so, collected (Amount?_____)   _____

Inspection of rental with property condition checklist   _____

Rental agreement signed and explained   _____

Keys issued   _____

House rules signed   _____

Additional agreements/addendums signed   _____

_____   _____

_____   _____

_____   _____

Welcome New Resident folder   _____

On-time payments emphasized/collection procedures   _____

Worry-free Auto Pay and Payday payment plans discussed   _____

Notice of accountability   _____

Office hours/maintenance request/repair policies explained   _____

Periodic inspections/Future Homebuyer program discussed   _____

Renter's insurance suggested/required   _____

If applicable, lead pamphlet and disclosure form given   _____

_____   _____

_____   _____

PART THREE

Collection and Violation Notices

Forms to Get Residents to Pay Money Due and Follow Your Rules

The vast majority of landlords think that if they find a good resident who's paying good (top market) rent, they've done all they need to do to have complete success. You have done well, because the average landlord has great difficulty getting both good residents and maximum rent. My goal for you is that you have not just partial, short-term success, but long-term landlording success, which means all of the following:

- Ideal residents
- Maximum income
- No management headaches (on-time rent payments and excellent property upkeep)

Doesn't that all sound good? Sure it does. And it is possible to obtain all three objectives. The following money-making management strategy focuses on the third objective.

WELCOME FUTURE HOMEBUYER

Most rental residents treat their dwellings like renters, not homebuyers. That's because rental residents think like renters in almost all cases. However, I've found it is to the landlord's advantage if residents think like future homebuyers. Residents who think like homebuyers:

- Take better care of property than average resident
- Pay rent on time and fulfill other obligations
- Handle minor repairs and needed maintenance
- Add upgrades and improvements

Therefore, from the very first month a rental resident moves in, one of my major management objectives is to change their mindset from renter to future homebuyer. In fact, my opening letter of introduction, or cover letter, to announce my rental policies starts off, "Welcome Future Homebuyer."

The process of changing a resident's mindset from renter to future homebuyer is not instantaneous, but can be gradual yet continual and very effective. Here's how I suggest you start the transformation.

■ *Tip Number* **24**

Offer residents an incentive for rental performance.

Welcome Future Homebuyer In the first month, welcome the resident as a future homebuyer and use that term in both oral and written communication. See the Welcome New Resident and Future Homebuyer form.

Give On-Time Thank You Vouchers At the start of the second month, after the resident pays the rent on time, send your resident a Future Homebuyer Voucher valued at either $50 or $100 good toward the purchase of a home, not necessarily the one he or she is living in, not even one that you own. However, the resident many receive vouchers toward the purchase of the home he or she resides in, if that is an option you would consider.

The first time your residents receive this voucher, they will probably not call you up in immediate urgency making plans buy your home. But this is the beginning of the transformation process from tenant to future homebuyer. The vouchers will start their minds thinking a little about the possibility of buying.

If a resident is ever late, any vouchers received up to that point are considered null and void. This point is spelled out in the rental agreement and on each voucher as a reminder to residents.

This is significant because when residents first start receiving the vouchers, it affects them. Even though they may not be sure if they will ever buy a home, most people don't want to lose out on something of high perceived value. Residents will keep paying you on time so they can keep getting the $50 or $100 vouchers.

The vouchers begin to add up to significant amounts after several months, up to $1,200 in a year. Residents don't want to simply throw that much money away or lose it. Some owners offer a one-time only, or once a year only, late payment without complete loss of the accrued voucher total. With a late payment, owners deduct a penalty of 25

percent or 50 percent off the accrued total instead of penalizing the full amount. Whatever method you use, the penalty should be significant to be effective.

Your residents will do everything within their power to keep paying the rent on time each month in order to keep from losing the possibility of using the vouchers. Don't be surprised if the residents begin paying a week to ten days early or request automatic debit from their checking account to ensure they don't come close to missing out.

By the middle of their first rental year, ask the resident to participate in a homebuying discussion. Many residents may have already indicated the need for such a discussion.

Hold homebuying discussions twice a year. They are an important part of the transformation process. During homebuying discussions, share with your residents the buying possibilities: outright purchase, lease option, land contract, etc. If you are considering selling your rental house, you should also mention your criteria for choosing to whom you would sell the home with favorable terms. Homebuyer criteria should include someone with good payment history and good maintenance and upkeep history.

Some landlords have said, however, "Wait a minute! What if I don't have enough positive cash flow to pay back a resident, or what if I don't want to sell my house?"

As part of the program, a participating resident can receive credit into a future homebuyer's account each month they paid rent promptly. After two or three years of renting, residents may accrue two to three thousand dollars into their homebuyer's accounts (depending on how much credit they receive each month), all of which can be applied toward the purchase of a house. But, there's good news for the landlord.

I suggest that landlords work in alliance with homebuilders or brokers who are willing to rebate/credit up to 3 percent of the purchase price to the buyer at time of closing. (A builder is discounting the price; a broker is simply reducing the amount of commission collected.) *Thus, the homebuilder or broker, not the landlord, actually pays for any money that accrues in the homebuyer's account.*

This program accomplishes two great objectives for the landlord. The owner is able to (1) offer a future homebuyers program for homes that he or she does not have to sell and (2) the owner does not have to take any money from rental income or cash flow to pay back the amount credited in the homebuyer's account. Yet the owner receives all the advantages of on-time rent payments and two-year or three-year residents who take excellent care of the rental. Similar programs offered throughout the United States require a renter's minimum residency of at least 24 months.

Landlords offering future homebuyer programs also report that such programs help to fill vacancies because they provide an added incentive to prospective residents who perceive they will not be wasting all their money and time as a renter, but instead will be working with someone who will help them buy their first home.

Mr. Landlord Challenge Consider offering some type of future homebuyer program to your residents that has benefits for the residents, home-builders/brokers, and you, the landlord!

THE PROBATIONARY RENTAL PERIOD

I often hear the argument that you can't always find ideal residents who do things the way you want. You are absolutely right. In fact, most of the residents you select will not respond the way you want them to if given a choice. *Choice* is the key word. An effective landlord does not let residents feel they have any choice in whether they will pay on time. As soon as residents feel they have the option, paying the rent will come second choice to an item on sale at the store, another pressing bill, or the resident may just do something or get something "they couldn't resist."

■ *Tip Number* **25**

Be tough during the first two to six months.

It is during the first two months of occupancy that conditioning and good habits should be established. You must stick with a set of firm ground rules that are clearly explained before you accept someone as a resident. By taking the time at the onset to explain ground rules clearly, you immediately put yourself in control, and you will get a good indication from the resident's reaction as to how much resistance you will encounter. I'd much rather have the resident tell me "Take a hike," and leave in the middle of explaining my ground rules than to have to deal with him or her over and over again in the next couple of months. Ground rules

should include sending a Notice to Pay Part or Quit immediately once a rent payment is not made.

Let residents know you mean business. Don't waste your breath with idle threats trying to stress the importance of timely payments. Strict enforcement of your penalties will stress the importance far better than anything you can say. Some landlords offer rent discounts; others have multiple late charges; while others have daily added rent tacked on each day in which payment is not made. Check state laws to see what is permitted. Whatever penalties you elect, make sure you enforce them.

GOOD EXCUSES LEAD TO THE POORHOUSE

Unless you've just started in the landlording business, you probably have found yourself in the following uncomfortable predicament. A resident notifies you that because of a very legitimate reason, the rent payment was not made on time. The excuses include a money order lost in the mail, a resident's check from employer or government agency is delayed, or the mail carrier may even admit to having handled the check that was sent to the residents but, because of confusion about the resident's whereabouts, the check was returned to sender.

Here's a tip. Turn the tables. At the beginning of the rental relationship, give your residents a list of excuses (see the Tenant Late Rent and Excuses form) and ask them to simply check the one most applicable (that they were considering to use), and mail it in with their on-time payment. As residents read the excuses they will chuckle. Inform them that whatever reason they may come up with, the management company does not accept excuses. You've just communicated a very serious point, yet in a light-hearted way.

The resident offers a valid excuse and assures you that as soon as the problem (which was no fault of the resident) is cleared up and corrected, he or she will give you your rent. Naturally, because the resident is not to blame, you will also be asked to allow payment without any late charge or eviction actions carried out.

At this point, strongly suggest to the resident, politely but firmly, that if he or she desires to continue residing in the residence, immediate alternate arrangements for getting the payment to you must be made. Perhaps through a loan from a friend, employer, or church. But, by no means should you not carry through with enforcing your agreement.

Afraid you'll be accused of being unreasonable? Or will you feel guilty about laying down the law on your innocent resident? If so, see the Ten Reasons Why You Should Not Feel Guilty about Evictions form.

■ *Tip Number* **26**

Do not accept any excuses.

Handle all nonpayment cases the same, whether good or bad excuses. I let my residents know right from the beginning what our procedure is when payment is not received. We also inform them that security deposits can never be used for future rent and are only for covering damages *after* the resident has moved or is evicted (that question seems to always come up as a way of temporarily covering the rent until the problem clears up). All of these policies are spelled out in the rental agreement.

GOOD OR BAD RESIDENT— IT'S YOUR CHOICE

There is no such thing as "bad" residents. Only *bad landlords.* I hope I'm offending you enough to motivate you to action today. Because changing that one perception of your landlording business can literally eliminate your resident worries and put the control of *your success* on you where it should be. After going around the country speaking to thousands of landlords and even listening to myself at times, I noticed how easy it is to blame our rental difficulties on our residents. This belief is one of the biggest downfalls of landlording, and I don't want you to fall into that trap.

A resident can be considered bad for 30 days. That's it! After that, the landlord is to blame. I'll define *bad* simply as violating one or more of the guidelines in your rental agreement. If the resident continues to violate the rental agreement and to display nonacceptable behavior beyond 30 days, a bad habit starts to develop. For example, sometimes our residents develop a bad habit of not paying the rent on time. And, it's easy to let this bad habit develop. Rent comes in a couple of days late, and you are happy to get it so you don't say anything about the late fee that should have been included. This happens once or twice more with rents now coming between the fifth and the tenth and you still say nothing, because after all the residents do not call you about problems and they're "nice" people. The resident is no longer to blame, but you are for allowing the resident to develop the bad habit, whether it is paying rent late, being guilty of poor rental upkeep, or any other nonacceptable behavior.

In fact, because you set the precedent of accepting payment without late fees over the past months, do not expect a judge to enforce your lease. A judge may not honor your request to evict the resident because of your bad habit of not strictly enforcing the agreement. If you have been guilty of being slack with enforcement of your policies, put your residents on notice that you will strictly enforce your rental policies. See the Notice of Strict Enforcement of Rental Policies form.

■ *Tip Number* **27**

Break your residents' bad habits.

Once you allow a resident to develop a bad habit, you need to correct the problem or clean house as quickly as possible. Now if a resident is doing *anything* that is not acceptable to you and that action or problem area is not addressed in your lease, you need to immediately change or strengthen your rental agreement before you just start changing residents, or the problem will keep surfacing.

Because I want the ability to stop a bad habit from developing, my rental agreements are on a month-to-month tenancy. See the customer loyalty program outlined later in this book that encourages residents to stay a minimum of three years.

■ *Tip Number* **28**

As long as it is legally permitted, make sure there is a significant (though legally acceptable/reasonable), payment difference between on-time payments and late payments.

Having a small $5 or $10 late charge or loss of discount for not paying on time is not enough to encourage residents to break a habit of paying late. I use to only charge a late charge of $25. However, when I discovered that my state law would allow me to charge a 10 percent late fee, I did so, which in many cases was nearly triple the late fee of what I had been charging, and in other cases, more than four times the previous charge. More importantly, since I did not want the small headaches of continual late payments, I noticed by increasing the amount it would cost the resident for paying after the due date, residents were much more likely to either break their bad habits and pay on time or simply move to another property where the owner or manager was more lenient, yet seemingly always dealing with problems. Some landlords even have a small per-day late charge to help encourage on-time payment. Again, check state laws for what is permitted in your state, at what dates charges can be assessed, and if there are any limits.

PREPARE FOR THE WORSE, EVEN IF YOUR RESIDENT DOESN'T

One wise landlord once said, "It's just a matter of time before something goes wrong, but as long as you know that's just part of this business and prepare for problems, your cash flow will outlast the amateur landlord and your real estate will be able to pay off well in good times and bad."

I'm sure *you* are prepared for the worse. However, as a landlord, the word of advice I want to share is that by preparing for the worse *for your resident,* you can add several thousands of dollars during their tough times.

Here's what I mean. When times get tough, residents become unable to pay. The average landlord may give good residents "more time to pay" for a while before realizing that is not much help and both of you are getting financially farther behind. And you have lost control of your cash flow.

Because you know it's only a matter of time before your residents may have financial problems, you can prepare ahead for it. How? Contact all possible agencies, organizations, or churches in your area which provide short-term financial assistance for housing. List them on a form.

■ *Tip Number* **29**

Develop a list of contacts of those who can provide emergency financial assistance.

In my area I can come up with a list of such agencies and churches so that I know if any of my residents were to have financial difficulty and they simply made the effort to contact those listed on my Financial Assistance Available form, the residents would be able to come up with enough

money to cover one month's worth of rent, and probably two, during a tough time.

For maybe a day's worth of effort calling around town to develop this housing assistance list, along with calling once a year to update the information, I receive numerous potential benefits to my bottom line:

- I'm able to keep more marginally good residents longer because even though they had financial difficulties, the problem could be solved with a month's worth of outside help. Plus they feel grateful to the assistance I provided and will bend over backwards to work with me in the future.
- I'm able to collect another month or two worth of rent from residents whom I would not have gotten anything else from once they ran into financial problems Note: I put agencies and churches on the list who pay the landlord directly when assistance is needed, because I know which organizations pay the landlord directly when assistance is needed. Because I know that this assistance is only a short-term solution, I've got a time of transition to encourage and help a "No-Hope" resident move to another place and find a new resident with limited loss of rental income. Under normal circumstances, by not using this strategy you can count on losing at least two months' income for what the resident was unable to pay before being forced to leave.
- I have no feelings of guilt whatsoever, if eviction becomes necessary, because I have given my residents a solution to their problem if they really needed help. (Yeah, I know, most of you have no problem with guilt anyway, but for the softhearted of you who are constantly getting yourself in trouble by being Mr. or Mrs. Nice Guy, this strategy will make you feel good and help your bottom line.)

Providing a list of possible financial assistance sources is not just for landlords of low-income residents. To ensure not losing a thousand dollars of rent, some landlords will even do the residents a favor and escort them down to the appropriate agency and accept the assistance check so the property won't be left unpaid.

One landlord was looking for a way to get past-due rent and looked at the original application the residents filled in and decided to contact the person listed as an emergency contact: the parents of a daughter who was having serious financial difficulty. (When rent is not paid, *that* is an emergency. Get authorization from the resident on the rental application to communicate with emergency contacts for financial assistance.) The landlord wrote to the parents (see the sample Letter to Emergency Contact). The landlord also sent copies of the promissory note (see the Promissory Note form) their daughter had signed. When writing to an emergency contact, put the following words on the outside of the envelope: "Extremely Important—Open immediately." Deliver the envelope via priority mail (for emphasis).

Within 72 hours, the landlord, who sent the letter to the parents, received a phone call from the very concerned mother, and within one week a check came from mom to satisfy her daughter's debt for the entire outstanding balance. Case closed!

Take the philosophy that *you* are ultimately responsible or in control of your cash flow—not your residents—and don't just wait and hope for results. Take steps now to prepare for the worse, for both yourself and your residents. And stay in control.

PAY OR QUIT AND PERFORM OR QUIT

Nonpayment of rent is one thing. Not performing one of the other terms in the agreement is another. When someone does not pay the rent, a landlord starts the legal proceedings by serving a pay or quit notice to his or her resident (see the sample Notice to Pay Rent or Quit form). Please note: This is one form where your state may require specific wording (or even size of wording) on the form, or your case may not be enforceable in court, which means you would have to start the legal process all over. Please consult a local legal professional.

■ *Tip Number* **30**

If you accept promises, require written performance dates, and always continue the legal eviction procedures.

If you accept any promises to pay, always get the promise in writing, and with specific performance dates. For example, refer to the Promise to Pay letter. Just because you agree to work with a promise

to pay schedule, does not mean, however, that you delay starting the eviction procedure. Why? Let's say the normal eviction process in your state takes approximately 45 days before you can legally evict a resident, and that is assuming there are no legal challenges by the resident. If you start the eviction process at the earliest possible date and the resident pays as promised, say within a four week period, you can dismiss the case, no problem. If the resident does not pay, you go to court as scheduled and resident is out of your place in 45 days. However, if a resident does not pay as promised, AND you had not already started the eviction process, you now have let valuable time go by – four weeks, without any payment. You now start the eviction proceedings that will still take 45 days beyond the four weeks you were waiting on the resident to pay as promised, before you can regain possession. You have allowed a minimum of 10+ weeks to go by before you can regain possession and get started again generating rental income with new residents.

A side note to the above scenario, please check state laws regarding accepting partial payments before the court date as part of a promise to pay agreement. In some states, accepting partial payments as part of a promise to pay will automatically nullify the eviction process (judge dismisses the case in favor of the resident) and you will still have to restart the eviction process. In some other states, you are able to accept partial payments without it affecting or delaying or nullifying the eviction process, (that is if a proper letter is sent to the resident, in some states called a reservation letter. Check state laws).

■ *Tip Number* **31**

Do not ignore or let slide small violations.

After doing this business for nearly 25 years, I've discovered that small rental headaches, if not addressed, will only become large headaches. Often landlords will share with me how a resident is giving them big headaches. If those same landlords were to look back over time and honestly evaluate the same resident's performance, there are almost always signs of smaller problems that the landlord ignored or let slide. If the smaller violations had been swiftly dealt with, it's a good chance the larger problems or headaches would not have occurred. So address any and all rental violations while they are small. There are forms included in this section to address violations, such as excessive utilities, garage, noise, unauthorized vehicle or pet, and more.

■ *Tip Number 32*

Do not delay when starting legal eviction procedures.

The Notice to Perform or Quit is used for terminating a tenancy because the resident is not doing something that he or she promised to do in the written rental agreement (other than paying rent). Some common breaches big enough to qualify as grounds for terminating the tenancy are assigning or subleasing the property without the landlord's written permission, unauthorized pets or persons in the premises, and misuse of the premises. This list is not inclusive and can be as long as your rental agreement.

When giving a perform or quit notice (see the Notice to Perform or Quit form), it is important that you clearly specify in the notice exactly where in the rental agreement (paragraph and portion thereof) are the terms that are being breached or the resident is not performing. For example, don't just say in the notice that "You must move the junker car in the driveway." Instead say, "You are in violation of the provision in your agreement (indicate article number, heading, or paragraph) that says, *All vehicles on the property must be operable, meet any required inspections, and display current city decals and state tags, or be removed."*

HOLD YOUR RESIDENTS ACCOUNTABLE

One of the absolute best ways to get residents to be cooperative is to hold them accountable for their actions. That sounds simple enough, but most (over 95 percent of) rental owners do very little to make residents think that the consequences of their rental conduct or actions, good or bad, will follow them after they move on.

One very effective way to do this, which I call the *Report Your Resident* strategy, is to notify new residents at the beginning of the relationship, and remind them throughout the term, that their rental performance while they reside in your property will be regularly evaluated and reported. Put residents on notice that you will let the world know about their performance with you. This is something most landlords fail to do.

■ *Tip Number 33*

Evaluate and report your residents' performance.

How do you measure up? Do you always get a judgment against residents who leave owing you money or cause unpaid-for damages? Do you try to collect what they owe after they leave? Do you report judgments to credit reporting bureaus? Do you turn them over to a collection agency? Do you report them to local and nationwide tenant reporting agencies? These are all steps you can take to show residents that they will be held accountable, and this section has the forms to help you do that (see the Good Tenant Letter, 72-Hour Warning to Report Poor Performance, and Sample Letter to National Credit Reporting Agency forms).

Evaluating and reporting your residents' performance can have positive benefits that help residents establish and/or keep a good credit report and reputation. One key to the success of using the Report Your Resident strategy is to inform residents at the beginning of the rental term that you do a review of resident's performance every six months and will provide a copy of a *good* performance report for residents who pay on time and follow all terms of the agreement. The residents can then turn around and provide copies of good reports to future landlords and lenders to help verify their creditworthiness.

Another key to the success of using this strategy is that you only rent to rental applicants who have a good credit history to protect! This strategy is far more effective in getting cooperation from residents who are concerned about keeping a good credit reputation. They will do what is necessary and do it promptly to avoid negative remarks placed on any of their records. This is especially true when you remind them, in a notice, that negative remarks can make it more difficult to rent or buy a home, get a car loan, or obtain any other financing or credit. Let residents know that the policy of many management companies states that just one negative report from a previous landlord can cost an otherwise qualified applicant the ability to rent an apartment.

If a resident breaks a rental term (e.g., nonpayment or upkeep violation), you immediately send a letter notifying the resident that he or she has 72 hours to correct the violation or the unfavorable information will be placed in their file and made available to any and all who inquire that the resident may seek to do business with in the future, including future landlords, mortgage companies, lenders, creditors, etc. making it more difficult to rent or buy a home or car in the future. If after sending out the 72-hour warning letter, the resident corrects the violation within three days, inform the resident that no unfavorable information will be placed in their file, and thank the resident for the prompt cooperation. Likewise, remind vacating residents that if they leave owing any money for rent, unpaid charges, or damages in excess of the security deposit, that you will not only seek a judgment against them and pursue legal means to collect money due, but you will also report their debt to all three major credit bureaus, which, again, will make it much harder to rent or buy a home or car in the future.

Mr. Landlord Challenge Put your residents on notice and hold them accountable for their performance (see the Notice of Accountability form in Part Two). If you start doing this consistently and follow through on what you say you will do, you will have far more cooperative residents and all the rest of us will be grateful. Who do you actually report the resident's performance to, should that be necessary? There are many nationwide tenant-screening agencies that you can work with, including one featured on MrLandlord.com.

WELCOME NEW RESIDENT AND FUTURE HOMEBUYER

From: _____

_____

_____

Date: _____

To: _____

_____

_____

Dear _____:

　　We would like to take this opportunity to welcome you as a new resident and most likely a future homebuyer. We are pleased that you have chosen our property as your new home.

　　We recognize that most rental residents sooner or later consider buying their own home. We wish to help if you will be looking to buy in the near future (within the next three years), and we are glad to let you participate in our Future Homebuyers Program. As part of our Future Homebuyers Program, should you desire at any time in the future to actually purchase the home you are moving into, we will be glad to discuss the buying options available to you. We also work with home builders and real estate brokers in the area so that you may be able to purchase from a wide selection.

　　We reward loyal residents and future homebuyers who pay rent on time by giving an "on-time" thank-you voucher with each punctual payment. Each voucher has a value of $ _____ and is good toward the purchase of the home you are moving into or one of the homes by the builders or brokers participating in our homebuyers program. The homes that you may be able to receive credit toward are: _____ . The credit vouchers can quickly add up to several hundred dollars, even over a thousand dollars, and make it easier for you to accumulate part or most of the down payment you will need for your purchase. Vouchers are also given each time we conduct a semiannual inspection of the property and you pass the inspection. The amount credited for passing each inspection is $ _____. All vouchers can be redeemed once a resident has participated in the Future Homebuyers Program for a minimum of _____ months (at time of closing).

　　Every six months we hold a homebuying discussion to update you on your buying options, answer any questions, and offer assistance as you come closer to the day that you will buy a home. If you wish to discuss buying options anytime, please do not hesitate to call us. The best time to call is between _____ and _____ on _____ . And again, welcome!

Rental Manager

FUTURE HOMEBUYER VOUCHER
Thank You for Your On-Time Payment and Property Upkeep

This is to acknowledge receipt of your recent payment on or before the due date or for passing the semiannual property inspection. As part of the Future Homebuyers Program, you are entitled to receive this voucher good toward the purchase of the home

_____.

The value of all vouchers received are added into your Future Homebuyer's account. Vouchers can be redeemed/ credited at time of the actual closing of the home you purchase. Please note that if any rent payment is received after the due date or you fail to pass a property inspection, all vouchers and total amount accrued up to that point are considered null and void. It is therefore important to continue your excellent payment record and properly maintain the property. Thank you once again for your on-time payment. The value of this voucher toward the Future Homebuyers Program is $ _____

FUTURE HOMEBUYER VOUCHER
Thank You for Your On-Time Payment and Property Upkeep

This is to acknowledge receipt of your recent payment on or before the due date or for passing the semiannual property inspection. As part of the Future Homebuyers Program, you are entitled to receive this voucher good toward the purchase of the home

_____.

The value of all vouchers received are added into your Future Homebuyer's account. Vouchers can be redeemed/ credited at time of the actual closing of the home you purchase. Please note that if any rent payment is received after the due date or you fail to pass a property inspection, all vouchers and total amount accrued up to that point are considered null and void. It is therefore important to continue your excellent payment record and properly maintain the property. Thank you once again for your on-time payment. The value of this voucher toward the Future Homebuyers Program is $ _____

RENT STATEMENT/INVOICE

From: _____

_____   For month of: _____

To: _____   Date due: _____

_____   Rental address (if different):

_____   _____

Current Amount Due: Plus Past Due: Total Due: Total Due:
                                              (if paid by _____) (if paid after _____)

$ _____ $ _____ $ _____ $ _____

Mail payment to: _____

Thank you for your prompt payment.

RENT STATEMENT/INVOICE

From: _____

_____   For month of: _____

To: _____   Date due: _____

_____   Rental address (if different):

_____   _____

Current Amount Due: Plus Past Due: Total Due: Total Due:
                                              (if paid by _____) (if paid after _____)

$ _____ $ _____ $ _____ $ _____

Mail payment to: _____

Thank you for your prompt payment.

RENT STATEMENT/INVOICE

From: _____

_____   For month of: _____

To: _____   Date due: _____

_____   Rental address (if different):

_____   _____

Current Amount Due: Plus Past Due: Total Due: Total Due:
                                              (if paid by _____) (if paid after _____)

$ _____ $ _____ $ _____ $ _____

Mail payment to: _____

Thank you for your prompt payment.

TENANT LATE RENT WARNING AND EXCUSES

(Note: To be given to new, renewing, and late tenants)

Dear Resident:

Your rent is due on the _____ day of the month. I'm sure you fully understand that we must start eviction proceedings instantly once a payment is late (no matter the reason) and report your late payment to both local and national tenant/credit reporting agencies. We still request, however, that you submit your reason for late payment for our records. For your convenience, and to avoid lengthy explanation, you may simply check the appropriate reason below and submit this form with your late payment. Hopefully, this form and your payment will be received before you're evicted. Even better, your payment will arrive on time and you will not need this form.

I'm sorry my rent is late but . . .

_____ A. The check I've been waiting for did not come in the mail or was late.

_____ B. I was in the hospital/jail and I couldn't get to you.

_____ C. I missed a week's work because I had to take care of my sick mother/son/daughter.

_____ D. I had to have some teeth pulled, and the dentist wouldn't start work until I gave some money.

_____ E. I was in an automobile accident and I won't have any money until my attorney works things out with the other guy's insurance.

_____ F. I had my billfold stolen when this guy jumped me on my way to the bank/post office/my office.

_____ G. Someone broke into my apartment and took my money. No, I didn't file a police report. Should I?

_____ H. I had to have my car fixed so I could get to work, so I could pay you.

_____ I. My mother/sister/uncle hasn't mailed me my money yet.

_____ J. I couldn't find your address. I put the wrong address on the envelope.

_____ K. I got laid off from my job, and I won't get unemployment for a couple of weeks.

_____ L. I was unable to get a money order, and I know you didn't want me to send cash.

_____ M. You didn't come by when I had the money.

_____ N. My husband/wife/boyfriend/girlfriend/roommate left, and I didn't have all the money.

_____ O. They garnished my check, and I don't understand it, because the guy told me it would be okay to just pay so much per month and I only missed a couple of payments.

_____ P. I told my friend to bring it or send it to you while I was out of town.

_____ Q. I haven't received my tax refund yet.

_____ R. I got a new job, and I had to work three weeks before I got my first check.

_____ S. I didn't pay the rent because my _____ is not fixed. No, I'm sorry I didn't tell you there was a problem before now. I didn't think about it until now.

_____ T. My car is broken, and I didn't have a ride to your office/the post office.

_____ U. I had to help my brother/sister/friend who had a serious problem.

_____ V. My grandmother died, and I had to go to the funeral.

_____ W. I didn't have, or I forgot to put, a stamp on the envelope.

_____ X. The check's in the mail. Didn't you get it?

_____ Y. I ran out of checks.

_____ Z. I'm dead!

_____   Please briefly explain if your excuse is not listed above:

_____

LATE FEE DUE

From: _____

_____

_____

Date: _____

To: _____

_____

_____

Dear _____:

Thank you for your rent payment. As stated in your rental agreement, however, when rent payments are not received by _____ , you must pay additional rent because of a late charge due or because you did not qualify for the rent discount. The required additional amount was not included in your payment, and is therefore now due.

Please send the additional required rent amount of $ _____ at once to bring your credit balance up to date because it is currently delinquent. This amount must be paid within _____ days from the date of this notice.

Thank you for your prompt cooperation.

Sincerely,

Rental Manager

NOTICE OF LATE RENT/LATE FEE/CHARGES

From: _____

_____

_____

Date: _____

To: _____

_____

_____

Dear _____:

You are hereby notified that your rent, which was due _____, has not been received and is now past due. This letter is to your notification that as of _____, a late fee of $_____ is now also due.

In addition (if applicable), a $_____ per-day late charge went or goes into effect beginning _____ and this will continue to accumulate until the total amount due is received, including the rent, the late fee, and accumulated per-day charges (as permitted by state law).

Check appropriate box: ☐ Per-Day charge will apply   ☐ Per-Day Charge does not apply

Please make payment as soon as possible to keep charges to a minimum. Payments should be delivered to

_____.

It should also be understood that if total payment is not received by _____, eviction proceedings are initiated against you, and once initiated, the total rent due must include court costs to stop the proceedings.

One additional reminder: If payment is not received by _____, eviction proceedings are initiated against you, and once initiated, the total rent due must include court costs to stop the proceedings.

One additional reminder: If payment is not received and a court judgment is entered against you for nonpayment, the debt will be recorded in the city/county you reside and notification of the debt will be reported to all three major credit bureaus, which may stay on your credit history for up to ten years. However, this letter is sent to you in hopes that payment will be promptly made and additional charges, eviction, and reporting to the credit bureaus can all be avoided.

Thank you for your prompt cooperation with this matter.

Owner/Management _____

NOTICE OF STRICT ENFORCEMENT OF RENTAL POLICIES

From: _____

_____

_____

Date: _____

To: _____

_____

_____

Dear _____:

Your rental agreement states that monthly rent payments will be paid the first of each month. In the past, we have accepted rent payments made after the due date as a courtesy to you, not as a modification to your rental agreement.

From now on, however, we must insist on prompt payment as stated in your rental agreement. This will allow management to properly budget and cover all mortgages and expenses to run and manage this property, so that we will not be subject to losing the property to foreclosure or additional charges by our creditors that will force us to have to raise the monthly rent. Please let this letter serve as written notification that, in the future, you must follow the terms of your rental agreement requiring monthly rent payments to be made on the first of each month or other date(s) mutually agreed to.

All provisions of the rental agreement will be strictly enforced. Beginning _____, your rent payment must be made on time pursuant to your rental agreement. Any payment made after the due date will be considered late. If monthly rent payments are made after the due date, you will be subject to additional rent or a late charge of $ _____. The management also reserves its right to take all proper legal action against you pursuant to the rental agreement and the laws of the state. May we suggest that you sign up for one of our auto-pay, worry-free methods of paying rent that will help to ensure that payments are made before the due date, and you will never have to worry about having to pay additional rent or late charges? If you have any questions, or wish to set up an auto-pay plan, please feel free to call our office: _____.

We look forward to your cooperation.

Rental Manager

RETURNED CHECK NOTICE

From: _____

_____

_____

Date: _____

To: _____

_____

_____

Dear _____ :

Your bank has returned your check to us in the amount of $ _____ . This check was payment for _____ . In addition, this makes your payment late, which disqualifies you for any rent discount, or subject to a late charge of _____ . Also, as your rental agreement states, there is a returned check fee for any payment that is returned for insufficient funds.

This makes your account past due and delinquent. You must immediately make arrangements to bring your account current by sending us certified funds (money order or certified check). The total amount now due is:

Regular rent payment	$ _____
Loss of discount or late charge	$ _____
Returned check fee	$ _____
Total amount due	$ _____

This amount must be paid within _____ days.

Thank you for your prompt cooperation.

Sincerely,

Rental Manager

NOTICE TO PAY RENT OR QUIT

Please note: This notice is provided only as an example of a typical notice that was used in the past in some states. Many states now have certain standards that MUST be followed in a legal termination notice, including specific wording or content. Some states have specific standards for the look, format, wording size and type. You must also check state statutes for the correct number of days residents must be allowed to pay rent or deliver up possession, which must be stated in the notice. All this is why when preparing such a notice, you should consult your local and state landlord-tenant statutes. Or obtain a state specific legal form that complies with landlord-tenant law for your state, so that your notice will be valid and enforceable. If not, a judge may simply dismiss the case in favor of your resident. It's recommended that you seek counsel, before proceeding, if you have never gone through the steps in the legal eviction process or if you have any questions.

To: _____,

and all other residents in possession of the premises at the following address:

_____

PLEASE TAKE NOTICE that according to the terms of your rental agreement the rent is now due and payable for the above-stated address which you currently hold and occupy Our records indicate that your rental account is delinquent in the amount itemized as follows:

Rental Period (dates) _____   Rent Due $ _____

Rental Period (dates) _____   Rent Due $ _____

Rental Period (dates) _____   Rent Due $ _____

TOTAL RENT DUE $ _____

Less partial payment of $ _____

TOTAL BALANCE DUE of $ _____

You are hereby required to pay said rent in full within _____ days or to move from and deliver up possession of the above address or legal proceedings will be instituted against you to recover possession of said premises; to declare the forfeiture of the Lease or Rental Agreement under which you occupy said premises; and to recover all rents due and damages, together with court costs, legal and attorney fees, according to the terms of your Lease or Rental Agreement.

Dared this _____ day of _____ ,20_____

Owner/Manager _____ Phone_____

PROOF OF SERVICE

I, the undersigned, being at least 18 years of age, declare under penalty of perjury that I served the above notice, of which this is a true copy, on the above-mentioned resident(s) in possession in the manner(s) indicated below:

__ On _____, 20_____, I handed the notice to the resident(s) personally.

__ On _____, 20_____, after attempting personal service, I handed the notice to a person of suitable age and discretion at the residence/business of the resident(s), AND I deposited a true copy in the U.S. Mail, in a sealed envelope with postage fully prepaid, addressed to the resident(s) at his/her/their place of residence (date mailed, if different from above date _____).

__ On _____, 20_____, after attempting service in both manners indicated above, I posted the notice in a conspicuous place at the residence of the resident(s), AND I deposited a true copy in the U.S. Mail, in a sealed envelope with postage fully prepaid, addressed to the resident(s) at his/her/their place of residence (date mailed, if different from above date _____

Executed on _____, 20 _____, at the County/City of _____

State of_____ Served by_____

RENT PAYMENT SCHEDULE WORKSHEET

Previous balance (prior to current month): $ _____

Current month (A) (now past due): $ _____

Late charge, month A: $ _____

Next month B rent: $ _____

Following month C rent: $ _____

Total Rent Due within Next 60 Days: $ _____

Number of paydays in the next 60 days:
(prior to due date for month C rent)   _____

Amount due each payday:
(divide total rent due by # of paydays) $ _____

Dates of paydays within next 60 days: Amount paid   On-time: Yes/No
(prior to due date for month C)

_____   _____   _____
_____   _____   _____
_____   _____   _____
_____   _____   _____
_____   _____   _____
_____   _____   _____
_____   _____   _____
_____   _____   _____

The resident agrees to pay rent monies due according to the above payment schedule. If the resident fails to pay amount due on or before any of the agreed dates, the owner has the right to continue the legal eviction procedure against the resident without having to serve another pay or quit notice. The resident has already been served. The resident has been given extra time to pay only as a courtesy. By granting this extension, the landlord does not waive any current or future rights granted in the rental agreement, especially as it relates to rights to terminate this agreement and eviction for nontimely payments of rents.

Resident's Signature: _____ Date: _____

Owner/Manager's Signature: _____ Date: _____

PROMISE FOR PAYMENT

Dear Owner/Management

I promise to pay you $_____ for rent and other charges now owing on the residence which I rent from you located at _____.

_____ a) I promise to pay you the full amount due on or before the following date: _____.

_____ b) I promise to pay you in two payments to cover the full amount due:
The first payment will be for the following amount $ _____.
It will be paid to you on or before the following date _____.

The second payment will be for the following amount $ _____.
It will be paid to you on or before the following date _____.

In order to make the payments promised to you, I expect to be receiving sufficient funds to do so from the following sources: (You have my permission to contact them and, I give my authorization to verify each of the sources listed below)

Individual/Agency/Company	Address	Phone	Amount Expected

If you are unable to verify that these funds are to be sent to me, or if I fail to pay as exactly as promised, I understand that you will immediately proceed to evict me, and that this promise will be used against me as evidence of my bad faith in paying what I owe.

I acknowledge that I have received a Notice to Pay or Quit as required by law to begin eviction proceedings. I understand that that Notice may show a balance owed which is different from the amount stated above, because a Notice to Pay or Quit may demand only delinquent rent. I also understand that the period mentioned in this Notice is being extended to the date(s) given above, at which time I promise to pay you all that is owed at this point. If I fail to pay on or before the promised date(s), you have the right to continue legal eviction procedures against me without having to serve me another Notice to Pay or Quit. I have already been served. I am being given the extra time to pay only as a courtesy and only this once.

Resident's Signature _____ Dated _____

PROMISSORY NOTE

Principal amount: $ _____ Date: _____

    I, (the undersigned) am/are a resident living at the following address _____.
Due to various reasons and uncontrollable events, I have been unable to pay the rent and/or damages that are now past
due on the above address. As of this date, I owe the above-stated principal amount for which I make the following promise.

    For value received, I (the undersigned) hereby jointly and severally promise to pay to the order of _____
_____ the sum of _____Dollars ($), together
with interest thereon at the rate of _____percent per annum on the unpaid balance. Said sum shall be paid in the
following manner: Payments will be made monthly/weekly on the following date/day _____ in the
amount of _____ until total due is paid in full. This note may be prepaid, at any time, in whole or in
part, without penalty.

    This note shall be at the option of any holder thereof and be immediately due and payable upon the occurrence of
any of the following circumstances: 1) Failure to make any payment due hereunder on or before its due date.
2) Breach of any condition of any security interest, pledge agreement, or guarantee granted as collateral security for this
note. 3) Upon the death, incapacity, dissolution, or liquidation of any of the undersigned, or any cosigner or guarantor.
4) Upon the filing by any of the undersigned of an assignment for the benefit of creditors, bankruptcy, or other form of
insolvency, or by suffering an involuntary petition in bankruptcy or receivership not vacated within thirty (30) days.

    If I, the undersigned, do not fulfill the above promise and default in the payment of the whole or any part of any in-
stallment, the entire unpaid balance with interest will become due and payable. If I am still residing in the premises,
I/we also promise to immediately vacate the premises and give the Owner of the premises the right to terminate any
rental agreement.

    In the event this note shall be in default and placed for collection, then the undersigned agree to pay all reasonable
attorney fees and costs of collection. Payments not made within five (5) days of due date shall be subject to a late
charge of _____percent of said payment. All payments hereunder shall be made to such address as may from time
to   time   be   designated   by   any   holder.

    The undersigned and all other parties to this note, whether as cosigners or guarantors, agree to remain fully bound
until this note shall be fully paid and waive demand, presentment, and protest, and all notices hereto and further agree
to remain bound notwithstanding any extension, modification, waiver, or other indulgence, or discharge, or release of
any obligor hereunder or exchange, substitution, or release of any collateral granted as security for this note. No modification or indulgence by any holder hereof shall be binding unless in writing; and any indulgence on any one occasion
shall not be an indulgence for any other or future occasion. Any modification or change in terms, hereunder granted
by any holder hereof, shall be valid and binding upon each of the undersigned, notwithstanding the acknowledgment
of any of the undersigned, and each of the undersigned does hereby irrevocably grant to each of the others a power of
attorney to enter into any such modification on their behalf. The rights of any holder hereof shall be cumulative and
not necessarily successive. This agreement shall be binding upon and inure to the benefit of the parties, their succes-
sors, assigns, and personal representatives. This note shall take effect as a sealed instrument and shall be construed,
governed, and enforced in accordance with the laws of the State of _____. Dated
this _____ day of _____ 20_____ .

Signed: _____

Signed: _____

Witness:_____

EXAMPLE OF LETTER TO EMERGENCY CONTACT (PARENTS)

(On application, residents gave permission to contact emergency contacts for financial assistance, if needed.)

From: _____

_____

_____

Date: _____

To: _____

_____

_____

Dear _____:

I write to you with regret because I have had so much difficulty trying to resolve the following matter on my own. Perhaps your wisdom and life experience will help to resolve your (son's/daughter's) failing creditworthiness before it is too late.

I rented an apartment to _____ on _____ .
As you can see from the attached paperwork, I have had difficulties trying to collect all the rent due during the tenancy. I sought to work with _____ through the financial challenges and even offered a list of churches and community agencies that may have been able to offer assistance. I am not a hard-nosed, noncaring kind of person, who is hard to get along with. My nature is quite the contrary.

It was mutually agreed by all of us that I would let the rental agreement be broken so that _____ could move to a less expensive rental. With a promise on my part to work with them to accept payment, I really believed in their honesty. The last thing I wanted to pursue was any legal action or eviction proceedings. Those legal matters do nothing more than cost everybody additional money and take up valuable time in our lives. I come from a family tradition that really believes in working with others if they stick to their promises and continue to make an effort to fulfill their obligations. But it seems that no such efforts were made in this case.

I have attached the most current letter I have been forced to send to _____ because I just have not had any response. You were listed on the original application as a reliable reference and emergency contact in case of any financial problems. With your experience in life, you know how devastating a negative credit report can be these days when it gets in the way of a young person trying to get ahead in life. Perhaps a word or two would help resolve this matter before the _____ deadline given on the attached form. I have done all I can to help so far. I will be more than happy to speak with you or you can write me at the address above.

Yours truly,

Rental Owner

NOTICE TO PERFORM OR QUIT
(Correct Rental Violation)

To: _____
      Tenant(s) in possession

Address: _____

City: _____ State: _____ Zip: _____

1. You are hereby notified that you have violated or failed to perform the following terms in your rental/lease agreement, which states that resident(s) agrees to:

_____

_____

2. You are in violation of that provision for the following reason(s):

_____

_____

_____

3. You must perform or correct this violation within _____ days after service of this notice. The violation can be corrected by immediately doing the following:

_____

Or if you fail to perform or correct the terms of the rental/lease agreement within the specified time, you must vacate and deliver possession of the premises to the landlord/manager.

4. **If you fail to correct or vacate within _____ days, legal proceedings will be initiated against you to recover possession, rent owed, damages, court costs, and attorney fees.**

5. It is not our intention to terminate the rental/lease agreement. However, all tenants must follow guidelines stated in the agreement. If you are unable to comply, the landlord elects to declare a forfeiture of your rental or lease agreement. You will also be subject to forfeit any security deposit given by you to cover any costs you are still liable for, and the landlord reserves the right to pursue collection of any future rental losses. We may be contacted at _____.

Thank you for your prompt cooperation in correcting this matter.

Owner/Manager's Signature: _____ Date: _____

RENTAL UPKEEP VIOLATION

From: _____

_____

_____

Date: _____

To: _____

_____

_____

Dear _____:

    We do regular inspections of the rental property managed by our company. Your rental agreement clearly states that tenants are responsible for the general upkeep of the residence, both on the interior and exterior. This includes:

_____

_____.

    On our last inspection of the premises, it was noticed you have broken your rental agreement regarding upkeep concerning:

_____

_____

    To meet rental standards and correct this violation, you must keep this condition neat and clean at all times as well as:

_____

_____

    Please correct this problem immediately or, if you prefer, or we see nothing done on your part within the next five days, we will hire someone to do it and bill you accordingly.

Thank you for your prompt cooperation.

Rental Manager

EXCESSIVE UTILITY USAGE

From: _____

_____

_____

Date: _____

To: _____

_____

_____

Dear _____ :

As stated in your rental agreement, our company pays for the _____ at your address. The agreement also states, however, any time your usage of this utility becomes excessive and exceeds _____ per month, you are responsible for payment above that amount, and is to be considered as additional rent due.

We have enclosed a copy of the last record of your usage and it shows that you went above the amount agreed on. You went over the limits stated in the rental agreement by _____ . Please send us $ _____ as part of your next rent payment to cover the excess amount. Nonpayment of the full rent amount due is a violation of the rental agreement and grounds for termination of the agreement and appropriate legal action will begin.

Thank you for your cooperation.

Sincerely,

Rental Manager

GARBAGE VIOLATION NOTICE

Date: _____

To: _____

_____

_____

RE: Garbage Violation (We Need Your Help)

It is not Management's wish to restrict your enjoyment of your residence. However, Management must consider the rights and privileges of everyone. We are informing you that your garbage has not been kept in a proper manner from time to time. The following is one such example: _____ _____ . This is in violation of the lease agreement.

Though it may not always be easy to keep garbage on the premises in a proper manner, we must ask for your assistance and cooperation. Remember that spilled garbage can attract mice and other animals, such as cats, dogs, and raccoons. Please put your garbage in a garbage can **with a lid on top.** Or tie garbage in a **plastic bag** (no paper bags are to be used). We cannot allow garbage to be spilled or left lying about the premises. We would greatly appreciate your co-operation in this manner.

Remember that you are responsible for your own garbage. You must keep refuse and garbage in a clean and sanitary manner. We also ask Residents and their guests not to litter on the premises. Do not let this jeopardize your lease.

We ask each Resident to keep the garbage pickup area clean at curb or alley and at the place of weekly storage. We realize that sometimes papers and debris that belong to someone else end up on the premises. Please help pick up these papers so the property is nicer looking. Thank you for promptly (daily) picking up newspapers or flyers that are placed on or near your door, which is part of each resident's responsibilities.

We trust that Management will not have to notify you about any more garbage problems. However, be aware that if it continues to happen and you fail to comply with the Rules and Regulations, you will place yourself in further default of your lease agreement. Of course, default is a serious matter that could result in legal action being initiated against you.

An additional note: If Resident forgets to place garbage out for the weekly pickup, Management requests that Resident immediately remove that garbage from the premises at Resident's own expense. Management will have the right to terminate the lease agreement for noncompliance.

Please remember to retrieve your garbage cans soon after the garbage is picked up. If applicable, residents shall use garbage bins in accordance with the city ordinances. If you have any questions, please call _____.

Your cooperation in this matter is greatly appreciated.

Rental Manager

NOISE VIOLATION NOTICE

Date: _____

To: _____

_____

_____

It is certainly not management's wish to restrict your enjoyment of your home/apartment. Management must, however, consider the rights and privileges of everyone.

Most residents have continued to cooperate in keeping the noise level down in their rentals and will soon be treated to a night out on the town by management (see below). If, however, the word *violation* is circled at the top of this page, please read the next paragraph carefully.

We are informing you that there was reported to our office an unusual amount of noise coming from your home/apartment as noted here: _____
_____.
_____.

Excessive noise or high levels during the wrong time of the day is a violation of your standard rental agreement, which states: _____
_____.
_____.

We trust management will not receive any complaints from neighbors or have to notify you about any more violations. However, be aware that if disturbances continue and you fail to comply with the noise rules and regulations, you will place yourself in further default of your rental agreement and the agreement may be terminated and/or not renewed. If you have any questions call _____ between _____ and _____.

Your cooperation in this matter will be greatly appreciated.

Rental Manager

PS: If you work with us in helping to keep a peaceful environment, and we do not receive any complaints about the noise level in your rental during the next twelve months, the management will pay your way for a night out on the town where you can celebrate with lots of noise. You choose the hot spot, and we'll cover the cost up to $ _____

AUTOMOBILE VIOLATION

From: _____

_____

_____

Date: _____

To: _____

_____

_____

Dear _____:

We do regular inspections of the rental property managed by our company. Your rental agreement clearly states that unauthorized, nonoperational, unregistered vehicles, or those not displaying required local or state decals/licenses, are not allowed on the rental premises, even on a temporary basis. This includes: _____.

On our last inspection of the premises, it was noticed that there was a vehicle on your premises with the following description: _____.

This vehicle violates your rental agreement for the following reason(s):
_____.

To be in compliance with your rental agreement and remedy this violation, you are hereby notified that one of the following actions must be done within 72 hours or this violation will lead to a notice to terminate the rental agreement.

A) The vehicle must be removed by _____ .
B) The vehicle must be in fully operational status and display all required local and state decals/licenses.

Please contact us at the following number, _____ , within 72 hours to inform us of your actions regarding this matter. We want very much to have your cooperation with this matter. Be advised that without your cooperation, a towing service will be instructed to remove the vehicle. If you do not wish to have the vehicle towed, remedy the violation by one of the methods stated above, or contact us to make alternative satisfactory arrangements. The cost of removal and storage of the vehicle will be the automobile owner's responsibility.

Thank you for your cooperation,

Rental Manager

NOTICE REQUESTING REMOVAL OF UNATHORIZED VEHICLES

Date: _____

To: _____

_____

_____

RE: IMMEDIATE REMOVAL OF VEHICLE

WARNING OF PARKING VIOLATION

Make/Model_____, License #:_____

Make/Model_____, License #:_____

You are hereby notified that a vehicle(s) listed below and parked on the property located at
_____ must

(a) be removed within _____ days or

(b) be registered with the owner/management or

(c) have the violation below immediately corrected.

VIOLATION(S)

_____Vehicle unregistered with the Owner/Management

_____Does not have proper registration/tags/stickers, decals, etc.

_____Parking in unauthorized area/parking space

_____Vehicle is inoperable or in disrepair

_____Repair or work on vehicle is not permitted on the premises

_____Oil or other fluid leaking from vehicle (Stain must be removed).

_____Parking rent past due - Over_____ days

_____Not a personal use vehicle

_____Other Violation _____

Please comply with the above request within _____ days or the vehicle will be subject to towing at the car owner's expense.

Sincerely,

Rental Manager

PET RULE VIOLATION

From: _____

_____

_____

Date: _____

To: _____

_____

_____

Dear _____:

   We do regular inspections of the rental property managed by our company. Your rental agreement clearly states that pets (unless specifically included in the lease) are not permitted on the rental premises, inside or out, even on a temporary basis. This includes _____.

   On our last inspection of the premises, it was noticed or brought to our attention that you have broken your rental agreement by allowing a pet/animal to occupy or remain on the premises.

_____

To be in compliance with your rental agreement and remedy this violation, you are hereby notified that one of the following actions must be done within 72 hours or this violation will lead to a notice to terminate the rental agreement.

A) The pet must be removed by _____ .
B) You may request an application to have the pet added to the rental agreement, subject to approval and additional monthly rent and deposit.

   Please contact us at the following number, _____ , within 72 hours to inform us of your actions regarding this matter. We want very much to have your cooperation with this matter. Be aware that animals on the property that are not listed on the rental agreement are considered stray, and are subject to removal by appropriate authorities, with any costs billed to the resident.

Thank you for your cooperation,

Rental Manager

GOOD TENANT LETTER
Semiannual Report of Resident's Performance

To: _____ Date: _____

Address: _____ City: _____, State: _____, ZIP: _____

Thank you! Your past six months' rental performance met all the terms of your rental agreement. A copy of this favorable report is being made available for your files.

The items marked below are the terms of the rental agreement you have successfully completed during the past six months, and we have provided you a copy of this report for your files so that you can offer this information to future landlords, lenders, and creditors who may be evaluating your performance potential. If you continue to meet all your rental terms, we'll provide a favorable report for your files every six months, which should make it easier for you to rent or buy a home of your choice in the future. (An unfavorable report can make it difficult to rent or buy in the future.)

The following rental obligations have been successfully completed in the last six months.

1. _____ Rent paid in full each month
2. _____ All payments received on or before the due date
3. _____ All repair bills paid (which were resident's responsibility)
4. _____ All utility bills paid (which were resident's responsibility)
5. _____ No noise complaints by neighbors
6. _____ No disputes with neighbors
7. _____ No unauthorized occupants reported
8. _____ No unauthorized pet(s) reported
9. _____ No unauthorized vehicle on premises
10. _____ No excessive junk on outside of building
11. _____ Passed six-month rental inspection
12. _____ No property damage
13. _____ No health or safety hazard/violation present
14. _____ No reports or evidence of illegal activity on the premises

Again, we want to thank you for your cooperation in following all the rental terms of your agreement. Because you have satisfactorily met the above terms, we've sent you a copy of this favorable report for your records, so that you can provide copies to future prospective landlords and lenders.

The reputation you establish with us will be with you for many years to come. You will be able to present or offer a copy of this report to every landlord or company who reviews your record in the future. This can help you when you may need assistance from banks, home mortgage companies, insurance companies, and other creditors with whom you wish to do business. It's to your advantage to continue to meet all the terms of your rental agreement. If you ever receive a notice from us to correct a rental violation, do so immediately so that we will not have to report unfavorable information about your rental performance. An unfavorable report can make it very difficult for you in the future to:

- Rent a home or apartment of your choice
- Buy a future house, new automobile, or anything requiring good credit
- Get a car loan, credit card, student loan, or home loan for you and your family

Landlord/Manager _____ Date Sent or Delivered _____

Notice was hand delivered (to whom) _____

72-HOUR WARNING NOTICE TO REPORT POOR PERFORMANCE TO NATIONAL TENANT REPORTING AGENCY
Your immediate action is required.

To: _____   Date: _____

Address: _____   Time: _____ ☐ AM or ☐ PM

City, State, ZIP: _____

Alert! Your Immediate Action Is Required
Poor Performance to Be Reported:

The poor performance of items marked below are about to be reported to a nationwide tenant reporting agency. The function of agencies receiving this information is to track and maintain records on residents, including information of your credit history and your performance as a resident. This information will be available to future landlords, managers, lenders, and creditors who request it. However, this notice is sent to you to avoid this action from being necessary, if you respond immediately.

The Following Poor Performance Is to Be Reported Unless You Take Responsive Steps

1. _____ Unpaid rent
2. _____ Late rent payment
3. _____ Returned check
4. _____ Unpaid repair bill
5. _____ Unpaid utility bill
6. _____ Excessive noise
7. _____ Unauthorized occupant
8. _____ Unauthorized pet(s)

9. _____ Unauthorized vehicle
10. _____ Excessive junk outside
11. _____ Rental upkeep violation
12. _____ Damaged property
13. _____ Health or safety hazard/violation
14. _____ Threats to landlord/others
15. _____ Other _____

If you satisfactorily resolve the situation(s) described above with the owner or manager within 72 hours from the date and time indicated at the top of this page, this information will not be reported to the national tenant reporting agency at this time. To satisfactorily resolve this matter, _____.

The reputation you establish here will be with you for many years to come. Every landlord or company who reviews your record in the future will have access to the unfavorable record you are establishing with us. It may eventually be reported to banks, home mortgage companies, insurance companies, and other creditors with whom you wish to do business and who request a report. An adverse report can make it very difficult for you in the future to:

- Get a credit card or loan
- Rent a home or an apartment of your choice
- Buy a future house, new automobile, or anything requiring good credit

You should also note that if you are a cosigner, you are **fully** responsible for performance of the entire lease, regardless of any other cosigners' lack of performance. Remember, a favorable record is a vital key to your future and requires your immediate action.

Signature of owner/manager _____

Date notice delivered _____   Delivered by hand (to whom) _____

Or was posted (where) _____   Or sent by certified mail _____

NOTE TO RESIDENT(S): To respond to or dispute this report, please call _____

FINANCIAL ASSISTANCE AVAILABLE

From: _____

_____

_____

Date: _____

To: _____

_____

_____

Dear _____:

    We understand that sometimes situations come up that are beyond your immediate control. When this occurs, it can create a serious financial challenge to meet all your obligations. Because having shelter is your most important financial obligation, I know that even when serious problems occur, you will do all you can to pay the rent and make sure that you will have a place for you and your family to live. To offer you assistance so that you hopefully will never have to be evicted, the management staff has contacted community agencies and local churches in the area that have previously been able to offer assistance to individuals facing financial difficulties. If assistance is soon or now needed in paying your rent, we suggest that you try contacting them immediately. While we can't promise that they will always be able to help, they have helped others in the past. These agencies and churches may need verification from the owner or manager regarding payment due, and we will be glad to respond to their requests. Have them contact us at the following number _____ if they need our assistance and we will also provide them with our address where they can send financial assistance for rent. Please understand, however, that although it's our policy to offer helpful suggestions, during the time you work with any agencies or churches to come up with the money, until rent is actually paid, our nonpayment and eviction procedures must still be followed. That is why we encourage you to make contact with these agencies, relatives, friends, and any others who may provide you assistance as soon as possible, so that you can come up with the money before final eviction takes place. And be sure to contact us as soon as you received funds for your payment due. Following are the names and numbers of agencies and churches that may be able to help you:

_____

_____

_____

_____

_____

_____

_____

_____

_____

PARTIAL PAYMENT ACCEPTANCE

Address: _____

City: _____ State _____ ZIP _____

Date: _____

Dear _____ :

We can only accept partial payment if you understand and acknowledge that your rent was due on _____ and that making partial payment does not waive our right according to the Rental Agreement to begin or continue with legal proceedings without further demand of notice.

We do appreciate your efforts in fulfilling your obligation, and it will help with your credit standing with our company. If your partial payment proposal is satisfactory, we will work with you. However, if this occurs more often or if you fail to do as you propose, we will immediately begin legal proceedings without further notice leading to your eviction.

As you know, your total rent now past due is _____ , which includes _____ .

How do you propose to pay this complete amount?

$ _____   Date: _____

$ _____   Date: _____

Please sign below, giving your agreement to the above terms and acknowledging that you understand that you have violated the lease agreement and partial payment does not stop us from continuing legal proceedings.

Resident's Signature: _____ Date: _____

Resident's Signature: _____ Date: _____

Owner's Signature: _____ Date: _____

NOTICE TO TERMINATE TENANCY

To: _____
                                Tenant(s) in Possession

You are hereby required within thirty (30) days from this date to vacate, remove your belongings, and deliver up possession of the premises, now held and occupied by you, being those premises located at:

House No.: _____ Street: _____ Apt #: _____

City: _____ State: _____ ZIP: _____

This notice is intended for the purpose of terminating the lease/rental agreement by which you now hold possession of the above-described premises. Should you fail to vacate and comply, legal proceedings will be instituted against you to recover possession, to declare said lease/rental forfeited, and to recover rents, damages, attorney fees, and court costs for the period of the unlawful detention.

Please be advised that your rent for said premises is due and payable up to and including the date of termination of your tenancy under this notice. This notice complies with the terms and conditions of the lease or rental agreement under which you presently hold said property. Please contact the office of the landlord/manager if you have questions regarding this notice or the requirements and procedure for getting back any deposits to which you are entitled.

Dated this _____ day of _____ , 20_____ .

Owner/Manager

PROOF OF SERVICE

I, the undersigned, being of legal age, declare under penalty of perjury that I served the notice to terminate tenancy, of which this is a true copy, on the above-mentioned tenant in possession, in the manner indicated below:

On _____ , 20_____ , I served the notice to the tenant in the following manner:

_____

Executed on _____ , 20_____ , at _____

By: _____ Title: _____

REQUEST FOR JUDGMENT

From: _____

_____

_____

Date: _____

Original court date: _____   Docket no: _____

To: _____

_____

_____

Dear _____:

Please take notice that the undersigned will move the _____ General District Court, Civil Division, located at _____ , for judgment against you according to the original summons now pending before the Court on _____ at _____ AM/PM.

Your security deposit of $ _____ was applied as follows:

Damages/repairs	$ _____
_____	$ _____
_____	$ _____
_____	$ _____
_____	$ _____
Less security deposit	$ _____
Still due	$ _____
Rent claimed on warrant	$ _____
Total claimed in this motion	$ _____

NOTICE OF JUDGMENT

From: _____

_____

_____

Date: _____

To: _____

_____

_____

On _____ , which was the court date concerning the balance you owed our company, possession of the property was given back to us. The court also issued judgment against you regarding this matter on the same date or a following date _____ .

We have enclosed a copy of the judgment issued against you.

Rent amount: $ _____

Court costs: $ _____

Other costs $ _____

Total judgment amount: $ _____

This amount must be paid within five days, or at least satisfactory arrangements made for a payment schedule. If payment or satisfactory arrangements are not made, we will take further legal action against you by garnishing your wages or attaching any personal property, including your automobile, to recover the amount due, plus additional legal costs.

Contact our office immediately to stop further costs and legal action against you.

Thank you for your cooperation.

Sincerely,

Rental Manager

COLLECTION LETTER
(To: Attorney or Collection Agency)

Date: _____

To: _____

_____

_____

Gentlemen:

Enclosed are the necessary documents relating to the EVICTION, POSSESSION, FORCIBLE DETAINER, and/or COLLECTION OF ACCOUNTS RECEIVABLE for the following property address:

_____

Name of Resident: _____

Social Security #: _____

Name of Resident: _____

Social Security #: _____

_____

The judgment included the following:

Unpaid Rent:	$ _____	which included _____
Other Charges:	$ _____	for _____
	$ _____	for _____
Subtotal:	$ _____	
Attorneys fees:	$ _____	
Court costs:	$ _____	
Total Due:	$ _____	

Please send **collection** letter first before beginning suit.

Please begin suit immediately.

Please do not sue—**collection only**.

Please send letter demanding tenant take action to cure default as listed.

Comments: _____

Please notify us of any actions taken by tenant as a result of your efforts. We will notify you immediately of any action or receipt of any funds on behalf of the tenant.

NOTICE TO FORMER RESIDENT
FINAL DEMAND FOR PAST-DUE PAYMENT

From: _____

_____

_____

Date: _____

To: _____

_____

_____

AMOUNT IMMEDIATELY DUE: $_____

CREDIT IS A VALUABLE ASSET

Dear _____

We are making a final attempt to collect money due from you before reporting your delinquent debt to all three major credit bureaus and/or turning this matter over to a collection agency. A collection agency may be retained to collect the amount stated above that is past due resulting from unpaid rent or other charges from your lease agreement at the following address:

_____.

Unless you pay this debt (or make satisfactory payment arrangements) within __ days, we will have no choice but to turn this matter over to a collection agency which may result in garnishment of your wages and/or your bank account and **this debt being reported to all three major credit bureaus**. Your credit report is important because future landlords, lenders, banks, and creditors who you contact to rent or buy a car or home will be able to see the debts you owe. To avoid all this, send payment in full to us by the following date _____. Or call us now at _____ to make satisfactory payment arrangements.

Send payment in full to the address below:

_____

As required by law, you are hereby notified that a negative remark on your credit report may be submitted to a credit reporting agency if you fail to fulfill the terms of your obligations.

Sincerely,

Owner/Management

NOTICE OF DEBT FORGIVENESS

_____ , Former tenant

Date: _____

Dear   _____ :

    This letter is to notify you that you owe $ _____ for past-due rent and/or other charges to _____ (previous landlord). You have 30 (thirty) days to pay said amount in full or contact me to make satisfactory arrangements for payment. If I have not received payment in full or other acceptable arrangements by the following date, _____, I will assume that it is your intention not to pay the amount due. After that date, I will cancel the debt and forgive the back rent and other charges.

    Please be advised that pursuant to the **Internal Revenue Service** code, that when indebtedness is forgiven, it becomes classified as income and taxes will be due then from you on this amount. Cancellation of debt must be reported to the IRS by the one whose debt is being cancelled. It would, therefore, be necessary for you to include said cancellation of income on your tax return so that you'll be able to pay the tax due without incurring any interest and penalties for failure to report said income.

    I will be submitting a 1099 form to the **Internal Revenue Service** in your name for $ _____ . I will mail this form and officially forgive the debt on the following date: _____ . Once this form is received, it may trigger a letter to you from the IRS and possibly a **complete tax audit.** This letter is being sent, however, in hopes that you will pay the amount due or set up an acceptable payment plan, so that the IRS will not have to be contacted on your regard.

    Be advised as well that if you are on any form of public assistance, this classification of income will also be reported to all public assistance programs that you may be participating in, and this might cause you to lose eligibility in the program or reduce monthly payments to you.

    Hopefully you will pay the debt so that a 1099 will not have to be filed. To make payment arrangements, please contact me by this date: _____ . The phone number to call is_____ or send the amount due to me to the following address _____ .

Thank you for your cooperation.

NOTICE TO RECLAIM PERSONAL PROPERTY

From: _____

_____

_____

Date: _____

To: _____

_____

_____

Dear _____ :

When you vacated the rental dwelling at _____ , the following personal property was left behind in the dwelling:

_____

_____

_____ .

These items have been placed in storage for _____ days. You may claim this property by contacting

_____ .

These items must be claimed, as well as storage and moving charges paid within _____ days of this notice, or the property will be either sold or disposed of, which is allowed by local law.

Thank you for your cooperation.

Sincerely,

Rental Manager

PLEASE BE ADVISED OF THE FOLLOWING
NO TRESPASS NOTICE

In reference to Court Case   _____

Plantiff(s)   _____

                             _____
vs.

Defendendents   _____

                             _____

No Trespass Notice

PLEASE BE NOTIFIED that on the _____ day of _____ , _____ , an order was entered in the above-captioned cause restoring possession of the premises commonly known as _____ to the property owner/manager, _____ . The property owner/manager was restored to possession of the premises as of the _____ day of _____ .

ANY PERSON INCLUDING, BUT NOT LIMITED TO, THE ABOVE-NAMED DEFENDANT(S) AND ANY GUEST OR INVITEES OF THE DEFENDANT(S) ENTERING AND/OR REMAINING UPON THE PREMISES ON OR AFTER THE _____ DAY OF _____ , _____ , SHALL BE COMMITTING THE OFFENSE OF CRIMINAL TRESPASS TO REAL PROPERTY. THIS IS A CLASS _____ MISDEMEANOR PUNISHABLE BY IMPRISONMENT FOR NOT MORE THAN _____ MONTHS AND A FINE OF NOT MORE THAN $ _____ .

Please consider this notice of No Trespass. Any person, including, but not limited to, the Defendant(s) and/or any guests or invitees of the Defendant(s) will be subject to legal action by this building's management and/or criminal prosecution. Copies of this notice may have been delivered to all tenants of the above-mentioned residence.

Owner/Manager: _____   Date: _____

TEN REASONS WHY YOU SHOULD NOT FEEL GUILTY ABOUT EVICTIONS!

Please Post as a Reminder to *Yourself!*

1. Always start evictions immediately. If the tenants need extra time, the court will give it to them.

2. You don't make a profit with evictions. You only cut your losses.

3. You've already supplied the "needy" tenant with free housing. You've done your charity work, give someone else a chance.

4. If the tenant doesn't have a friend or relative to help out, doesn't that say a lot about the tenant's character?

5. If anyone asks you how you could put someone out on the street, ask the questioner to pay the rent so you won't evict the tenant.

6. The tenant has illegally kept possession of your house and is stealing from you. The tenant has stolen your home, stolen utilities, stolen your hard-earned investment, and stolen your services. The tenant is a thief. Do you see stores letting your tenant go in and take from them?

7. Letting a tenant stay in your house while not paying rent is like giving your tenant your charge card or a blank check and telling him, "Feel free to spend it because I really don't care. I like loaning money out interest free, even if I'm not sure I'll get paid back."

8. How would you feel if you worked all week and your employer said, "I don't have a paycheck for you"? Guess what, your tenant has told you that! Do you work for nothing?

9. If you want to give your apartment away or provide free rent, you should be the one who decides who gets it, not your tenant. There are a lot of people more deserving.

10. Your tenant is taking money that provides for your family needs. And the sad thing is some tenants live better lifestyles than their landlords. It's easy when the landlords let them live rent free! Picture yourself trying to tell your child you could not give him or her what he or she wanted because you had to pay a stranger's rent so the stranger could buy a gift for another child.

PART FOUR

Maintenance and Management

Forms to Get Residents to Take Proper Care of Your Property

WHAT "TITLE" DO YOU COMMUNICATE TO YOUR RESIDENTS?

■ *Tip Number 34*

Introduce yourself as the rental or property manager, not the owner.

When residents see you as the manager of the property and not just a mom and pop landlord, it provides you with several advantages. 1) Residents will be less likely to try to get you to bend the rules. And if they do, I simply respond, "John, sorry about your circumstances, if it was left up to me, you wouldn't have to pay any rent at all." 2) As a manager, you do not have to make any hasty decisions on the spot. If residents try confronting you to get an immediate answer about an issue, since you are only the manager, you can always respond that you have to get back with the resident, once you discuss it with the rest of management. This allows you to have time to "think" before responding with a promise or emotionally charged comment that may not be to your best benefit, or that you will regret saying later, or allows you time to think and gather all the facts, before giving a wrong response altogether. 3) Sometimes you will have to respond to a residents request contrary to what the resident wanted, or in a strict manner to enforce the rules of the lease. As a manager, the resident will be less likely to see you as the "bad" guy, since you are simply doing your job, just another working "joe" like they are. 4) Residents tend to try and take advantage of a landlord's "niceness" and are quicker to get really upset if you are the "rich owner" and can't help them out. And many owners do not want to be seen as unsympathetic to a person's problems or even fear retaliation, so they allow residents to play on their sympathies or fear and make allowances toward due dates, additional charges or lease rules, which actually trains residents to develop bad habits and perform worse. However, once residents realize that everything is run "by the book" and always professionally by you as the manager, (instead of a mom or pop landlord who could be swayed or played), residents will be much more prone to pay on time, not make excuses, and follow all the rules of the agreement. And even when residents fail to abide by the rules and face possible eviction, residents are far less likely to retaliate in a negative way toward you, toward the property, or toward your personal residence because they understand that it is not anything personal, just what has to be done. Though as a side note, have all of the correspondence with residents, including leases, always have the "company's" business P.O. box or street address, never your home address.

WHOM DO YOUR RESIDENTS CALL WHEN THINGS GET "HOT"?

A few years back, I experienced one of the most nerve-racking calls I've had in twenty years of rental management. It was about three o'clock in the morning. It just so happened that I was awake and near my in-home office when the call came in, so I monitored the call as the caller talked to my answering machine. The following is a transcript of what was said. And this was all that was said.

"Mr. Taylor, this is Mike. I live next door to one of your houses. Uh . . . Uh . . . I don't know if there is any way to let you know or not . . . [pause] You probably won't get this message until tomorrow, but one of your houses caught on fire. [pause] They got it under control now. It's out, but the people that live there . . . [long pause] It's the house on L Ave, not the brown duplex, but the two story. I don't know what else to say. [pause] I don't know. [pause—hang up]

I threw on some clothes and went dashing out toward the property to inspect the situation. All kinds of questions were racing through my head, and I was anxious about the current status of the residents, the property, and my insurance coverage (I know, it's kind of late to wonder if I should have updated my insurance coverage). Were the residents alive? How much of the property was gone? Would I be sued? Was this my signal to get out of the rental business? Could I sell the property? Who would

want it? Maybe, have a fire sale? Obviously my thoughts were running wild at that point, as I tried to use humor to counteract fear of the unknown. It was one of the longest ten-minute drives of my life.

The moment I turned the corner where the property was located I strained to see if my building was even standing. It was! The firemen had left. One upstairs window had been broken out. Smoke stained walls in the corner of one upstairs room, where a pile of clothes had burned (Those clothes were now laying on the grass on the front lawn.) The residents were standing out front—all okay. The bottom line to my early morning trauma was that very little damage was done, more emotional than physical to both my residents and me.

The outcome could have been different, and I could have suffered a tremendous financial loss. I believe there are very simple management strategies I implement with my residents at the beginning of the relationship that helped me save thousands of dollars and can assist you under similar circumstances. The simplicity of each idea is why some landlords don't think to implement them.

■ *Tip Number* **35**

Inform residents of all emergency/maintenance contacts.

First, inform (train) all residents to call the appropriate person or agency in case of an emergency. Give your residents a list of emergency numbers when they move in (see the Emergency Numbers and Regular Maintenance Numbers form). Guess whose name is *not* on the list? Yours. Be very direct in verbal and written communication. *In case of fire, call 911.*

Also, for every rental that you own, you should develop a good business relationship with at least one neighbor who will work in conjunction with your residents and you. A neighbor living next door can be "on watch" of your property day and night. Whether your residents are home or not, neighbors provide you with the back-up personnel for dealing with emergencies. In addition, any situation on your properties that needs your attention, if left unchecked, may become worse and cost you hundreds or thousands of dollars (e.g., residents moving out in the middle of the night or drugs creeping in).

The three o'clock phone call I received did not come from a resident not knowing whom to call. It came from my back-up personnel, the neighbor who was alerting me to what was going on. Of course, I made a point of asking that any future messages be a little more complete.

■ Tip Number 36

Educate residents on how they can protect themselves (and you!) Recommend, if not require, renter's insurance.

I have been notified a couple more times over the years of fires in my rentals. Thankfully, none of the occurrences have resulted in tragic loss or major damage. However, there has been damage to residents' personal belongings and some minor damage to the property. In each case, the resident was found to be negligent; in one instance, leaving something cooking on the stove.

Do your residents know that the owner's property insurance will not help them recover losses of personal belongings in case of fire or theft on the premises? Some residents are not aware of this and do not realize the tremendous risk they take by not obtaining a relatively low cost renter's insurance policy. We include a form (found back in Part 2) that informs residents of such risks.

Educate your residents to increase their understanding regarding this matter and to the fact that if they were found at fault for a fire, the resident would be liable for all damages, loss, and injuries to themselves, guests, and neighbors. Without proper insurance protection, such a scenario could financially ruin a resident. I now strongly recommend renter's insurance of all residents, and am actually transitioning to the point where renter's insurance will be required. It is to my advantage, and yours, to have the residents' insurance pay for damage to the property which is why you will also find a sample letter in Part 2 requesting that the renter's insurance company add the owner as an additional insured on the policy.

MAINTENANCE GUARANTEE

Over and over again, landlords tell me they believe the best way to keep residents happy is to promise to fix any needed repairs immediately. If you agree with that statement, read the following secret to keeping residents happy (you'll never fear maintenance emergencies again).

The secret to customer service is not what you do. Instead, whenever possible, always look for ways to help customers feel that they are winners.

You may ask then, "Well, don't residents feel that they lose when I provide slow service?" Following the strategy I'm about to present and using the Maintenance Guarantee form when you are slow to fix a repair, your residents will get happier each day the repair is not done.

Let residents know that all repairs that you are responsible for, that are outlined in the lease, will be taken care of within three days after the resident notifies you, *or the resident will receive free daily rent,* after the third day until the problem is fixed.

Without this type of service guarantee, your resident will continue to get upset each day a problem goes unrepaired, and possibly call the local housing, building, or health inspectors which complicates your problems even more. You will continue to feel enslaved to your property as you jump every time your residents say jump.

Using the maintenance guarantee suggestion, you can take up to three days to repair a problem, doing it at your convenience. Your resident only makes one phone call to you and has no desire to complain to anyone else. Instead the residents get happier with each day that goes by, actually hoping you do not fix the problem for at least three days because they have an opportunity to win free rent.

■ Tip Number 37

Offer free rent if promised service is not performed.

For you skeptics reading this, I do understand that if the maintenance problem is creating a life or death situation, even free rent won't make a resident happy. However, 99 percent of the maintenance requests that a landlord receives are not life or death situations and this guarantee will keep your residents working with you, instead of against you.

■ Tip Number 38

Seek the assistance of contractors who are referred by other landlords.

I'm often asked by landlords, "How or where do you find a reliable contractor or handyman to work on your properties?" The short and best answer I know is to get recommendations or referrals from other landlords in your area. You'll discover in this chapter a questionnaire to use with other landlords when seeking the recommendation of a contractor. There is also a form for receiving and comparing quotes from the contractors who are recommended.

LANDLORD'S RIGHT TO ENTER

Though the landlord has a right and responsibility to periodically inspect a residence to make sure it is being properly maintained, there are procedures to follow when doing so. Most states have access laws giving a landlord the legal right to enter to inspect, handle repairs, and show the property to prospective residents or buyers. However, in most cases, the access laws require that the landlord or manager give advance notice to the resident of the intent to enter, usually at least 24 hours. Respect the resident's right and, unless there is an absolute emergency, always give as much advance notice as possible (beyond state minimum requirements). Communicate your intent to enter in writing. A sample form is included in the forms in this section.

■ *Tip Number* **39**

Respect a resident's privacy.

While you have a legal right to enter, always ask for the residents' cooperation and work within their time preferences. In addition, when coordinating time schedules for contractors to perform repairs on the property, again notify residents of the need to enter the premises and seek their cooperation. This shows that you respect their rights and privacy.

RENTAL REPAIR RECEIPT

It's important to know that work is done after a maintenance request is made. Residents are the best persons to confirm that work was completed. So after any repair is completed, have the resident sign a Repair Completion Receipt form. The repairs can be anything from a broken light to clearing a drain. The form is completed for all repairs and signed by the resident.

■ *Tip Number* **40**

Determine who is at fault for maintenance problems.

However, if the problem was due to a resident's negligence, that is also indicated on the form by the person who performed the repair. The resident is then billed for the repair, including materials and labor. The resident is notified at move-in and reminded at the time of the repair that if the problem was created by the resident, the resident will be billed. This type of form was suggested by a "Mr. Landlord" subscriber who reported a 90 percent success rate when billing residents. A copy of the repair receipt is kept in the resident's file. These receipts may come in handy if a resident challenges the landlord in court about not completing repair requests.

HOME "TUNE-UP"

Every spring landlords have an opportunity to do something to help retain residents. In case you don't know, when the spring season brings warmer weather, your residents are thinking of moving. Late spring is the peak time of the year when rental residents begin looking for new places to move. Residents are tired of the same old rentals. Your residents greatly desire a feeling of newness, or at least an improvement in their homes or apartments that most landlords mistakenly do not offer. Most landlords don't realize they are losing good residents until it is too late. There is a very simple strategy to keep your residents happy and increase your profits during a time when millions of other landlords are losing their residents. As warm weather overtakes the last strongholds of winter, and the sun starts shining more, realize it is natural for people to want to shed old things and desire the new and improved.

Spring cleaning and improvement projects are widespread during the spring season. People on average will spend a minimum of $200 during this time of year to clean up and/or improve their environments. Put simply, this is the time of year when people are seeking improvements in their homes.

At this time more than any other throughout the year, up to one-third of your rental residents are willing to spend a reasonable amount of money to improve their environments. Some are even willing to spend a thousand dollars or more in total moving costs to change apartments.

■ *Tip Number* **41**

Long term residents often desire and deserve change or minor improvements, so offer it to them.

If your residents want change, offer it to them, plus increase your resident retention, on-time payments, and your cash flow in many cases. Let me share a successful strategy to implement every spring when Americans have a strong desire to improve their home environment. This is not a phenomenon to ignore but one to profit from before the fleeting high desire dissipates.

Offer all your rental residents a free spring home tune-up. To encourage long-term residents, offer a different level of improvements based on how long a resident has been with you. Provide a list of 10 to 12 possible home improvement options from which your resident can choose. One-year residents who've been with you a minimum of 12 months may select one free tune-up item or improvement. Two-year residents select two. Three-year or longer residents select three. Your residents will appreciate the tune-up and look forward to staying with you and receiving better tune-ups each spring.

The benefits of this strategy do not stop there. One out of every three or four residents will like the tune-up idea and the improvements you offer so well that they will be willing to pay you to provide a *major* home tune-up that includes their choice of four improvements in addition to the free items(s) they are entitled to. Therefore, offer each resident the option of a major tune-up for a total one-time cost of $125 or $150 or add a small $15 or $25 to their monthly rental amount. See our Free Spring Home Tune-Up form for a sample listing of items you may offer residents.

The expense and income from the major tune-up may mean that you only break even the first year, but after that you are receiving nothing but profit and your resident has paid for the cost of the improvements! The improvements may cost you slightly more than the $150 to $300 your resident pays you. Compare that to how much it will hurt your cash flow if your resident moves, not to mention how your peace of mind suffers and the risk of nightmares a new unknown resident may bring. An average vacancy can easily cost you $1,200 or more in fix-up expenses, rental income loss, advertising-related expenses, and the value of your time in finding a new resident.

Therefore, even if it costs you $100 above what the resident pays you, you are still way ahead from a cash-flow standpoint. Take a look at the list of improvements I suggest. These are the type of things

an owner or manager would do for a good resident for no charge.

This book also includes special letters to give to your residents during other seasons. For both the summer and winter months, letters are provided for landlords to give instructions to residents on how to best maintain and safeguard their properties during that time of year.

RESIDENT GRIEVANCE PROCEDURE

Has a resident attempted to sue you lately? I've conducted surveys with many "Mr. Landlord" subscribers, and one out of every four rental owners I have interviewed has had a resident contact an attorney about the possibility of a lawsuit. It's a real good chance that one of your residents may think of contacting an attorney before the year is over. Let me put it another way. Each year you own rental property, the odds are greater that you may have to fight or risk losing a million-dollar lawsuit.

A person who calls an attorney has been programmed by our society to think that suing someone is the best option if anything goes wrong and someone else can be found at fault. Your residents are no different. If you looked inside their heads, you'd see a big *Call the Attorney* button firmly implanted, which will be activated if anything occurs (or does not occur) at your rental that affects the resident in a negative way.

How do you control the actions of your residents? Sure, I've suggested that landlords always consider how cooperative residents will be when selecting future residents, and avoid those who seem to have a chip on their shoulder against landlords.

There is always a chance, however, that your good residents may think you've made a mistake in handling their housing needs (and perhaps you have). Your residents may feel they have a justified grievance against you. What, then, is to stop the resident from immediately calling a lawyer and attempting to sue you for everything you own?

Because a potential problem is greatly escalated when a resident calls an attorney, the suggested solution is to get the resident to call the landlord *first* if the resident feels he or she is owed something.

A resident who takes the time to call an attorney is doing so in hopes of being compensated. So you let residents know, when they first move in, in the form of a lease addendum, that you have a grievance procedure, and a mediation procedure (if necessary), for residents to use if they feel they have a grievance with the owner. In addition, if the owner quickly determines that the resident has a legitimate grievance or that the landlord is at fault after going through a mediation procedure, the resident is entitled to compensation.

■ Tip Number *42*

Try to resolve disputes without lawyers or lawsuits.

For this grievance plan to work, the resident must feel that the grievance procedure is fair and not slighted in the landlord's favor.

If the landlord is wrong, and if an attorney was involved, a lawsuit might force the landlord out of the landlording business. With the residence grievance procedure (see the Resident Grievance form), the resident first contacts you, not the attorney. Let's say the landlord is wrong. Under a grievance procedure you set up, you may elect to give rewards of up to three months' rent compensation to residents who have been treated unfairly or damaged because of your action.

To the average resident (not your professional deadbeat), three months of rent sounds like great compensation, and therefore gives the resident good reason or an incentive to call the landlord instead of the attorney. Anytime your resident calls you first, instead of an attorney, you're a winner.

Even if the grievance the resident has is legitimate and you recognize your mistake or you're found at fault, you come out way ahead in this scenario. It is far better for you to compensate a resident with three months' worth of free rent than to have had the resident contact an attorney, take you to court, and you lose. Giving a resident three months' worth of free rent is far less than what you would pay if your resident calls an attorney and wins a lawsuit against you. The attorney fees alone may be ten times more than three months of rent.

You may now be thinking, "But Jeffrey, what if I, the landlord, am not found at fault, even after a mediation procedure, but yet my resident decides to go ahead and contact his attorney and sue me?"

You still are far ahead in the game by having the resident contact you first instead of the attorney. While hearing a resident's concerns and going through a mediation procedure, your resident will lay all the cards on the table. You have the opportunity to see how valid the grievance and supporting claims are. Because the resident called you first instead of an attorney, you have an opportunity to "preview" possible court arguments. This is of tremendous benefit to you because you can make an intelligent decision, not based on fear, whether it's better to try to simply settle out of court or to let the resident pursue his lawsuit.

Mr. Landlord Challenge Consider outlining a fair grievance procedure for your residents to follow before they consider whether they are going to call an attorney to sue the pants off of you, because being nice is not enough of a safeguard against a lawsuit. Landlords in various cities nationwide have shared how they have identified mediation services in their local areas who are willing to listen to landlord-tenant disputes. The landlords then put in writing, in the form of a lease addendum, or as a clause in the rental agreement, that both landlord and resident agree to use the services of the designated mediation service to handle any grievance or dispute they can't solve, and to abide by the rulings of said service.

Mediation services, while providing a fair service to both parties, are especially beneficial for the landlord because most mediation services will not reward excessive compensation. A rental clause requiring both parties to agree to use a mediation service may not be enforceable in some locales. However, having such a clause may still encourage 99 percent of all residents to utilize your suggested service, instead of calling an attorney.

The key or secret to reducing the chances of a lawsuit and having residents not call an attorney is changing the residents' mindsets when they first move in. You let them know from the beginning what procedures to follow if they ever have a grievance. Convey the fairness or impartiality of the procedure, and the possibility for compensation (three months of free rent). If you wait until a dispute or grievance occurs to introduce a grievance procedure, it's too late. The resident's mindset has probably already locked in on the big "lawsuit button" in his or her head, and the attorney has probably already been called. I recommend that within the next 30 days you talk with your attorney regarding this discussion and the sample form in this book and draft an addendum or rental clause you can include or attach to your rental agreement that can literally save you tens or hundreds or thousands of dollars.

YOUR PROPERTIES ARE TOO VALUABLE TO BE LEFT ALONE

■ *Tip Number* **43**

Conduct annual inspections.

An annual inspection of each long-term resident's rental home can uncover needed repairs (leaky faucets, cold radiators, etc.), as well as provide an opportunity to know what the resident's needs and wishes are. When conducted with the right attitude (you are not checking up on the resident—you are assuring good service), such a visit makes the resident feel cared for. During such a visit, the resident will often reveal what, if anything, will make it more likely that he or she will remain in the rental home. Within reason, meeting such desires can pay off with a high retention rate.

If your property goes uninspected, residents may try to get away with poor upkeep. Yearly inspections are good for long-term residents, but it is suggested that you do an inspection every six months (see the Inspection Due form) during the first two years of a resident's tenancy. It should only take 15 minutes per property to do an inspection. Try to do all your inspections in one day or over one weekend. No sense having this drag out over more days than necessary. You will be able to see very quickly if there are any holes in the walls, or if the faucets are leaking, etc. Just the fact that the residents know you are coming by will mean that they will probably take care of anything that you would be concerned with before you get there. It is suggested that you actually give your residents an inspection checklist of the things you will be inspecting when you come. That helps the residents feel more comfortable about inspections, because they don't have to guess what you will be looking for.

PROPERTY CONDITIONS AND VALUES CAN CHANGE QUICKLY

■ *Tip Number* **44**

Conduct periodic drive-by inspections.

Once a month, it is advisable to simply drive by your rental properties to make a quick inspection. What you are checking for is whether there are any unauthorized vehicles, unauthorized animals, damage to the exterior of the property, excessive loitering, local or community violations, or health or safety hazards or violations. Use a Drive-by Rental Inspection Notice to notify your residents of any problems.

■ *Tip Number* **45**

Identify and recognize residents who take extra care of your properties.

As you have learned or will see, it is important to identify and notify residents who violate your lease and maintenance policies. However, it is equally important to identify and recognize residents who are taking excellent care of your property and demonstrating extra efforts toward the upkeep and maintenance of the property. Recognition does not have to be elaborate, just a short note of appreciation (see example in this chapter), can convey to your residents that you recognize their efforts. Small notes of appreciation can go a long way toward encouraging and reinforcing the type of actions you want repeated, plus cultivating long-term relationships. People tend to remain in an environment and repeat actions where they are recognized in a positive manner.

HANDLING RESIDENTS WHO VIOLATE THE LEASE

■ *Tip Number* **46**

Document all violations in writing.

There are several types of rental violations other than slow or nonpayment of rent. Therefore, this book provides different types of violation notices regarding various rental issues, including noise, excessive utilities, garbage, automobile, pet, and upkeep. Whenever a resident violates one of your rental terms, start a paper trail of written notices concerning the problems. Amateur landlords only give verbal notices. In addition to any notices, document police calls, complaints from other residents, neighbors, etc. All this may be helpful if you need to evict the residents and must prove your position in court. From the very first sign of a problem, get going on your paperwork and be sure to put copies in the resident's file.

PROPERTY MAINTENANCE ISSUES MUST BE ADDRESSED

■ *Tip Number 47*

Offer residents an incentive for money-saving maintenance.

If you want residents to cooperate, explain your policies and then give them an incentive to abide by those policies. For example, if residents are making too much noise that disturbs neighbors, not only should you notify your residents that they are violating the terms of their agreement, but also consider offering an incentive for their cooperation. When notifying residents that their actions may result in termination of the agreement, mention that if they keep the noise level down, keep the peace, and there are no complaints from neighbors for the next six months, you will treat them (*and* the neighbor who made the initial complaints) to dinner at the restaurant of their choice.

Another idea to generate resident cooperation is in regard to water usage in a small multifamily building where the owner pays the water bills (this concept also works for other utilities the owner pays for). Inform residents that you have set a water budget for the building. Every month that the residents use less water and bring the utility bill under budget, the management will reward the residents with cash back for the difference. This is a win-win arrangement and motivates residents to use less water and report costly leaks. This type of communication to your residents can save you hundreds of dollars.

Those are the type of incentive-based concepts that are incorporated into some of our management forms in this book. Other forms included in this section address issues such as mold, safety, smoke detectors, satellite dishes, security, accidents, suspicious activity, and crime.

INTRODUCTION TO PROPERTY MANAGEMENT COMPANY

Date: _____

Dear _____:

    This letter is a friendly and official notification that the property you are residing in at _____ _____ has come under new management. We would like to take this opportunity to introduce ourselves and the major rental policies we use in working with residents. The name of our management company is _____ . Our phone number is _____ . Please call this number regarding any major concerns. Our office hours are _____. Our business address is _____ . Below are a few of our main rental policies.

On-Time Payments. We expect payment by the _____ of each month. There is a late charge of _____ for any payments received after the due date. We begin legal proceedings on the _____ of the month if we still have not received payment.

Pay by Mail. We ask that you please send your rent payment postmarked at least three days before the due date to avoid paying late charges to the business address above. We do not pick up rent checks in person. Please send check or money order only, not cash. Make checks payable to our company. This is for your protection as well as ours.

Rental Agreement. We have either enclosed a new rental agreement or we will have one of our managers stop by to meet you and explain the standard rental agreement we use with all residents and give you a copy for your records.

Deposits. Our office must have a deposit from all residents equal to _____ . To avoid misunderstanding later, we also must verify that the amount on file from your former owner/manager is what you think it should be. If we've included a questionnaire with this mailing, please fill it out and include the deposit you originally gave so we can confirm our records.

Property Manager. We have assigned a very capable individual to handle the management responsibilities for the buildings in your area. _____ will be contacting you in the near future to answer any questions you may have. We look forward to your cooperation in helping to make this management transition a smooth one.

Sincerely,

Property Manager

MAINTENANCE GUARANTEE

Attention all new and current residents. We now offer a maintenance guarantee to all residents. To help ensure your satisfaction with our rental home and the service that we, _____ , are responsible for, as outlined in your lease, major repairs (that are not caused by resident neglect, misuse, or abuse) will be addressed within three days (72 hours) *after* you notify us, so that problem does not continue to create a hardship for you or your family.

Examples of major items that we are responsible for include:

_____

_____

_____

If the problem or hardship is not addressed within the three-day period, you will have *free rent until the problem is corrected* on a per-day basis following the third day after we received notification of the problem. Your free rent will be awarded in the form of a rent rebate following your next on-time rental payment that we receive.

Resident: _____

Address: _____

City: _____ State_____ ZIP_____

Move-In Date: _____

Approved By: _____

EMERGENCY NUMBERS AND REGULAR MAINTENANCE NUMBERS
(For Your Information)

Dear Resident:

Welcome as a 3-Star resident to your home. We are pleased that you have chosen one of our houses/apartments as your new home, and we look forward to meeting your home-related needs during the next three years, and to assisting you in buying a house should you decide to buy in the future.

Below is a list of IMPORTANT numbers you may need to call during the time you are residing at your new address. These numbers include our office number, emergency numbers, and the names and numbers of workers who have been preapproved by the owners to do work on the premises. As your lease indicates, all work on the premises, including maintenance areas the resident is responsible for, must be done by preapproved licensed workers. If you prefer to use other licensed workers than those listed below, please first request written approval from the owners/management. Using nonapproved workers is a violation of the lease agreement and grounds for termination of the agreement. Thanks for your cooperation in the matter.

Office Number and Hours: _____

Emergency Numbers (in case of):   Call:

Fire: _____

Police (criminal activity on/near property): _____

Ambulance/Paramedic: _____

Gas Leak: _____

Water Line Break (need to shut off): _____

Loss of Electricity (other than nonpayment): _____

Emergency Property Repair: _____

(no heat, air conditioning, sewer back-up, roof leak):

Regular Maintenance (resident's responsibility) Preapproved workers

Plumbing (clogged drains): _____

Lawn Care: _____

Pest Control: _____

Appliances: _____

Broken Window: _____

Carpet Cleaning: _____

Other: _____   _____

LOCK-OUT ASSISTANCE RECEIPT

The following resident, _____, has requested assistance in getting into his/her residence because he/she is locked out of the premises located at
_____.

Date of request: _____

Time of request: _____

The resident is locked out because of the following reason:
_____.

The resident understands the owner or manager must check identification, review files, and verify individual requesting lock-out assistance is indeed a valid resident and current lease holder. Nonresidents are not permitted entry. The following was shown/given as proof the individual was a current resident:
_____

The resident understands and agrees to the following fees in regard to lock-out assistance:

Charge for lock-out assistance during business hours: $15 from 10 AM to 5 PM.
Charge for lock-out assistance outside business hours: $30 from 5 PM to 10 AM.
There is an additional charge of $ _____ if the resident's key is lost and/or the lock has to be completely replaced. All fees are due and payable at time assistance is provided.

Payment received from: _____

Amount received $ _____

If payment is not received, resident agrees that the following amount of $ _____ is owed and this amount will be immediately considered as additional rent due, and paid by the following date, _____ , or the resident is subject to eviction for nonpayment.

It should also be noted this is the _____ time the resident has needed lock-out assistance. If assistance is requested more than _____ times, the following additional terms may also apply:
_____

Resident's Signature: _____

Landlord/Manager's Signature: _____

NOTICE – NEW LOCK MUST BE INSTALLED

From: _____

_____

_____

Date: _____

To: _____

_____

_____

It has come to our attention that a new lock on your house or apartment has been changed without the owner's/management's authorization. In case of an emergency, it is essential that management have access to your home or apartment and therefore management must at all times have a set of keys to your home. Without access to all rentals, there is a substantial safety risk to all residents and to the property. In addition, if you lock yourself out or lose your keys, management will be able to allow you access to the home.

We have a standardized lock system in place, and to maintain this system we require that all locks be ones authorized by us. We are therefore giving you notice that a new lock must be installed on the property in the upcoming week. There will be a service charge of $ _____ for the lock replacement that you will be responsible for.
Please contact our office by calling _____ between _____ and _____ during the week, so that we can coordinate with you to arrange this and to provide you with a new set of keys.

Sincerely,

Management

INSPECTION DUE

From: _____

_____

_____

Date: _____

To: _____

_____

_____

Dear _____:

It is time for one of our regular inspections of the dwelling in which you reside. We will be sending one of our staff over during the next week. Please contact our office to set up an inspection date and time that is convenient for you. If we do not hear from you, someone will be by for inspection at either of the following times:
_____ or_____ .

Remember that, as part of the Future Homebuyers Program, you may earn $ _____ credit toward the purchase of a home if you pass the inspection, which will be added to your Future Homebuyer's account. Not passing the inspection means losing all credit previously accumulated and starting again. To help you pass the inspection, I've included some of the key items of property upkeep and maintenance that we will be checking for:

1. _____
2. _____
3. _____
4. _____
5. _____
6. _____
7. _____
8. _____
9. _____
10. _____
11. _____
12. _____
13. _____
14. _____
15. _____

Thank you for your cooperation.

Sincerely,

Rental Manager

NOTICE OF INTENT TO ENTER

Resident: _____

Address: _____

City: _____ State _____ ZIP _____

    According to your rental agreement, owner/manager may enter the property you are renting to perform part of the management duties. This is only done after giving a reasonable notice of at least 24 hours in advance.

    We are therefore sending this letter to notify you at least 24 hours in advance the owner/manager intends to enter the premises you are renting at the address noted above for the purpose of:

_____.

Approximate time of entrance: _____

Estimated duration of stay: _____

    If you will be available at the above time, please let the owner/manager know. However, it is not necessary you be on the premises at the time of entry. Owner/manager, after knocking to determine if anyone is home, will use a passkey to gain entrance.

    Change of Lock Notice: If the landlord/owner or designee is unable to enter because the resident has changed or rekeyed locks, landlord will use a locksmith to open the door and locks will be rekeyed. A new key will be given to resident, who will be charged for the service.

    You are always welcome to be present at the time of entry. If you have any questions, or if the date or time listed above is inconvenient, please notify us by the following date _____ so we can attempt to schedule an alternative time better for you. You may call us between _____ and _____ on the following days _____. Our phone number is _____. Though we will need to enter the dwelling no later than _____.

Thanks for your cooperation.

Signed: _____ Date: _____

Delivered in person by: _____

Signed: _____

Date: _____ Time: _____

DRIVE-BY RENTAL INSPECTION NOTICE

Dear Resident,

A recent drive-by inspection of your residence found:

_____ Unauthorized or nonworking vehicle parked on the property or without proper registration

_____ Unauthorized animal on the premises

_____ Window or screens broken/damaged on the _____ of the building

_____ Too many occupants loitering or actually residing in the property

_____ Items left on the outside of the premises, yard, porch, or balcony that are a violation of community, health, or safety standards

_____ Excessive noise coming from the property

_____ Further explanation of above: _____

_____

_____ Other rental agreement violation: _____

_____

    We did not know if you were aware of the above conditions, and we know that you desire to abide by all terms in the rental agreement so as not to jeopardize that agreement. Please correct above conditions by the following date: _____.

Thank you for your cooperation,

Owner/Manager

NOTE OF APPRECIATION

From: _____

_____

_____

Date: _____

To: _____

_____

_____

Dear _____:

Please accept this note of our appreciation. We wanted to take a moment to thank you for your outstanding efforts in the maintenance and upkeep of your property located at_____ demonstrated by _____ _____.

To show our appreciation we are pleased to give you a gift certificate that can be used at the following restaurant or store below: _____.

Again our sincere thanks,

_____

Management Team

FULL INSPECTION REPORT

Address: _____ Date: _____

City: _____ State _____ ZIP _____

We are scheduled to do our semiannual home inspection of your premises on the following date: _____
_____. We will be inspecting the following areas and items to see if they are in the same clean satisfactory condition as when you moved in. We again thank you for your cooperation.

	Satisfactory				Satisfactory	
	Yes	No			Yes	No
Entrance Door				*Bedroom #1*		
Knocker/bell	___	___		Ceiling	___	___
Peephole	___	___		Walls	___	___
Deadbolt lock	___	___		Floors	___	___
Living Room				Windows	___	___
Ceiling	___	___		Screen	___	___
Walls	___	___		Elec. fixtures	___	___
Floors	___	___		*Bedroom #2*		
Windows	___	___		Ceiling	___	___
Screen	___	___		Screen	___	___
Elec. fixtures	___	___		Floors	___	___
Dining Room or Bedroom #3				Window	___	___
Ceiling	___	___		Screen	___	___
Walls	___	___		Elec. fixtures	___	___
Floors	___	___		*Bathroom*		
Windows	___	___		Ceiling	___	___
Screen	___	___		Walls	___	___
Elec. fixtures	___	___		Floors	___	___
Kitchen				Windows	___	___
Stove	___	___		Screen	___	___
Refrigerator	___	___		Elec. fixtures	___	___
Cabinets	___	___		Medicine cabinet	___	___
Sink	___	___		Mirror	___	___
Countertops	___	___		Toilet	___	___
Ceiling	___	___		Tub	___	___
Walls	___	___		Sink	___	___
Floors	___	___		Shower	___	___
Windows	___	___		*General*		
Screen	___	___		Porch/balcony	___	___
Elec. fixtures	___	___		Heating system	___	___
General				Water heater	___	___
Back door	___	___		Front yard	___	___
Mail box	___	___		Back yard	___	___
				Garage/driveway	___	___

Special Remarks (cleaning or repairs needed): _____

Resident has been given a copy of this report and can provide any explanation if he or she so desires on the back of this form. Tenant will be held responsible for any detriment or damage to the property reported that was not present at original move-in date.

INSPECTION FAILURE REPORT

Date: _____

To: _____

_____

_____

Dear _____ :

During my recent inspection of your residence, the following conditions were found to be below the standards as defined in your Lease Agreement and listed on your Inspection Due letter. Corrective action must be taken within ten (10) days of receipt of this letter. If you do so, your Future Homebuyer's account will not be completely reduced to 0, but instead only be deducted by $ _____. Failure to correct the problem not only completely deletes your Future Homebuyer's account, but your neglect will leave us no alternative but to take the actions allowed us in your Lease Agreement to terminate the tenancy. We hope that will not be necessary.

_____ Health, safety, or fire hazard found in: _____

_____ Pick up and remove trash from: _____

_____ Cleaning needed for the following area(s): _____.

_____ Remove excessive materials stored on premises: _____.

_____ Replace or replace broken light bulbs, fixtures, or outlets and switch plates.

_____ Tighten all loose hardware on _____ and replace lost or damaged items.

_____ Replace furnace filters or air conditioner pads and/or smoke detector batteries.

_____ Remove mildew buildup in bathroom and cleaning needed for: _____.

_____ Remove the inoperative automobile you have stored on the premises.

_____ Repair or replace windows, screens, or doors.

_____ Clean up after animals. Municipal ordinances prohibit these unsanitary conditions

_____ Lawn needs care. Water, fertilize, trim edges, and mow lawn to prevent damage.

_____ Other: _____

Thank you for your cooperation.

Rental Manager

FREE SPRING HOME TUNE-UP
For 3-Star residents who paid their rent on time during the last year

One-year residents may select any one tune-up item or service below.
Two-year residents may select any two tune-up items or service below.
Three-year, or longer, residents may select any three tune-up items or services below.

Special Major Home Tune-Up Offer

You have the option of having FOUR additional home tune-up items or services as part of a major home tune-up. The value of a major tune-up with four items, as you can see below, can range up to $350. However, as one of our 3-Star residents, you may have a major tune-up done to your home or apartment for a $150 one-time charge, or just agree to add only $20 to your monthly rent amount for the next 12 months. The sooner you call _____ , the quicker we can schedule to have your free tune-up done and a major tune-up for those who want to take advantage of our special spring offer.

Home Tune-Up Items/Services
(Major tune-up, your choice of any four—only $20 added to rent)

1.	Choice of any approved wall color painted in any one room	$ 75.00
2.	Carpet cleaning for any two rooms	$ 60.00
3.	One ceiling fan installed	$ 60.00
4.	Two sets of mini-blinds installed	$ 60.00
5.	Wallpaper border added to any room (removable type)	$ 75.00
6.	Any three windows cleaned	$ 60.00
7.	Oven cleaned	$ 60.00
8.	Strip and wax kitchen floor	$ 60.00
9.	One time maid service—entire unit	$ 75.00
10.	One closet—additional shelves added	$ 75.00
11.	Additional phone jack added to one room	$ 75.00
12.	Additional door lock installed on both front and rear door	$ 75.00
13.	One-time pest control treatment provided to the entire unit	$ 75.00
14.	Spot painting/touch-up entire home or apartment	$ 90.00
15.	One-time yard maintenance/landscaping (single family home)	$100.00
16.	_____	$ _____

SUMMER CHECKLIST FOR RESIDENTS

Will you be traveling out of town during the summer months? We would like to recommend the following steps to help prevent any problems from occurring in regards to your residence. We will be glad to even check on your property if you will be away for an extended vacation period.

Notify management of your absence. Call and inform us of any dates when you will be away from your rental for an extended period (beyond three days). Leave an emergency number where you can be reached.

Prepay your rent. Prior to leaving, prepay rent, especially if you are traveling near the rental due date. This way, you can avoid late fees and preserve your excellent payment and credit history. Reminder, we offer the special automatic draft or electronic transfer payment plans that allow you to focus on your trip and not worry about mailing payments and possible late fees.

Purchase automatic timers for your lights (or receive them as a free gift). Lighted windows give the impression that someone is home. We will give you two as a free gift when you sign up for the automatic draft prepayment plan. Your automatic timer can turn on your lights in the evenings and off in the morning.

Yard Maintenance: If your rental agreement states that residents are responsible for yard maintenance (regular lawn cutting), be sure to make arrangements for someone to cut the grass during your absence. Owner reserves the right to hire someone to cut the grass if left unattended for two weeks, and bill the resident for the charges.

Stop newspapers and mail delivery. Stop all routine deliveries, so that there is no evidence that you are away. Items accumulated at your front door, on your yard, or in your mailbox are signals that you are not home.

Inform your immediate neighbors. Designate and ask at least one neighbor to keep an eye on your property during your absence. Give that neighbor our management number, in case a problem should arise. Please give the management the name and phone number of the designated neighbor.

Secure all doors and windows. Weather changes can damage your carpet, drapes, and furniture. Close and lock all doors and windows. Be sure we have duplicate keys to all locks.

Avoid insect problems. Eliminate the possibility of returning to an insect infested home. Empty all trash containers and garbage bags and remove them from the home. Secure open food containers, and put them in your refrigerator.

Disconnect appliances. Avoid leaving any appliances plugged in, including your television, computer, microwave, iron, toaster, and other small appliances. Check all cords for fraying to insure a fire will not occur while you are away.

Check your gas stove burners and oven. Before leaving your premises, always take a final check of your stove to ensure the burners are off to eliminate the possibility of a gas explosion.

Water all houseplants. Prior to an extended absence, water all houseplants and place them in the kitchen sink. Make arrangements for a friend to water your plants.

Telephone message. Do not leave messages on your voice mail system or answering machine that reveal you are on a vacation or away for an extended period.

Do not leave any animals unattended. If your lease permits a pet, do not leave pets in the residence unattended while you are gone.

PREPARATION FOR COLDER WEATHER

Dear Residents,

Cold weather will soon be here, and we'd like to share a checklist that will help keep your heating bills down this winter and make your home warmer and safer for you and your family. Planning ahead can save you money and frustration. As per your rental agreement, any preventable damage (such as freezing pipes) is the tenant's responsibility.

Outside Preparation

_____ Check and close all the vents to the crawl space under the building.

_____ Unhook your garden hoses.

_____ Prevent water lines from freezing by wrapping exterior pipes; newspapers covered with a waterproof material work.

_____ When the temperature forecast drops below freezing, leave outside faucets running slightly (a small steady stream of water). But don't allow outside faucets to flow into the street or onto sidewalks and other areas where people may walk. Should pipes freeze, don't use open flames to thaw out lines. This may catch the house on fire, or worse, create an explosion caused by expanding steam between two plugs of ice. Pipes don't always burst the first time they freeze. However, should a pipe burst, locate your water shutoff quickly at the main valve. (If you don't know where the shut-off is, let us know now, before any trouble occurs.) If the pipe break is a hot water line, close valve on the top of the water heater also. A plumber may need to be called. Please use plumber(s) previously approved by us: _____ .

_____ Check to ensure the caulking around the outside windows and any weather stripping around door frames is still in place to stop cold air.

_____ Don't forget to close storm windows.

_____ Make sure storm chains, if present, are attached on any storm doors. This prevents strong winds from blowing the door off or damaging the door.

_____ Keep the gutters cleaned out if they are clogged with leaves. The water will overflow and cause the house to rot or back up under the roof and into the house.

Inside Preparation

_____ Make sure the heat never goes below 50 degrees, even when you are not home.

_____ If the temperature is forecast to drop below freezing, leave at least one inside faucet dripping lukewarm water so both hot and cold pipes are involved.

_____ During periods of cold weather, leave cupboard doors open in the kitchen and bathroom so pipes inside will be exposed to heat. If you will be away for more than two consecutive days this winter, please let us know at least one week in advance so we can check on your rental if a sudden freeze occurs. We also want to be able to reach you in case of an emergency.

_____ Changing the heating/air filters monthly can make a big difference in your bills.

_____ Make sure the attic access door is in place.

_____ If you have a fireplace or a wood stove, the chimney needs to be cleaned each year. Chimney fires are common if this is not done. Call a professional who can do a complete job and also check the safety of the chimney.

_____ Test your smoke alarm(s). There are more fires in the winter, and the smoke alarm is one of your best safety features. If you don't have one, or it doesn't work, let us know. This is important for your family's safety. Make sure your smoke alarms have a working battery. You might want to consider buying a small fire extinguisher for your kitchen and garage.

We greatly appreciate your efforts in helping to make sure your residence is kept as warm and as safe as possible during the upcoming winter months.

CHRISTMAS TREE SAFETY TIPS

Dear Residents,

Your safety and the safety of your family is our concern. If you have placed a Christmas tree in your home or you will be buying a Christmas tree for your home, one of the most important things to remember when decorating your Christmas tree is to use safe tree lights. Some lights are designed specifically for indoor use.

The larger tree lights should also have some type of reflector rather than a bare bulb and all lights should be listed by a nationally recognized testing laboratory. Never use electric lights on a metal tree.

Follow the manufacturer's instructions on how to use tree lights. Any string of lights with worn, frayed, or broken cords or loose bulb connections should not be used.

Always unplug Christmas tree lights before leaving home or going to sleep.

Never use candles to decorate a tree, and never burn candles in the home.

If you have a live tree, try to keep it as moist as possible by giving it plenty of water.

Do not purchase a tree that is dry or dropping needles.

Choose a sturdy tree stand designed not to tip over.

When purchasing an artificial tree, be sure it is labeled as fire-retardant.

Children are fascinated with Christmas trees. Keep a watchful eye on them when around the tree and do not let them play with the wiring or lights. Store matches and lighters up high, out of the reach of children, preferably in a locked cabinet.

Carefully plan where your tree will be positioned. Make sure it is at least three feet away from any source of heat, and do not place the tree in front of or near your exit. Also try to position it near an outlet so that you do not use extension cords and so that cords are not running long distances.

Safely dispose of the tree when it begins dropping needles. Dried-out trees are very dangerous and should not be left in a garage or placed against the house.

Thanks for your cooperation,

Management Team

MAINTENANCE REQUEST

Date: _____

Address: _____

Resident: _____

Phone (Home)_____ (Work/Cell) _____

Problem (Be Specific): _____

When did this start and how long in this condition? _____

How bad is the situation right now? _____

Are there any others who were affected by this situation? _____

Time and day we can inspect: _____

Can we enter if you are not there? _____

What is the one most important thing you need at this time? _____

DO NOT WRITE BELOW THIS LINE

Date Received _____ By: _____

Action Taken: _____

Date Completed _____ By: _____

What was done: _____

Labor Cost: _____ Materials Cost: _____

Total: _____

MAINTENANCE REQUEST AND WORK ORDER–A

Date request received: _____ Time: _____ Date work order given: _____

Rental address: _____

Resident's name_____

Home phone_____ Work phone_____ Cell: _____

Permission given to enter home? Yes _____ No _____ Anytime _____ Only if occupant present_____

Maintenance appointment scheduled. Date_____ Time_____

Maintenance Request or Concern _____

_____

_____

Special instructions _____

Work assigned to: _____

Date and time work began_____

Job status at end of day: Complete_____, How many hours ?_____, Incomplete _____ because of

_____

Will return to complete on following date and time_____

If work is complete, what was done (please be specific)?_____

_____

_____

Materials used/purchased_____

_____

Total cost _____ Material cost_____ Labor cost_____ Other costs_____

Explanation of other costs_____

Signature of person performing work (once completed): _____

Verification of work completed by owner, manager, resident, or other _____,

Authorized Signature_____ Date completed_____

QUESTIONS TO ASK OTHER LANDLORDS ABOUT PROSPECTIVE CONTRACTORS

Date:_____ Contractor's Name:_____

Type of Job Needed:_____

Hello. My name is _____. Mr. or Ms._____ listed you as a reference, stating that he/she performed work for you. May I ask you a few questions regarding this contractor's work?

1. How long have you known Mr./Ms._____?

2. How did you first hear about him or her?_____

3. What type of work/jobs did he/she perform for you?_____

4. On a scale of 1-10 with 1 being poor and 10 being excellent, a) how would you rate the quality of the work performed?

Why do you give it this rating?_____

5. How promptly was the work completed, early, on time, or late?_____

6. While the work was in progress, did you feel that you had to check behind what was done?

_____

7. Could you rate the cost and quality of the materials that were used?_____

8. How would you rate the cost of the work in comparison with similar work performed by others? Lower, similar, or more expensive?_____

9. Did he or she request any payments upfront or all once the job was completed?

_____

10. Did he or she have any others working with or under him or her? And if so, how would you rate the work of those working with him or her?_____

11. When the job was completed, did you have to request for anything to be corrected or more fully completed?

_____

12. Overall, was the value of the work worth the cost in your opinion? _____

_____

MAINTENANCE REQUEST AND WORK ORDER–B

Property Address _____

Work Needed _____

Time Frame Needed _____ Approximate Budget_____

Contractor #1 _____ Phone_____

    Labor _____ Cost_____

    Materials _____ Cost_____

    Other Comments_____

_____

Contractor #2 _____ Phone_____

    Labor _____ Cost_____

    Materials _____ Cost_____

    Other Comments_____

_____

Contractor #3 _____ Phone_____

    Labor _____ Cost_____

    Materials _____ Cost_____

    Other Comments_____

_____

Contractor #4 _____ Phone_____

    Labor _____ Cost_____

    Materials _____ Cost_____

    Other Comments_____

_____

INDEGENT CONTRACTOR AGREEMENT

Address of property where work will be performed:

_____

City:_____State:_____ZIP:_____

The work to be performed on this property, including all terms, is fully outlined in a separate agreement.

I, _____, hereby acknowledge and agree I am an independent contractor under IRS regulations and will be fully and solely responsible for any damage, loss, or injury the owner or any and all others may suffer or incur either directly or indirectly as a result of my work. I will be fully responsible for myself and all others associated with me for any damage, injury, or loss of any kind whatsoever.

Though the owner will request certain work to be performed, I am ultimately responsible and have the authority to determine the method of work, hours worked, and means of performing the work on above premises and control the work of those working under me. The rental owner shall not interfere in this regard and control, direct, or supervise my employees or subcontractors. The owner does reserve the right to inspect the work being performed to determine whether it is being performed in a satisfactory and "workmanlike" manner. I will warrant all work for a period of _____ months following completion.

I agree I will obtain and provide my own equipment, tools, and all necessary materials for any work the owner contracts with me to perform.

I agree to provide the rental property owner with written and itemized invoices for all work performed.

I agree I am not and will not become an employee, partner, agent, or principal of the rental owner while this agreement is in effect. I understand I am not entitled to the rights or benefits afforded to any employee benefits, including disability, unemployment insurance, worker's compensation, or medical benefits.

I may, at my own expense, employ assistants or subcontractors as may be necessary for performance of work. I acknowledge and agree I (not the rental property owner) am responsible for paying any wages, taxes, unemployment, and withholding taxes, and providing any permits and licenses for myself, my employees, and subcontractors required by local or state law.

I acknowledge I am fully insured and my coverage includes workman's compensation, disability, and liability insurance for work performed for myself, employees, and subcontractors, and will name the rental property owner as an additional insured. I have attached a copy of my Workman's Compensation and Certificate of Insurance.

I will furnish owner appropriate releases or waivers of lien for all work performed or materials.

I shall defend, indemnify, and hold the rental property owner harmless from all lawsuits, accidents, or claims made by any entity for payment of any damages or harm incurred because of my actions or those of my assistants, employees, or subcontractors.

Contractor's Signature: _____   Date: _____

KEY RELEASE

Date: _____

Resident: _____

Address: _____

City:_____State:_____ZIP:_____

The above resident has requested something be checked in their rental residence. The owner or manager will schedule to respond to this request by entering (or having someone else enter) the premises to check on the situation on the following dates and times listed below. If the resident will not be present, he or she must agree to the following terms:

I, _____, (resident) am unable to, or choose not to, be present when entry is required in my residence. I authorize the landlord and or manager to release a key to my residence to the following individual and/or company: _____ on the following date(s) and time period(s): _____.

I fully understand the landlord and/or manager is in no way responsible for damages or theft to my residence or my belongings. And I reserve the right to have the locks changed at my expense (by a locksmith or personnel approved by the landlord), should I feel it necessary after entry by above person or company. If so, the owner or manager will be notified and given a copy of the keys for any new or changed locks.

Resident's Signature(s) _____

This notice must be signed and on file with the owner or manager prior to permitting any requested work done on your residence, if you are unable to be present when entry is required.

Thanks for your cooperation.

Rental Manager

TIME ESTIMATE FOR REPAIR
(A letter to give to residents, informing them of the status of their maintenance request.)

Date: _____

Resident: _____

Property address: _____

City: _____ State: _____ ZIP: _____

Thank you for promptly notifying us in writing on the following date: _____.

You have notified us of the following situation with your rental home:

_____

_____

_____

_____

We expect to respond to the situation by the following date: _____.

The following reasons affect when and how the situation will be responded to:

_____

_____

_____

_____

We want to remind you if there is a delay in responding to your notification, we will honor our maintenance guarantee to rebate rent (prorated) on a daily basis. The guarantee goes into effect if there is a delay beyond _____ days after your initial notification date. Rent rebate begins from that point and will be sent after the next on-time rental payment is received.

Be sure to provide us, or any contractors working with us, access into your property. If there is any problem getting access into the property, our maintenance guarantee is voided.

We appreciate your cooperation with this matter.

Sincerely,

Landlord, Manager

SORRY WE MISSED YOU!

From: _____

_____

_____

Date: _____

To: _____

_____

_____

We were asked by the management, to check on a maintenance issue or concern that either you or they had.

We came by on the following date and time: _____

☐ When we came by to check on this and/or to respond to the requested service call, we found no one home. Since you had given your permission for us to enter, or we believed the maintenance issue or situation could possibly cause further problems or damage to the home, we went ahead and did the following within the home in response to your concern.

_____

_____

_____

☐ Since we did not have your prior permission, we will await a call from you to reschedule another time to respond to the maintenance concern or your service request. Please call _____ to reschedule and be sure and give your name and address and confirm if we will have your permission to enter if for any reason you are not there when we arrive.

Thanks for letting us serve you.

_____

_____

REPAIR COMPLETION RECEIPT

Date: _____

Resident's name: _____

Resident's address: _____

City: _____ State: _____ ZIP: _____

(Following to be completed by repair person.)

I, _____, hereby performed the following repairs in a workmanlike manner at the above-mentioned address. I have also listed under each repair what I believe to be the cause of the needed repair, and checked if in my judgment the problem was caused by the resident's action or negligence (as opposed to normal wear and tear).

Repair 1: _____

Cause: _____

Was cause of the problem tenant related?   Yes _____   No _____   Partially _____   Not sure _____

Based on what finding? _____

Repair 2: _____

Cause: _____

Was cause of the problem tenant related?   Yes _____   No _____   Partially _____   Not sure _____

Based on what finding? _____

Both signatures below are required as acknowledgment of satisfactory completion of said repairs and full understanding of all terms of this receipt.

Repair Person: _____   Date: _____

Resident: _____   Date: _____

Owner reserves the right to bill residents for any repairs that were a result of their negligence or were beyond normal wear and tear. Any unpaid repair bill will be treated as unpaid rent.

Repair Completion Billing (Following to be completed by the management.)

Per the terms of the repair completion receipt, you are hereby being billed for the following repairs:

1. _____ $ _____

2. _____ $ _____

The above charges include both labor and materials. Please remit the total of $ _____ to the following address _____ within 10 days of the date below, which will be considered as additional rent due. If you have any questions, please feel free to call our office at_____.
Note: Failure to comply with this request for payment can result in termination of your lease.

Thank you for your cooperation.

Owner/Manager

ACKNOWLEDGEMENT OF RENOVATION TO BE DONE

(To be given to rental residents prior to renovation or repair activity but no more than 60 days before beginning renovation activities in any residential dwelling unit built before 1978. Residents should also be given a notice describing the general nature and locations of the planned renovation activities, and the expected starting and ending dates. Renovation is defined as any activity resulting in the disturbance of more than two square feet of paint per building component, including removal of large structures such as walls, ceiling, replastering, and window replacement, and surface preparation activities such as sanding, scraping, or other activities generating lead paint dust.)

_____ I have received a copy of the pamphlet "Protect Your Family from Lead in Your Home," informing me of the potential risk of lead hazard exposure from renovation activity to be performed in my dwelling unit. I received this pamphlet before the work began.

Property address: _____

City: _____ State: _____ ZIP: _____

Printed name of resident: _____

Signature of resident: _____

Date: _____

Please note: When an occupant refuses to sign the acknowledgment of receipt of the pamphlet, the owner/manager can certify delivery. The owner may fill in the following section.

_____ I certify that I have made a good faith effort to deliver the pamphlet "Protect Your Family from Lead in Your Home" to the unit listed below at the dates and times indicated, and that the occupant refused to sign the acknowledgment. I further certify that I have left a copy of the pamphlet at the unit with the occupant.

Property address: _____

Attempted delivery dates and times: _____

Printed name of owner/manager: _____

Signature of owner/manager: _____

Date: _____

If resident is unavailable for signature, the owner may fill in the following section.

_____ I certify that I have made a good faith effort to deliver the pamphlet "Protect Your Family from Lead in Your Home" to the unit listed below, and that the occupant was unavailable to sign the acknowledgment. I further certify that I have left a copy of the pamphlet at the unit by sliding it under the door.

Property address: _____

Attempted delivery dates and times: _____

Printed name of owner/manager (person leaving pamphlet): _____

_____

Signature of owner/manager: _____

Date: _____

SAFETY LETTER

Dear Resident:

As part of our management program, we make regular inspections of your residence so it remains safe for you, your family, and guests. Please allow one of our managers to view the interior of your home during the next safety check scheduled for the week of _____.

We also need your assistance in helping to keep your home safe. Let us know of anything you see in or around your home that may be a hazard or dangerous to you, a family member, or guests. We will then inspect your residence and do all we can to make your home safer. After your home is inspected for safety, one of the managers will have a copy of this letter for you to sign. If, right now, everything appears safe to the best of your knowledge, please sign below and mail this letter back to us with your next payment. If there are any unsafe conditions, let us know as well. Mail this letter to the following address:

_____ .

Thank you for your cooperation,

Rental Management

_____

The following to be checked by the resident and returned to the management.

_____ As of this date there are NO unsafe conditions in or around my home.

_____ There is a condition that I believe is unsafe. That condition is described as follows:

_____

_____

Resident's Signature: _____ Date: _____

Address: _____

City: _____ State: _____ ZIP: _____

RESIDENT RELEASE FOR USE OF RECREATIONAL ITEMS
(for properties with items such as a pool, swing set, jungle gym, etc.)

To: _____ , owner

Re: _____ , address

I, _____ , resident of the above address, wish to use the recreational items located on the premises.

Those items include: _____ . The use of these items is NOT part of the rental agreement between myself and the owner.

I hereby agree to bear sole responsibility for its setup, structure, maintenance, and ongoing upkeep.

I agree to bear sole liability and responsibility for any and all direct and indirect costs, damages, and expenses incurred as a result of any physical or other injury sustained or caused to myself, members of my family, or guests resulting from the use of the above recreational item(s).

I further agree not to hold the owner or managers responsible in any way for any injury or damages that may occur. I have also purchased liability insurance which provides up to $ _____ in coverage for possible injury or damages.

Resident's signature: _____ Date: _____

Owner's signature: _____ Date: _____

ELECTION TIME IS NEAR - NOTICE REGARDING CAMPAIGN SIGNS

From: _____

_____

_____

Date: _____

To: _____

_____

_____

Election time is upon us again. With each campaign season, the management grants permission to certain candidates to post yard signs at various property locations that we manage. As such, you will likely see some of these campaign signs popping up on the property, both during the Primary season, as well as again during the General Election season this fall. Please do not remove any properly authorized signs. If you have any questions about whether a particular sign has our authority or not, just give us a call (number above on this letter) during the following hours _____ and we will let you know.

Please note that only those signs authorized by the management of this property are permitted to be placed on the property. Any unauthorized signs will be removed. As in years past, we thank those of you who have cooperated in this matter.

Sincerely,

Management Team

SMOKE DETECTOR CHECK

Dear _____ :

We would like to take a few minutes of your time to double-check the condition and safe operation of the smoke detectors in your home. According to our records, smoke detectors should be located at all of the locations shown below. Please take a minute, now while you think about it, to complete this survey. Please sign and return to us. We will return a copy to you for your own information. Here are some facts you should know:

1. The battery (or batteries) in each of your smoke detectors should be replaced at least once a year. If they are older (or if you are unsure), they MUST be replaced. It's important that you replace them with batteries of the same type. Let us know if you are unsure of the type.

2. The smoke detectors should be tested by pushing the test button now, and then again once each month.

3. If smoking is permitted in your rental agreement, an additional smoke detector should be installed in the bedroom—even if no one smokes in bed. This is extremely important and we will be happy to install one without charge.

4. If you are having trouble with smoke detectors going off from kitchen odors or from someone smoking, let us know. Do not remove the batteries. A detector with a silencer can be installed.

Smoke Detector #1

Location: _____

Date battery changed: _____

Smoke detector tested: _____ OK _____ Didn't operate

Smoke Detector #2

Location: _____

Date battery changed: _____

Smoke detector tested: _____ OK _____ Didn't operate

Tests performed by: _____ Date: _____

Does anyone in the household smoke? _____ Yes _____ No

REMINDER, IN CASE OF FIRE, your personal belongings and furniture are not covered under the company's fire insurance. Be sure and have renter's insurance.

Do you presently have renter's insurance? _____ Yes _____ No

Would you like us to send you an application? _____ Yes _____ No

SATELLITE DISH AND ANTENNA ADDENDUM

1. **Number and size.** You may install only one satellite dish or antenna within the premises that are leased to you, for your exclusive use. A satellite dish may not exceed 39 inches in diameter. An antenna or dish may receive but not transmit signals.

2. **Location.** The location of the satellite dish or antenna is limited to: (1) inside your dwelling, or (2) in an area outside your dwelling such as a balcony, patio, or yard of which you have exclusive use under your lease. Installation is not permitted on any parking area, roof exterior wall, window, windowsill, fence, or common area, or in an area that other residents are allowed to use. A satellite dish or antenna may not protrude beyond the vertical and horizontal space that is leased to you for your exclusive use.

3. **Safety and noninterference.** Your installation: (1) must comply with reasonable safety standards; (2) may not interfere with our cable, telephone, or electrical systems, or those of neighboring properties; (3) may not be connected to our telecommunication systems; and (4) may not be connected to our electrical system except by plugging into a 110-volt duplex receptacle. If the satellite dish or antenna is placed in a permitted outside areas, it must be safely secured by one of three methods: (1) securely attaching it to a portable, heavy object such as a small slab of concrete; (2) clamping it to a part of the building's exterior that lies within your leased premises (such as a balcony or patio railing); or (3) any other method approved by us. No other methods are allowed. We may require reasonable screening of the satellite dish or antenna by plants, etc., so long as it does not impair reception.

4. **Signal transmission from exterior dish or antenna to interior of dwelling.** You may not damage or alter the leased premises and may not drill holes through outside walls, door jams, windowsills, etc. If your satellite dish/antenna is installed outside your living areas on a balcony, patio, or yard of which you have exclusive use under your lease, signals received by your satellite dish or antenna may be transmitted to the interior of your dwelling only by: (1) running a "flat" cable under a door jam or window, (2) running a traditional or flat cable through a preexisting hole in the wall (that will not need to be enlarged to accommodate the cable), (3) connecting cables "through a window pane" similar to how an external car antenna for a cellular phone can be connected to inside wiring by a device glued to either side of the window without drilling a hole through the window, (4) wireless transmission of the signal to a device inside the dwelling, or (5) any other method approved by us.

5. **Workmanship.** For safety purposes, you must obtain your approval of: (1) the strength and type of materials to be used for installation, and (2) the person or company who will perform the installation. Installation must be done by a qualified person or company that has worker's compensation insurance and adequate public liability insurance. Our approval will not be unreasonably withheld. You must obtain any permits required by the city for the installation and comply with any applicable city ordinances.

6. **Maintenance.** You have the sole responsibility for maintaining your dish or antenna or all related equipment. We may temporarily remove the dish or antenna if necessary to make building repairs.

7. **Removal and damages.** You must remove the satellite dish or antenna and all related equipment when you move out of the dwelling. You must pay for any damages, and for the cost of repairs or repainting that may be reasonably necessary to restore the leased premises to its condition prior to the installation of your satellite dish or antenna and related equipment.

8. **Liability insurance and indemnity.** You are fully responsible for the satellite dish or antenna and related equipment. Prior to installation, you must provide us with evidence of liability insurance to protect against claims of injury and property damage related to your equipment. The insurance coverage must be no less than $ _____ and must remain in force while the satellite dish or antenna remains installed. You agree to defend, indemnify, and hold us harmless from the above claims by others.

9. **Deposit increase.** A security deposit increase (in connection with having a satellite dish or antenna) is required. Your security deposit is increased by an additional sum of $ _____ to help protect us against possible repair costs, damages, or any failure to remove the satellite dish or antenna and related equipment at time of move-out. A security deposit increase does not imply a right to drill into or alter the leased premises.

10. **When you may begin installation.** You may start installation of your satellite dish or antenna only after you have: (1) signed this addendum, (2) provided us with written evidence of liability insurance referred to in this addendum, (3) paid us the additional security deposit, and (4) received our written approval of the installation materials and the person or company who will do the installation.

Resident's Signature: _____   Date: _____

Owner/Manager's Signature: _____   Date: _____

LEAKAGE LETTER

Dear _____:

    I am writing to ask for your help in keeping expenses to a minimum by simply completing the lower portion of this letter and returning it to me with your next rent payment.

    The City of _____ has what is called a Sewer User Fee. This is a fee charged (to owner) for the use of the city's sewer system and is paid in addition to the water bills. The amount of the Sewer User Fee is determined by the amount of water used during the winter months. Needless to say, the lower the water consumption, the lower the Sewer User Fee.

    Therefore, to keep expenses (and, ultimately, your rent) as low as possible, I am asking you to check to see if your toilet runs continually and check each of your water faucets, as well as those not in your living areas (e.g., basement or exterior faucets) for leaks. Circle the appropriate faucet below, along with any notes about the problem, and return the lower portion of this letter to me at _____ . If you find none of your faucets leak, please circle yes on the last question and return it. If the form is not returned, it will be necessary for us to have someone inspect your apartment or house.

Thank you, in advance, for your cooperation

Sincerely,

Owner/Manager

_____

Your address: _____

Any leaks?	Which faucet?		Approximate amount of leakage? How long?
Kitchen sink	hot	cold	_____
Bathroom sink	hot	cold	_____
Bathtub/shower	hot	cold	_____
Toilet		cold	_____

Other (e.g., drain) Specify location: _____

All faucets okay? _____ Checked by: _____ Date: _____

Resident's Signature: _____ Date: _____

UTILITY BUDGET NOTIFICATION

From: _____

_____

_____

Date: _____

To: _____

_____

_____

Dear _____:

   As stated in your rental agreement, our company pays for the following utility _____
for your building. Our company has budgeted our expenses so we may continue to offer you the best fair market rent
possible with minimum rent raises each year. We would like to announce or remind you of our Resident's Utility Reward
Program, to show our appreciation to you every time you help us best serve you. Our monthly or quarterly budget for
the above stated utility is $ _____.

   As part of our Resident's Reward Program, every month or quarter you (and other residents in the building who use
this utility) use LESS utilities than the amount we have budgeted, we will reward you (and all units in the building) by
offering you rent credit for the difference. If applicable, you will be notified of the amount of rent credit within five days
after we receive each utility bill. The rent credit/discount can be applied toward your next rent payment due. This is just
another part of our 3-Star Resident Program. We will continue to inform you of ways you can be rewarded as we work
together to make renting from our company a rewarding experience.

Thanks for your cooperation.

Rental Manager

STORM PREPARATION NOTICE
Effective Immediately

Date: _____

To: _____

_____

_____

Due to the upcoming storm projected for our area on _____,
all residents must do the following:

Remove all items from the yard or from near parking areas, such as garbage cans, lawn chairs, toys, and other objects.

Remove all small items on your porch or balconies and secure them in a safe area. This will help to ensure safety for our residents and neighbors and keep buildings from being damaged by flying objects. In addition, please do the following regarding your specific home or apartment:

_____

_____

_____

If instructed by city, state, or federal officials to vacate the property, please do so after securing your possessions and the property and inform us of where you will be temporarily relocating. While it is too late for this storm, it is recommended that you obtain renter's insurance before there is another storm that may impact our area if you have not done so already. Let us know if you need a recommendation of a company that offers renter's insurance. We will be glad to suggest a contact to call.

In addition, please call, fax, or email us to provide at least two phone numbers that we may use to contact you, including cell phone numbers and/or phone numbers of relatives or friends.

You can reach the management at the following contact information.

Phone :_____ Fax: _____

Alternative phone number(s):_____

Email address:_____

Thank you for your cooperation,

Property Manager

FREEZE WARNING

Dear Residents,

Take precautions for the coming freeze! (Suggested steps to take to prevent damage when anticipating below freezing temperatures).

Protect Your:

Pipes: _____

_____

_____

Faucets: _____

_____

_____

Water shutoffs: _____

_____

_____

Plants: _____

_____

_____

Vehicles: _____

_____

_____

Emergency number: _____

Procedure following a freeze: _____

_____

_____

_____

SECURITY NOTICE

Dear Residents,

Take precautions to prevent a crime on your property. A drive-by inspection of your residence found:

_____ Door left open/unlocked (front, back, patio)

_____ Windows left open/unlocked/broken

_____ Window screens off/damaged

_____ Items left on porch, patio, or balcony

_____ Other: _____

_____ Other: _____

We did not know if you were aware of the above conditions, and we know your safety and the safety of your property is important.

Thank you for your cooperation.

Rental Manager

ACCIDENT/INCIDENT REPORT

Type of Incident: Accident _____   Fire _____   Medical emergency _____   Crime _____   Other _____

Address of where happening occurred: _____

State details regarding any injuries or damages that occurred (use back of page if needed):

_____

_____

_____

Name of residents involved: _____

Were there any individuals involved who are not current residents of the above address?
_____ If so, why were they on the premises? _____

Names, addresses, and phone numbers of any individuals other than residents of the premises:

_____

_____

Any witnesses? If so, please give their names, addresses, and phone numbers:

_____

In your opinion, do you know what may have caused the incident or accident? If so, what?

_____

Please give the reasons why the cause may have been what you suspect:

_____

_____

_____

Name of insurance company and policy numbers of all parties involved (including yours):

_____

_____

Has insurance company been notified?   _____ Yes   _____ No   _____ By mail   _____ By phone
Date and time insurance company was notified: _____

Was the incident documented by use of the following?   Photos _____   Videotape _____

Date and time fire department, police, or emergency personnel were contacted: _____
_____ Who was contacted? _____
Date and time someone responded to the situation: _____

Follow-up action to be taken by owner or manager: _____

_____

Resident reporting the above incident: _____

Resident's signature: _____ Date: _____

Up to

$500 REWARD

Paid for Information Leading to the Arrest
and Conviction of Any Person or Persons
Damaging or Marking on Walls, Stealing,
or Otherwise Committing a Crime
on These Premises

To Collect Reward

1. Call police. First person to report crime receives first $50 of reward.
2. Get another witness. Or take picture of criminal committing crime.
3. Call building manager at (_____) _____.

Building owner will pay reward as follows:

Day of conviction
    $50 paid to person first reporting crime.
    $50 divided among any witnesses who testify against criminal.

For each month the criminal spends in jail
    $50 paid to person reporting crime.

Maximum reward will be $500 to all persons.

Parents are responsible for crimes committed by their children!

SUSPICIOUS ACTIVITY RECORD
(For Residents and Neighbors)

Date: _____ Time: _____

Location where activity took place: _____
_____

Was activity on the street, sidewalk, or private property? _____

Describe the activity you saw: _____
_____
_____
_____

Name(s) and/or address(es) of the person(s) you saw (if known): _____
_____
_____
_____

Describe the person(s) you saw (circle the one that applies):

    Male / Female   White / Black / Hispanic / Other: _____

    Height: _____   Weight: _____   Eyes: _____

    Other characteristics: _____

Describe their clothing: _____
_____
_____

Describe vehicles:

    Make: _____   Model: _____

    Color: _____   License: _____

Location where drugs were seen or stored: _____
_____
_____

Your name: _____
Your address: _____
Your telephone number: _____

If you prefer not to give your name, address, or phone number, that is okay. If, however, you do provide this information, it will remain confidential and will not be released to anyone without your permission.

Thank you very much for helping to make your community safer.

PROPERTY MANAGEMENT AGREEMENT

A. Parties

This Agreement is between _____ , Owner, and _____ , Manager. Both parties enter into this agreement for property management services provided by Manager for the properties owned by Owner listed below.

B. Property(ies) to Be Managed

_____
_____ . Manager will not/will be renting unit _____ of the property under a separate written rental agreement that is in not contingent upon or related to this agreement.

C. Dates/Terms

Manager will begin work on _____ . This agreement is for a term of month to month. Owner or Manager may cancel this agreement at anytime, though if at all possible, both parties agree to give the other a minimum of _____ advance notice. This agreement may be terminated immediately for any one of the following reasons: _____

D. Responsibilities

The Owner hereby assigns the Manager as agent to handle the following responsibilities (items left unmarked remain the responsibility of the Owner):

1. Leasing units
- ____ advertise rentals
- ____ answer phone inquiries about vacancies
- ____ show vacant units
- ____ accept rental applications
- ____ run credit checks
- ____ select tenants
- ____ accept initial rents and deposits
- ____ negotiate rental rates
- ____ sign leases and sign property condition checklist
- ____ give required disclosure forms
- ____ offer residents optional upgrades and payment plans
- ____ other (specify) _____

2. Property turnover
- ____ inspect rental when tenant moves in
- ____ conduct anniversary meetings and send thank you letters
- ____ inspect rental when tenant moves out
- ____ general cleaning of unit after tenant moves out
- ____ clean floors, carpets, and rugs
- ____ paint walls, baseboards, ceilings, lights and built-in shelves
- ____ clean kitchen cabinets, countertops, sinks, stove, oven, and refrigerator
- ____ clean bathtubs, showers, toilets, and plumbing fixtures
- ____ repair doors, windows, window coverings, and mini-blinds
- ____ other (specify) _____

3. Rent collection

___ collect rents when due
___ promote and establish auto draft and electronic payment plans
___ sign and send rent receipts
___ maintain rent-collection records
___ collect late rents and charges
___ inform Owner of late rents
___ prepare late rent notices
___ serve late rent, pay or quit, and unlawful detainer notices on tenants
___ serve rent increase and tenancy termination notices
___ deposit rent collections in bank
___ other (specify) _____

4. Maintenance

___ conduct monthly drive-by inspections
___ conduct semiannual interior inspections
___ provide monthly report of maintenance, repairs, and utility expenses to Owner
___ give rental violation notices when applicable
___ vacuum and clean hallways and entryways (for buildings with common areas)
___ replace light bulbs in common areas
___ drain water heaters
___ clean stairs, decks, patios, façades, and sidewalks
___ clean garage oils on pavement
___ lawn care, trim bushes, and rake leaves
___ clean up garbage and debris on grounds
___ shovel snow from sidewalks and driveways or arrange for snow removal
___ other (specify) _____

5. Repairs

___ accept tenant complaints and repair requests
___ inform Owner of maintenance and repair needs
___ categorize and maintain written log of tenant complaints
___ plumbing stoppages
___ garbage disposal stoppages/repairs
___ faucet leaks/washer replacement
___ toilet repairs
___ stove burners/hinges/knobs repair or replacement
___ appliance repair
___ light switch and outlet repair/replacement
___ heater thermostat repair
___ window repair/replacement
___ painting (interior/exterior)
___ key replacement
___ handle all other routine maintenance and repairs
___ coordinate repairs with contractors if needed (with owner approval for jobs over $ _____)
___ other (specify) _____

6. OTHER RESPONSIBILITIES

___ Provide his or her number to tenants so they will have an emergency contact number. Within reason, manager should be able to respond at any time to an emergency.

___ Meet or call Owner weekly (or monthly) to consult on the job priorities and give updated reports on status of residents and management priorities.

___ Submit weekly/monthly time sheets to the Owner detailing daily/weekly activities, materials purchased, and receipts.

___ Manager will keep the following day(s) and times available for routine maintenance:

_____

_____

___ Additional responsibility: _____

_____

E. Hours and schedule

Manager will be available to tenants during the following days and times:

_____

_____

If the hours required to carry out any duties may reasonably be expected to exceed _____ hours in any week, Manager shall notify Owner and obtain Owner's consent before working such extra hours, except in the event of an emergency. Extra hours worked due to an emergency must be reported to Owner within 24 hours.

F. Payment terms

1. Manager will be paid:

   ___ $ _____ per hour (guaranteed weekly minimum of _____ hours and work will not exceed _____ hours weekly without the consent of the owner, unless to handle an emergency)

   ___ $ _____ per week

   ___ $ _____ per month

   ___ Other (e.g., percentage of rental income received): _____

   ___ Additional compensation or bonuses: _____

2. Manager will be paid on the specified intervals and dates:

   ___ Once a week on every _____

   ___ Twice a month on _____

   ___ Once a month on _____

   ___ Other: _____

G. Additional agreements and amendments

Owner and Manager additionally agree that:

_____.

All agreements between Owner and Manager relating to the work specified in this Agreement are incorporated in this Agreement. Any modification to the Agreement must be in writing and signed by both parties.

H. Signatures

Date:_____   Owner: _____

Date:_____   Manager: _____

POWER OF ATTORNEY

KNOW ALL MEN BY THESE PRESENTS, THAT I, _____ , the Undersigned hereby make, constitute, and appoint _____ my true and lawful Attorney for me and in my name, place, and stead and for my use and benefit for all transactions concerning the property described as follows:_____ .

Said attorney in fact is authorized:

A. To ask, demand, sue for, recover, collect, and receive each and every sum of money, debt, account, legacy, bequest, interest, dividend, annuity, and demand (which now is or hereafter shall become due, owing, or payable) belonging to or claimed by me, and to use and take any lawful means for the recovery thereof by legal process or otherwise, and to execute and deliver a satisfaction or release therefore, together with the right and power to compromise or compound any claim or demand;

B. To exercise any or all of the following powers as to real property, any interest therein and/or any building thereon: To contract for, purchase, receive, and take possession thereof and of evidence of title thereto; to lease the same for any term or purpose, including leases for business, residence, and oil and/or mineral development; to sell, exchange, grant, or convey the same with or without warranty; and to mortgage, transfer in trust, or otherwise encumber or hypothecate the same to secure payment of a negotiable or nonnegotiable note or performance of any obligation or agreement;

C. To exercise any or all of the following powers as to all kinds of personal property and goods, wares, and merchandise, chooses in action and other property in possession or in action: To contract for, buy, sell, exchange, transfer, and in any legal manner deal in and with the same; and to mortgage, transfer in trust, or otherwise encumber or hypothecate the same to secure payment of a negotiable or nonnegotiable note or performance of any litigation or agreement.

D. To borrow money and to execute and deliver negotiable or nonnegotiable notes therefor with or without security; and to loan money and receive negotiable or nonnegotiable notes therefor with such security as he shall deem proper;

E. To create, amend, supplement, and terminate any trust and to instruct and advise the trustee of any trust wherein I am or may be trustor or beneficiary; to represent and vote stock, exercise stock rights, accept and deal with any dividend, distribution, or bonus, join in any corporate, financing, reorganization, merger, liquidation, consolidation, or other action and the extension compromise, conversion, adjustment, enforcement, or foreclosure, singly or in conjunction with other of any corporate stock, bond, note, debenture, or other security; to compound, compromise, adjust, settle, and satisfy any obligation, secured or unsecured, owing by or to me and to give or accept any property and/or money whether or not equal to or less in value than the amount owing in payment, settlement, or satisfaction thereof;

F. To transact business of any kind or class and as my act and deed to sign, execute, acknowledge, and deliver any deed, lease, assignment or lease, covenant, indenture, indemnity, agreement, mortgage, deed of trust, assignment of mortgage or of the beneficial interest under deed of trust, waiver of priority, hypothecation, bottomry, charter-party, bill of lading, bill of sale, bill, bond, note, whether negotiable or nonnegotiable receipt evidence of debt, full or partial release or satisfaction or mortgage, judgment and other debt, request for partial or full reconveyance of deed of trust, and such other instruments in writing of any kind or class as may be necessary or proper in the premises.

GIVING AND GRANTING unto my said Attorney full power and authority to do and perform all and every act and thing whatsoever requisite, necessary, or appropriate to be done in and about the premises as fully to all intents and purposes as I might or could do if personally present, hereby ratifying all that my said Attorney shall lawfully do or cause to be done by virtue of these presents.

WITNESS my hand this _____ day of _____ , 20_____ .

STATE OF _____ , COUNTY OF _____ .

On the _____ day of _____ , 20_____ , personally appeared before _____ , signer of the foregoing instruments, who duly acknowledge to me that she executed the same.

_____ Residing at: _____ .

My Commission expires: _____ NOTARY PUBLIC

PART FIVE

Retention, Turnover, and Advertising

Forms to Keep Residents Longer and Fill
 Vacancies Quickly

RESIDENT RECORDS

Rental owners often fail to update information about their residents at least once a year or when renewing a lease. When a resident initially enters into a lease agreement, he or she must provide the landlord with certain information, such as employment, occupants, pets, and emergency contacts, requested on the rental application.

■ *Tip Number* **48**

Update and verify resident information annually.

The landlord should ask residents to fill out an "updated" resident information form (see Updated Resident Information) once a year. Consider making it a condition of receiving the anniversary gift. It is likely the resident will provide more complete, accurate facts in order to receive the gift. This document can help determine information that may be missing or outdated from the initial application.

It is especially important to update employment information. This is helpful in the event a resident does not complete the term of the lease, but vacates the unit and still owes money. If the court renders a judgment in favor of the owner, the landlord can begin a wage garnishment proceeding against the former resident to collect money owed.

Your application should request the license number, model, and year of a resident's vehicle. This eliminates any confusion as to the ownership of vehicles on the property. In addition, this provides a way for landlords to track residents who vacate prior to the end of their leases.

Personal contacts that residents list in case of an emergency may not be accurate a year or two later. This information is not only important in emergency situations, but also in the event a resident leaves without properly ending the lease. An address or telephone number of a relative or friend may be vital in finding former residents.

This form has another benefit that is valuable to owners who have a manager or management company handle most of the duties. The information provided directly from the residents can serve as a crosscheck against the records the owner has received from a manager or management company.

DEVELOP A CUSTOMER LOYALTY PROGRAM

In regard to resident retention, our biggest goal is to change residents' mindsets so that they don't think that after one year, they have to make a decision about staying or moving. Here's just one example of what you may do to change your residents' mindsets.

When you accept your next new residents and explain the rental agreement, from day one, let the residents know that you are so pleased to have the privilege to rent to them and invite them to participate in a special 3-Star Program.

Let residents know that as part of this special 3-Star Program, after their first year, you will give them a ceiling fan; after the second year, they will have their carpet cleaned or receive a new appliance; and after three years, their apartment or home will be repainted with choice of wall color in one room. These are only suggestions for improvement; the type of improvements is not the important factor. What's important is that first you reward the residents in some way after each year. And second, even more essential, is that you emphasize from the beginning that whatever improvements you promise are part of a three-year program. That's why I use the term *3-Star* and provide residents long-term benefits over three years.

■ *Tip Number* **49**

Offer a 3-Star Program.

When you send letters or any communication to residents, remind them that you are glad they are part of the 3-Star Program. Anytime someone does work on your property, make them aware that your residents are part of a 3-Star Program. Tell all contractors to let residents know that they (the contractors) are there to provide excellent service for 3-Star residents.

After 10 or 11 months of the resident staying in your rental, residents don't need to be asked if they want to renew. Instead send them a letter (see the 3-Star Program Anniversary Increase form) thanking them for the privilege of serving them for the first year of their 3-Star Program and say that you look forward to serving them for another two years. This is all part of the plan to change and reinforce a new mindset in each of your residents.

If you follow this plan from day one, your residents will not move in with the mindset that they will only be with you for one year before deciding whether to stay another year. Instead, when your residents move in, they will have the mindset that they'll be with you for at least three years. Guess what, they will! Especially as you reinforce the 3-Star Program throughout the rental term.

You have now effectively prevented one of the major management headaches, resident turnover, by changing your resident's mindset.

Mr. Landlord Challenge Make it a priority to change and create the right mindsets in your residents by developing a customer loyalty program similar to the 3-Star Program. You will have long-term success as you are able to keep good residents happy through every situation.

ANNIVERSARY AGENDA

It can be to your advantage to talk with your resident once a year near their anniversary date. I recommend that you send an Anniversary Agenda Checklist, along with a thank you letter, for participating in the first year of their 3-Star Program. The checklist informs residents that they have an opportunity to discuss any concerns and new options available during next year of their 3-Star Program.

■ *Tip Number* **50**

Ask your residents what they would like to discuss.

The checklist asks residents to select the topics from the agenda. Each topic a resident selects gives the landlord the opportunity to meet the changing needs of the resident. Equally important, as you offer options to meet the resident's needs and concerns, *each topic on the agenda will also give you the opportunity to increase your cash flow, plus increase the customer satisfaction level of the resident.* See the sample Anniversary Agenda Checklist.

RAISE RENTS WITHOUT FEAR

Let's talk about annually increasing the amount of rent you get. This book provides three types of rent increase letters. I'm going to reveal an effective rent-raising strategy. You will never again be afraid to ask your residents for more money.

I often get asked, "Jeffrey, I have a couple of good residents. Do I raise their rent and risk losing them or just keep the rents the same and not have to worry about dealing with turnover? For a few extra bucks, is it really worth the possible loss?"

I hear landlording instructors mistakenly suggest to rental owners not to raise rents on good residents, and if you do raise their rents, keep them slightly lower than market rents. The concern about limiting rental increases on good residents is all based on fear that you will lose residents who don't like the amount of the increase, and this is a fear that in most cases is unwarranted, costing you lots of cash flow.

Here's how I suggest you raise rents in the future, so that you never have to have a sleepless night. First, determine how much rental adjustment you desire. Let's use $20 as the desired amount you want to achieve. In your letter notifying residents of an increase, you *do not* state your desired amount ($20) as the new increase amount. Instead, state an amount greater, up to double the actual desired amount. So in this example, you would state $40 in your letter to the resident as the proposed increased.

In the same letter you thank the resident for being a 3-Star resident (see the 3-Star Program Anniversary Increase form), inform the resident that if the stated rental increase ($40 in our example) is too much or more than they can handle because of personal circumstances or financial difficulties, please contact your office within the next five days. What are your residents going to do after they get the letter? Call and say, "It's too much for me to handle." What do you say?

■ *Tip Number* **51**

Let residents have a say in rent negotiation.

It is important that you let your residents feel that they have a say in the negotiation when possible. This creates more of a win-win relationship. In our example, you, the landlord, do not arbitrarily respond to the resident by stating a new figure of

$20. Instead, ask the resident, "Mrs. Jones, what would you consider a fair middle ground?" Nine times out of ten, Mrs. Jones will respond, "twenty." In the rare instance she says a figure too low for you to accept, you together negotiate upward toward an acceptable rate.

The point is, when you let residents determine the amount of the increase, who is happy afterwards? Everybody! Your resident walks away happy because he or she played a part in the negotiation. When the resident quotes you an acceptable rental increase, you admit that your company can work with that. How does the resident feel about the rent increase? Great, because he or she won! How do you feel? Great. You got what you originally hoped for. You are happy and so is the resident. Mission accomplished. The next time you go to raise the rent, does the resident get angry? No, because, your resident feels he or she plays an active role in determining the amount of the raise.

Every now and then, after you send out your letter notifying the resident of the rental increase (the higher $40 amount) the resident will *not* call you and accept the large increase. In that case, however, I suggest you add one or two small upgrades to the rental (e.g., ceiling fan, microwave oven, or, better yet, whatever they indicated on the last resident survey they would like to have added to the property). The upgrades should be ones that you can cover the cost of within three months with the extra rent you are receiving. Providing the upgrade will help justify the higher rental amount in the resident's mind, even in multifamily buildings where neighbors have a tendency to compare rental rates. You will have neighbors to the residents where you just added upgrades, calling you to get the same upgrade "Mrs. Jones got." This gives you the opportunity to raise the rents on another resident. This strategy is a great way to turn a potentially negative situation of neighboring residents comparing rental rates into an opportunity for more cash flow.

HELP RESIDENTS WITH MOVING PLANS

■ *Tip Number* **52**

Show residents that moving costs a lot.

If residents are considering moving, send them a move-out budget worksheet (see the Planning to

Move? form) to help them clearly see how much up-front cash and expense they will need to move. Use the form to convince residents that it costs a lot to move (in case they may want to reconsider). Finish the letter with a reminder that there are many good reasons not to move and for residents to call you if they change their minds and to see if they still qualify for the anniversary bonus.

HAVE RESIDENTS GIVE NOTICE IN WRITING IF THEY INTEND TO MOVE

Landlords should require more than just a verbal notice from residents who state that they plan on moving. Insist that they provide you with a written notice of intent to move. A sample of such a form is included in this section of the book. Unfortunately, countless numbers of residents say to their landlord that they are planning to move, only to later change their minds, often at the last minute (for various reasons). If the landlord had gone ahead and had begun the process to rerent the property (based merely on the verbal notice), it could create not only an awkward situation, but a very costly one for the landlord. This is especially true if there is a new resident wishing to move in and trying to hold the landlord accountable for moving costs, temporary housing, and storage fees because the landlord could not deliver the premises on the date promised.

■ *Tip Number* **53**

Always require an exact date of a resident who plans on moving.

Insisting on a written notice with an exact date from the resident who claims to be moving may help in two ways. From a psychological standpoint, the resident is far more likely to follow through with the move if a written and signed statement has been given. From a legal standpoint, the landlord has a much stronger case against the holdover resident should he or she seek to sue the resident for damages (expenses owed to the new resident) for not moving on the date as agreed.

MOVE-OUT CHARGES

Avoid misunderstandings over why money was deducted from a resident's security deposit. More importantly, give a list of move-out charges before a resident actually moves so that they will be motivated to do everything necessary to get their full deposit back.

All types of business establishments have list prices for the various services they offer. When you go to the barbershop, dry cleaner, or a fast food restaurant, you can see a list price for items or services available. In each of these cases, you find out in advance how much the item or the work will cost.

Why not do the same thing with your routine move-out costs? Let your resident know in advance of moving just how much your move-out costs really are. If they know what charges they face at move-out time, they'll be less argumentative when you start deducting certain sums from their deposit. They'll be expecting to pay $12 for a towel bar and $75 for having the refrigerator painted.

■ *Tip Number* **54**

Give the residents your list prices for move-out charges.

Try it and see what happens. Itemize as many of the things you might have to do to a place when residents move out, and assign a dollar figure to each (see the Receive Your Full Deposit Back When You Move! form). Adjust the figures to fit your circumstances. Then, give this list of prices to your residents when they first rent from you and later when they give you notice that they're moving, and you'll detect a difference in their attitude when you give them an accounting of their deposits. They'll be less defiant and you won't have to be so defensive about your charges. You will find that more of your expectations will be met, because the resident has been forewarned of what it will cost them not to meet your expectations of how the property should be returned.

This book includes several forms related to a resident vacating the premises, so that the transition is as smooth as possible for all parties involved. The forms provide very clear instructions on what is expected of vacating residents and how they can get their deposit back, even if they are leaving on short notice.

Give residents the opportunity to know in advance what is needed to get their full deposit back.

Here's an idea. Send a contractor or handyman over to the property where someone will soon be vacating to do a "pre-move-out" inspection. The person you send should be someone who is very familiar with what condition the property must be returned in order for the person to get their full deposit back. Not only should the person be familiar with your lease expectations and requirements, but also capable of actually doing the work if needed to assist the resident in getting the property back into move-in condition, minus any normal wear and tear. This contractor does the inspection with the resident and points out any needed repairs if any, painting, etc., that is needed to qualify for a full refund of deposit. He also offers his services (at a reasonable and even discounted price) if the resident would like to him to complete the work. One of the selling points in using the contractor's services is that he reminds the resident that the management offers a $50 or $100 bonus on top of whatever deposit the resident is entitled to, if a prospective resident sees the place, likes it, applies, and qualifies, before the last day of the current resident's occupancy. Therefore, the contractor wants to help get the place ready for show as soon as possible to help the resident get the full deposit back PLUS bonus money.

This idea has advantages to both resident and you, the owner. The resident has the assurance that they will get their full deposit back and have work completed at a reasonable price, which they probably would not have been able to complete themselves or could not have hired someone else at a lower price. And, there is the possibility that the resident may get back a bonus if the place gets rerented in time.

You, the owner, now have your property ready to show to prospective residents BEFORE the last day of occupancy of the current resident. You will even have the support and cooperation of the resident in the process, allowing you access to show it, keeping the place looking move-in ready, and even saying a positive word about the home or community when called upon. This all increases the odds that you will rent the place faster and thereby cutting out costly vacancy and turnover time. Sure, the cost

of the repairs would have come from the resident either way, but residents are far happier with this scenario than if you had simply deducted money from their deposit after they moved out, which most often leaves them feeling cheated. This suggested way, residents feel like a winner. A sample letter requesting the right to a "pre" or initial move-out inspection is included.

LEASE CANCELLATION

■ *Tip Number* **56**

Allow residents to move out early for a price.

If you are using a standard one-year lease term, there will be occasions when a resident must terminate a lease early. They may ask your permission to cancel the lease. You may agree to do so by offering the residents the opportunity to cancel or "buy out" their lease. As part of the buy-out agreement, you may establish certain conditions. For example, in exchange for the resident paying a fee, you (the landlord) release the resident from any further payment obligations for the rest of the lease. This does not include payment for any property damages the resident may be responsible for. You, however, take the responsibility of finding a new resident and any marketing expenses or loss of future income that occurs because of the early move-out.

The terms and conditions to cancel a lease are negotiable. A sample form is included in this section. You may wish to require a fee equal to two months' rent (an amount you consider fair to cover costs of rerenting and loss of rent before finding a qualified resident replacement). In the agreement, specify the date the property is to be vacated, and give clear instructions on how the property is to be left, where the key is to be returned, and how to leave the resident's forwarding address. Before accepting a cancellation fee or returning the security deposit to the forwarding address of the vacating resident, inspect the property.

TRACK YOUR VACANCIES AT A GLANCE

It's often easier to keep track of vacancies and make-readies if you can visually see at a glance what you have. We have included a sample Vacant Units Checklist. With this form, you can keep track of make-ready progress of your rentals and quickly see what each property or unit still needs. You can make big circles for uncompleted items and slash through the circles when an item is completed.

TURNING VACANCIES INTO PROFIT CENTERS

What is often the most stressful time for a landlord can instead become one of the most profitable opportunities of the year, especially if you are actively seeking to buy or lease more rental properties.

The next time you have one of those "rare" instances when a property becomes vacant, use the opportunity to not only sell the idea of renting it to new prospective residents, but also sell yourself or your company to neighbors who may be selling or losing their property in the near future. Statistics show that, on the average, at least three of the homeowners on the same or adjacent block to your rental will try to sell or rent their home within the next year.

When you have a home that becomes vacant, your first thoughts may be to run a classified ad and put a Rent Me sign on the front of the building. I want to recommend to you not to overlook perhaps your most profitable advertising contacts—neighbors to your rentals. When you have a vacancy (or even better, right after receiving a 30-day vacating letter from a resident), send a letter to all the owners of the properties next to and near you rental. I'll call this a Hello, Neighbor Letter. Start the letter off by introducing or reintroducing yourself, or merely remind them that you are the owner or manager of the particular property.

In your Hello, Neighbor Letter (see the included sample), compliment the neighborhood and mention your commitment to maintaining neighborhood property standards in the residents you choose. Seek the neighbors' help in finding qualified residents, possibly giving a bonus for assistance (if state law allows). The active investor should most importantly mention in the letter that he or she "would like to buy another property in the neighborhood" or "lease on a long-term basis" for owners who don't want to worry again about vacancies, maintenance, and midnight calls (all the ugly images—scare the uneducated rental owner). Finish the letter with a PS telling homeowners that you'll be glad to let them know how much you may be willing to pay to buy or lease their homes, without any obligation on their part, if they give you a call.

If most of the neighbors are nonowners (which you should avoid when buying), you can get the mailing addresses of the owners from the local tax assessor. Information on where tax bills are mailed is available to the public.

The first time you mail out a set of letters and each time after that should cause your phone to ring. Granted it won't ring off the hook, but it only takes one really motivated seller to create big profits. Each time I use this strategy, sure enough I get one or two sincere calls from someone thinking of selling their property and interested in how much I'm willing to pay. How you handle the calls is another whole discussion.

Most of the calls will not be from sellers who really need to sell and are open to "flexible" terms, but I usually don't have to spend a lot of my time to find the one serious caller willing and ready to negotiate. If you work this wealth-building strategy and wait for the right callers, you will come across those deals that can produce a $200 a month or more cash flow or a minimum $10,000 turn around profit margin, which will be well worth the minimum effort you put forth.

■ *Tip Number* **57**

Ask neighbors for assistance and purchase their homes.

You can use your vacancies to go a step further in building relationships and profitable contracts with neighbors. After you've done all the extra touch-ups to the exterior and interior of the rental, along with your neighbor letter, send an invitation to a rental open house. Let the neighboring owners know that you would like to meet them and personally give them an emergency number to call if they ever have a problem with your resident. In the invitation, mention refreshments will be provided. And offer to talk seriously to anyone who may be thinking about selling a home, and you'll be glad to tell them what you would be willing to pay to buy or lease their house. Do your homework ahead of time and have contracts available at the open house.

Have a guest register available at the rental open house and be sure all neighboring owners who attend sign the register. This will become a prime mailing list for sending follow-up letters every four months. In those letters, remind them that you have rentals available, in case they know someone looking to move, and of your interest in buying other homes. Ask if their house-selling plans have changed.

AGGRESSIVELY MARKET YOUR RENTALS

In addition to traditional advertising, like classified ads and For Rent signs, also advertise on the Internet for free at <www.mrlandlord.com>. Rental owners are also advised to utilize marketing letters and flyers to reach qualified applicants.

■ *Tip Number* **58**

Take your advertising to where your ideal prospects are.

Many landlords who are successful in filling their vacancies reveal that their secret is that they target their marketing efforts. This book includes samples of flyers and marketing letters to neighbors, brokers, colleges, and businesses. It is very important however, that you do not send any letter to a company, college, hospital, etc., without first calling and establishing an informal relationship with a contact person who is actually in a position to be able to refer others to you and who will be expecting your letter. Address your letter to the contact person and be sure to follow up with the same person systematically. Your goal is to develop a network of contacts who continually refer your name to prospective residents, which makes your phone ring often with qualified applicants.

CERTIFIED PROFESSIONAL LANDLORD

I want to commend my fellow professional. No, I'm not talking just to the brokers, attorneys, and other professionals who may be reading this book. I'm talking to every one of you who owns at least one rental home.

My definition of a professional includes the following:

- Participates *for gain* or livelihood in an activity or field of endeavor often engaged in by amateurs
- Takes part in an activity requiring specialized knowledge or training
- Maintains high standards and has high goals

This definition describes the vast majority of the readers of this publication. See if I'm right. Take a minute now, go back, and test yourself. Do you match up to all three characteristics? Are you a *professional* landlord or landlady?

The term *for gain* in the first part of the definition quickly separates the pro from the amateur. In landlording terms, professional landlords operate properties with positive cash flows. Amateurs operate properties with negative cash flows.

Professionals are often highly paid for their activities, and professional landlords are like doctors. They know how to operate on a dying patient or poorly managed property and by using specialized knowledge (tricks of the trade) give it new life. Professional landlords with trained effort can take their learning and generate income by turning negative properties into positive cash cows. As a result, they can buy more properties from amateur landlords and increase their gains further. Professionals of all types have success because they're constantly setting high standards for themselves, learning all they can, and practicing improved techniques to reach their goals.

Most landlords, unfortunately, are amateurs and do not fit any of the above descriptions. Amateur landlords remain amateurs because they never fully realize that they are taking part in an activity that requires specialized training and knowledge. Doctors, lawyers, and other professionals know that they must learn certain things to produce good results and that learning must constantly stay updated. Millions of individuals who become landlords because of unplanned circumstances figure they'll learn as they go and pick up knowledge through hearsay and friends. Amateur landlords ask, "How difficult can it be to rent a house?" And they are always asking for a free form. They'll get professional help if things get really difficult. By that time, it's too late and thousands of dollars are lost.

■ *Tip Number* **59**

Always run your business in a professional manner.

Here's my final point and money-making principle. Your perception of yourself directly affects your productivity and income. Even though you recognize the need for specialized information, nine out of ten do-it-yourself landlords still see themselves as amateurs, and not as professionals in the field of landlording. Most see it as simply a side job or activity to generate some extra income. The doctor or attorney on the other hand clearly sees himself or herself as a professional and expects to generate more and more income from his or her activity.

This perception of average landlords consciously and unconsciously limits the desire to reach higher goals, and they don't operate as real estate professionals in their business dealings. At one point you may have had the goal of large financial gains through real estate. Have you doubled the value of your properties? Are your properties running at maximum efficiency? Or do you evade the entire landlording subject when others ask what you do for a living?

You probably had or still have high goals for real estate. You bought this book. Many of you have bought several real estate books, tapes, or study courses. You were on your way to becoming a highly paid professional with tremendous financial gain. But you no longer see yourself as that high-paid professional. You are not practicing the skills you've learned. Your study materials are on a shelf. Instead of seeing yourself as a real estate pro, you are thinking as an amateur with lower goals. You are getting trapped in a 9-to-5 activity, working as a hired hand, helping someone else's dream come true. Don't get me wrong, many jobs provide great ways to use your talents or pay well so that you can use money gained to put into your own investments.

I want to speak hard to those of you who at one point had higher goals and standards for real es-

tate. Unfortunately your day-to-day activities keep you preoccupied with merely existing. You're not where you want to be financially and *it's your fault*. Do I need to give you a swift kick in the pants? I have to give myself one often. Raise your goals higher. Refuse to think as an amateur. Say to yourself, "I'm a real estate professional," and attack your goals and life in a professional manner. (By the way, it is okay to have more than one profession, so I'm not suggesting you stop engaging in other profitable professions.)

A professional attitude not only motivates you, but it's communicated to all those around you. You will attract better residents, get more of your rent payments on time, and get favorable cooperation in all your dealings.

I consider you a professional. In recognition of your professional status and as part of my promise to motivate you toward higher achievement, I want to award you with a professional designation—C.P.L., Certified Professional Landlord—for commitment and desire to continued learning in the field of landlording (demonstrated by your purchase and study of this book). A copy of this certificate is included herein (see the last form in this section) for you to have as an encouragement and continual visual reminder to keep your standards and goals high. This certificate recognizes that you are a professional landlord!

UPDATED RESIDENT INFORMATION
(Annual Review to Update Records and/or Cross-Check Management)

Address: _____

City: _____ State: _____ ZIP: _____

Phone: _____ Cell: _____ E-mail: _____

Name: _____ Social Security #: _____

Name of Spouse: _____ Social Security #: _____

Please list all other individuals living in the dwelling, their relationship to you and ages:

_____

_____

_____

How many pets: _____ Please describe: _____

Current rent per month: _____ Last time you had a rent raise: _____

Do you pay other than monthly?   Yes _____   No _____   If not, how often? _____ How much? _____

Rent is due by what date? _____ If paid after due date, how much? _____

I pay my rent with: Cash ____   Money orders ____   Checks ____   Electronic transfers ____   Other _____

What date is late charge added? _____ How much is late charge? _____

Have you paid any late charges this year? _____ Which months? _____

I pay late charges with: Cash ____   Money orders ____   Checks ____   Are you given receipts? _____

My payments are: Mailed ____   Dropped off ____   Picked up ____   By whom? _____

Do you owe any back due rent/late charges right now? _____ How much: _____

Date of the last time you made a rent payment: _____ For what month: _____

Have you been requested to pay any charges this year for bad checks? _____ How much? _____

Any additional charges/fees paid?   If so, amount: _____ For what? _____

When did you first move in? _____

I paid an application fee in the amount of: _____ Refundable _____ Non Refundable _____

Any other move-in fees?   If so, what? _____ Refundable _____ Non Refundable _____

If you moved in this year did you receive a move-in special/bonus?   Yes _____   No _____   N/A _____

Describe the move-in special, bonus, discount, or gift you were given: _____

Amount of original security deposit: _____ Any deposit still/now due? _____

Have you been told any money has been deducted? _____ For what? _____

Do you pay for any utilities?   Yes _____   No _____   Which ones? _____

Appliances (that are part of the rental agreement): _____

Any other extras that have been added: _____

Do you currently have renter's insurance? _____ With what company? _____

Have you received a referral fee or extra tenant bonus of any kind this year?   Yes _____   No _____

If so, how much? $_____ For what? _____

Have you received satisfactory service this year from management?   Yes _____   No _____

If not, what is one thing we have neglected to do? _____

Employer: _____ Phone: _____

Address: _____

Supervisor: _____ Gross income: _____ Weekly: _____ Mo: _____

Spouse's Employer: _____ Phone: _____

Address: _____

Supervisor: _____ Gross income: _____ Weekly: _____ Mo: _____

Other income by either resident: _____ Weekly: _____ Mo: _____

From what source: _____

Current bank: _____ Phone: _____

Checking: _____ Savings: _____ Account #: _____

Make of automobile(s): _____ License: _____

Person to contact in case of an emergency: _____ Phone: _____

Resident's Signature: _____ Date: _____

YEAR-END RESIDENT SURVEY

Please answer the following questions so we may better serve you. Complete each question and return in the enclosed or attached self-addressed stamped envelope. In thanks, you will receive the following, as our holiday gift to you,

_____.

1. We have lived here: ___0-6 months ___6-12 months ____ 1yr___2 yrs___3 yrs or longer

2. How did you first find out about the residence you are now living in?

_____

3. What two things do you most like about your residence or the area you live in?

       1. _____

       2. _____

4. What do you like the least about your residence?

_____

5. How have your concerns or requests been taken care of? _____ satisfactory _____not satisfactory

6. Is there a concern that has still not been taken care of? If so, what?

_____

7. Name three local stores/businesses you go to often (e.g., supermarket, laundromat, dry cleaner, medical office, pharmacy, barber/beauty salon, hardware store, bottled water supplier):

    1. _____   2._____   3. _____

8. Which school does your child or children attend?

_____

9. Name two places you go for recreation (rec center, health spa, club, restaurant, country club, theater, library, book store, church socials, bowling alley, etc.):

    1. _____   2. _____

Of the following rental extras or upgrades, check the items or services that you would like us to offer next year and would be willing to pay extra rent or a service fee for each month.

Computer	_____	Internet access	_____
Ceiling fan	_____	Mini satellite dish or cable TV	_____
Additional door lock	_____	Garage/extra storage	_____
Water filter system	_____	Membership at local gym	_____
Closet organizers	_____	Weekly house cleaning	_____
TV or surround sound	_____	Phone answering service	_____
Microwave oven	_____	Lawn service	_____
Choice of wall color	_____	Grocery home delivery	_____
Extra phone jack or fax	_____	Flood lights front/side	_____
Washer and/or dryer	_____	Alarm monitoring service	_____
Screen door or added AC	_____	Renter's insurance	_____

10. When you do eventually move, what will be the main reason for moving?

_____

11. Give us the name of a friend, relative, or co-worker who may be looking for a new home or apartment.

_____

If they rent or buy from us, you may qualify for one of the free property upgrades above.

SPECIAL THANK YOU NOTE

Dear _____ :

We are offering a special thank you to our 3-Star residents who continue to reside in one of our properties for an additional year. Take your pick of the following upgrades which we will be glad to add to the property in order to customize your home. We are providing you a choice of one of the upgrades below without any additional charge.

1. _____

2. _____

3. _____

4. _____

Select one thank-you gift, and contact us at the following number to inform us of your selection:

_____

Whichever item you select, it becomes a permanent part of your custom rental home and will remain with the home if you should ever move, unless otherwise noted: _____.

Sincerely,

Rental Manager

(Note to rental owners: Examples of upgrades may include ceiling fan, mini-blinds, additional door lock, dimmer switch in dining or bedroom, choice of wall color in one room, outside motion-detector light, or choice of a garden plant.)

STATEMENT TO RESIDENT OF INTEREST EARNED ON SECURITY DEPOSIT

From: _____

_____

_____

Date: _____

To: _____

_____

_____

Good news! The purpose of this notice is to inform you your security deposit in the amount of $ _____ has been held in a checking or savings account at _____ Bank and you are now entitled to _____ annual interest in the amount of _____.

Enclosed is a check in the above amount.

Thank you again for being one of our 3-Star residents.

Rental Manager

HAPPY HOLIDAYS

--- $25 --- $25 --- $25 ---

We wish you and your loved ones a happy holiday season!
We appreciate you are renting from us. To help celebrate the holiday season
and to show our appreciation to you as one of our 3-Star residents,
we want to give you this $25 rent certificate.

To use it, simply return it with your _____ rent payment.
This entitles you to deduct $25 from your normal rent due.
Your normal rental rate is $ _____ .
With this certificate, your payment due is $ _____ .
Please note: This certificate is good only for the month stated
and only if payment is made on or before the due date.

Again, thanks for being a 3-Star resident.
We hope you can take advantage of this certificate.
We wish you and your family well!

--- $25 --- $25 --- $25 ---

HAPPY NEW YEAR

From: _____

_____

_____

Date: _____

To:_____

_____

_____

We hope that you and your family are having a happy holiday season and have a Happy and Healthy New Year!! Thank you to everyone who has paid their rent on time during the year and to those who have kept their homes nice both inside and out. To show our appreciation to those who paid on time and kept their homes nice during the entire year we are providing them with the following:

_____.

TO HELP MAKE IT EVEN EASIER TO MAKE ON-TIME PAYMENTS ALL NEXT YEAR, WE INVITE YOU TO TAKE AD-VANTAGE OF OUR PAYDAY PAYMENT OPTION PROGRAM. THAT PROGRAM ALSO HELPS SOME RESIDENTS TO BUDGET BETTER AND AVOID LATE CHARGES.

More Good News! We will soon have **RENT CONTESTS**, where we will have a drawing with all those who paid on time, and with each drawing, a winner will receive a free gift.

DON'T FORGET, YOU CAN MAKE SURE YOUR RENT PAYMENT IS ON TIME ALL THE TIME WITH OUR DIRECT DEPOSIT PROGRAM.

Call us today to take advantage of either the payday payment option or direct rent deposit program. We hope that you stay with us for a long time. Thank you for all of your help in keeping your home nice. To sign up for the Pay Day or Direct Deposit program, call us at: _____.

BEST WISHES FOR THE NEW YEAR!

Management

NOTICE OF CHANGE
AMENDMENT TO RENTAL AGREEMENT

Date: _____

To: _____

This letter is to notify you that there will be a change or amendment to the terms of tenancy under which you occupy the property located at: _____.

As of the following date, _____, there will be the following changes or amendments:

_____

_____

_____

The changes or amendments are due in part for the following reasons:

_____

_____

_____

We look forward to your continued participation in our 3-Star Resident Program. Also, we would like to remind that your next 3-Star resident benefit will be as follows:

_____

_____
        Owner/Manager

ANNIVERSARY AGENDA CHECKLIST

We like to meet with residents at least once each year to help ensure we continue to meet their housing needs and make sure they are aware of all the housing options available. We want YOU to select the agenda for the meeting. Tell us what you would like to talk about. We can discuss just one of the following topics or we can discuss as many of the topics as you select. Or, if you prefer not to meet at this time, just let us know.

The meeting will take place at your residence on one of the following two dates. Please let us know which date and time is most convenient for you to meet with us. Return this checklist to us within the next three days so we can schedule the meeting. Mail or deliver it to the following address:

_____.

Which meeting date and time is best for you?

_____ or _____.

Select which topics you would like to discuss at the meeting.

_____ Different rent payment plans available. Some residents prefer to pay every two weeks instead of monthly. It is possible to change your payment terms.

_____ Future Homebuyers Program. You may want to buy a home within the next three years. Ask us how you can receive monthly vouchers good toward a homebuyer's account.

_____ Any concerns about your current rental home?

_____ Receive $100 annual security deposit refund for passing inspections.

_____ New upgrade options available for the next year of your 3-Star Program.

_____ Transfer location if you're considering a move to another size rental home.

_____ Prices and rental policies of other homes in the area.

_____ Negotiate new rental amount for the upcoming year.

_____ Tell-a-Friend Referral Program. How to get free rent or an upgrade.

_____ Your evaluation or comments about our maintenance guarantee program.

_____ Special services and advantages of out VIP Resident Program.

_____ Other topic: _____.

_____ No need to meet at this time. Everything is satisfactory. Thanks!

THANKS FOR LETTING US SERVE YOU FOR THE FIRST YEAR OF YOUR 3-STAR PROGRAM

(Sample letter for landlords to send to residents when they are nearing their rental anniversary. This letter is sent instead of the customary renewal and rent increase notice.)

Date: _____

Dear _____:

    I want to personally thank you for the privilege our company has had to serve you and your family for the first year of your 3-Star Program. We look forward to serving you for the next two years of your 3-Star Program.

    As mentioned at the beginning of your rental term, the rental amount is adjusted on an annual basis. The amount of adjustment for the next 12 months, to take effect in 60 days or more, beginning _____, will be an increase of $ _____ per month. We do, however, seek to work with residents and any unique circumstances as much as possible. If, at this time, you are having financial difficulty or other personal circumstances making this rental adjustment too much for you to handle, contact our office within the next five days.

    Again, we look forward to serving you throughout your 3-Star Program. And, as promised, as part of your 3-Star Program, as soon as we receive your written permission, we will arrange to provide the following benefit to you:

_____ .

Give us written permission below to provide you this benefit as soon as possible. Mail this letter back to us with your next rental payment.

Sincerely,

Rental Manager

Resident's signature granting permission to provide above benefit: _____ .

Phone number and best time to contact you, if needed: _____ .

NOTICE OF RENT INCREASE

Date: _____

To: _____

    This letter is to notify you there will be a change to the terms of tenancy under which you occupy the property located at: _____.

As of the following date, _____ , your rent will be adjusted by _____ per month. The new rent amount will be _____ per month, payable in advance. The increase is due in part for the following reasons:

_____ ,

_____ ,

_____ .

_____

            Owner/Manager

PS: To help keep future rental increases to a minimum, your cooperation continues to be appreciated with on-time payments, excellent property upkeep, and in the following matter(s):

_____

_____

RENEW EARLY—SAVE MONEY

Address: _____

City: _____ State: _____ ZIP: _____

Dear _____ :

    Your current lease will expire within the next 90 to 120 days, on _____. Each year your rent is adjusted; however, we let residents help determine how much the rent increase will be. For the upcoming year, your rent increase will be between $10.00 and $100.00. Again, the good news is that you get to determine if the rent increase will be small or large. This increase is necessary because of increasing operational expenses, taxes, and utilities. Because you are a 3-Star resident, we want to keep your increase to a minimum, so we encourage you to respond to this letter as soon as possible. The rent increase will be small, only $10, if you renew your agreement early; however, the small increase of $10 is guaranteed only until the following date: _____, after which your rent is subject to an additional increase of $1.00 per day until you decide to extend your agreement, up until your anniversary date.

    The maximum rent increase is $100. Here's how you can save up to $90 off that increase. If you renew now, at least 90 days prior to your anniversary date, save $90 off your monthly rent increase. Instead of an increase of $100, the increase is only $10 per month. If you wait and renew 60 days before your anniversary date, save $60; your increase will be $40 per month. Wait longer and renew 30 days prior to your anniversary, you save $30, making your rent increase $70 per month. As you can see, the earlier you renew your agreement, the more you save and the lower your rent increase will be.

    The reason we offer the savings is because the sooner we know if you will be staying in the property, the less we have to prepare to possibly advertise and rerent the premises. The sooner we know, the easier you make our job, and so we offer greater savings for letting us know early.

    Please sign below and return this letter as soon as possible to the following address: _____, no later than: _____, to take advantage of the biggest rent savings and discount. The date we actually receive this letter is the date we use to calculate your savings. We value your tenancy and hope you plan to stay and save as much as possible. After this letter is returned to us, we'll send back a copy for your records and an addendum to your rental agreement with the new rental rate. If you have any questions regarding your renewal savings, please call me at _____. Thank you for your cooperation.

Yes, I wish to renew/extend my lease an additional year. I also wish to save as much money as possible on the rent increase. My goal is to that you receive this letter at least _____ days before my anniversary date, so I can reduce my monthly rent increase by that same amount.

Resident's signature: _____ Date: _____

Owner/Manager's signature: _____ Date: _____

LEASE EXTENSION AGREEMENT

This extension made this date, _____ , by and between _____
_____ as owner, and _____
_____ as resident:

The parties hereby have previously entered into a lease regarding the premises located at _____
_____ . The term of that lease shall expire on _____ .

1. The term of the lease shall now be extended as follows:
2. The rental during the extended term shall be by the resident's choice (please check one):

_____   I wish to extend the lease for **36 months** with a monthly rental rate of $ _____

_____   I wish to extend the lease for **24 months** with a monthly rental rate of $ _____

_____   I wish to extend the lease for **12 months** with a monthly rental rate of $ _____

_____   I wish to extend the lease for **6 months** with a monthly rental rate of $ _____

Rent will be due in advance of the first day of each month of the extended term.

Please note: resident pays a higher rental rate for flexibility of having a shorter term and pays a lower rental rate for agreeing to stay for a longer term. If the resident vacates sooner than the time period agreed to below, resident agrees to pay a lease cancellation fee of $ _____ .

3. Upon execution hereof, the Lease Extension Agreement, this addendum shall become an integral part of the lease. All other terms and provisions of the lease shall remain in full force and effect.

Resident's signature: _____   Date: _____

Owner/Manager's signature: _____   Date: _____

_____   If resident will not renew the existing lease on premises noted above and will vacate the property on or before expiration date of lease as noted above, please check here and sign below.

Resident's signature: _____   Date: _____

Owner/Manager's signature: _____   Date: _____

RENTAL AGREEMENT EXTENSION AND OFFER FOR UPGRADE

FROM: _____

_____

_____

Date: _____

Dear: _____

I want to personally thank you for the privilege our company has had in serving you as a ___ year Resident at _____. We look forward to serving you many years into the future.

Your present Rental Agreement will expire on _____. We have included a new Rental Agreement form for you to sign to continue living in your current residence.

It is customary for our company to update the yearly rent when each Rental Agreement is extended. We pride ourselves on implementing cost saving techniques to keep rent increases to our Residents at a minimum. The amount of the adjustment for the next twelve months, to take effect on _____ will be an increase of _____ per month to make your annual rent, when paid in monthly installments equal to _____ per month..

It is our policy to offer an upgrade to any Residents who elect to extend their Rental Agreement for each additional year they reside with us. As you mentioned in the survey you previously filled out, you would be interested in having a _____ as an upgrade. These items are more costly than our usual extension upgrades. However, there will be no additional charge as an Anniversary gift for extending your rental agreement. This upgrade will / will not (circle one) become a permanent addition to the dwelling. If you are not interested in that upgrade at this time please contact us for a list of Rental Agreement Extension upgrades we offer at no charge.

Again, we look forward to serving you throughout your residency. And as promised for extending your Rental Agreement, we'll arrange for the installation of the upgrade of your choice. Please give us written permission to provide you this benefit as soon as possible. Mail your signed Rental Agreement Extension form in the self-addressed stamped envelope by _____. If you do not wish to extend your agreement, please call or write us as soon as possible. Please call me if you have any questions.

Thank you,

Rental Manager

Resident signature granting permission to provide above benefit _____

Phone number and best time to contact you if needed _____

LEASE EXTENSION REMINDER

FROM: _____

_____

_____

Date: _____

Dear: _____

_____

_____

We have not yet received your response to our invitation for a new one-year lease extension. Perhaps you have overlooked returning your response sheet. Please return your response to us as soon as possible. We want to remind you that we need to hear from you by the following, date, _____.

If we have not heard from you by that date, we will begin to make arrangements for another resident to move into the home or apartment. Should you decide after that point that you indeed wish to continue residing in the property, that option may no longer be possible, because we may have another applicant desiring to move in, or other immediate plans for use of, or work to the property. After that point, if it is not too late, and we are able to still offer you the opportunity to extend your agreement, you may have to pay an additional amount to reimburse us for expenses for marketing, legal fees, or other costs spent in preparation for ending your rental tenancy and preparation for our next residents. Some costs may be charged, even if you decide not to extend the agreement, but wait until after the date to let us know. So again, please let us know your response as soon as you can, and especially by the above date.

We hope you decide to extend your lease and stay at your current home. With all the cost-involved in moving these days, it probably will save you a lot if you don't have to move at this time. We look forward to meeting your housing needs for another year. If we can further assist you in helping to make your decision, please do not hesitate to call us at _____.

Owner/Management

RESIDENT'S NOTICE OF INTENT TO VACATE

From: _____, Resident

Date: _____

To: _____, Owner/Manager

_____

_____

Dear _____, Owner/Manager

This letter is to notify you I will be moving from the following address:
_____.

I intend to move out and vacate the premises no later than the following date: _____.

This notice is to provide you with at least _____ days written notice as required in the rental agreement. (Unless special arrangements are being requested, which may include a buy-out payment, to cancel or terminate the agreement early.) I plan to fully cooperate with the management in regards to the following:

a) To allow Owner to show the premises to any prospective residents, and I understand if I can't be reached after the Owner or Manager has made a good-faith effort to do so, Owner or Manager may enter and show the rental.

b) To promptly return the keys to Owner and completely move and vacate the premises on or before the date stated above.

c) To leave the rental in a clean condition and free of any and all damages.

d) To pay an additional buy-out fee, if applicable, to get the rental agreement cancelled early and/or without sufficient advance notice provided to the owner or manager.

e) To provide a forwarding address to Owner prior to vacating the rental, so the security deposit can be returned, provided that I have complied with the above terms, that I have no unpaid outstanding charges of any kind, and that there are no damages to the property.

Resident's Signature: _____   Date: _____

PLANNING TO MOVE?
Checklist of Moving Expenses

Below is a list of expenses you may need to plan for if you are preparing to move. The costs are only estimates but may be helpful guidelines. If we can be of any assistance to you when you move, let us know and, if you decide to rent from us for a longer period of time, contact us as soon as possible so we will not make arrangements for someone else to rent your residence.

_____ First month's rent in advance   _____

_____ Security deposit that will be required   _____

_____ Additional rent or deposit   _____

_____ Moving company/hired help   _____

_____ Utilities/deposit(s)   _____

_____ Telephone installation/connection/deposit _____

_____ Time and trouble of packing/unpacking   _____

_____ Cost of lost/broken items during move   _____

_____ New blinds, drapes, or curtains   _____

_____ Miscellaneous items for new location   _____

_____ Loss of income while taking off work to take care of moving,
      going to utility companies, new school, etc.   _____

_____ Other costs _____   _____

Total Estimated Cost   _____

Any move works far better if you know ahead of time how much your total costs may be. Many residents make the mistake of thinking it does not cost much to move and then have big headaches when they realize it costs more than they thought. Many wish too late they would have stayed where they were a little longer. Remember, if you decide to extend your lease, let us know before it's too late. It may save you a lot of money.

NOTICE TO VACATING RESIDENT

Address: _____

City: _____State: _____ZIP:_____

Dear _____ :

We received notification on _____ you will be vacating the above address by _____ . We want to remind you the property must be returned to us in the same condition it was given in order to receive your full security deposit back. Please refer to our Minimum Charges form for charges deducted from your deposit if we have to restore different aspects of the property back to the same condition.

Return all keys to our office, because, unless otherwise agreed on, you remain responsible for rent payment each day until the keys are received by us. After keys are received, we will make one final inspection with you to see if the property has been reasonably cleaned and without any damage. If all checks out well, your deposit will refunded to you within _____ days.

We have immediately begun advertising for new residents. Let us know if you have any change of plans on your move date or know someone you can recommend, because we will be scheduling a new resident to move in the day after you vacate. Also, if we can provide you with a larger rental or in another location better suited to you, let us know because we do have other rental homes that will soon be available.

Thank you for your cooperation.

Sincerely,

Rental Manager

PS: Please keep rental looking good so when we show it to prospective tenants they will be impressed. Remember, if we sign up a new resident before you move out, you receive an additional $50 bonus in moving assistance, on top of whatever deposit you are entitled to. We also ask for your cooperation in permitting us to show the property to prospective residents while you are still residing on the premises. If you know someone who may be interested in renting the home, please call us as soon as possible at: _____.

RESPONSE TO VACATING
WITH SHORT NOTICE

Address: _____

City: _____State: _____ZIP:_____

Dear _____:

We have received your request for permission to vacate the above address without giving proper notice. Under normal circumstances, and as stated in your rental agreement, you are requested to give a minimum 30-day written notice prior to the date you desire to move out in order to receive your security deposit back.

We understand that sometimes circumstances arise that you are unable to plan for. The reason 30-day notices are required is to give both parties advance notice to plan for the change. In our case, the notice gives us enough time to find another tenant to take your place. Without sufficient time we may have days go by with a vacant dwelling and loss of income, which is why your security deposit is not refunded. However, if you assist us by recommending a friend or coworker to take over the dwelling as soon as you move out, we do not lose rental income and we can, therefore, return your deposit to you, minus a small transfer fee of only $50.

We will also do all we can to get the place rerented promptly. If we do so prior to you moving, we will return your deposit to you minus the transfer fee plus advertising costs we incurred. This will still provide you with a return of part of your deposit that I'm sure will be helpful to you, wherever you are going.

Thank you for your cooperation.

Rental Manager

END OF LEASE NOTICE

From: _____

Date: _____

To: _____

      _____

      _____

Dear _____:

    Your present lease has already ended or will end in less than _____ days.
One of the following actions is now required by you. Please indicate your response and notify us as soon as possible.
We can be reached by calling _____.

_____ To continue living at this residence you must sign and return a new lease or lease extension agreement that we have sent you, or the tenancy will end as of _____.

_____ You would like to discuss remaining in the home and extending the lease, but only for a short-term basis of _____ months. Contact us immediately to see if this option is available, which would be at a higher monthly rent.

_____ You do not intend to renew or extend the agreement and therefore you are asked to be completely out of the dwelling by _____ so that we can make preparation to return the security deposit that is due you. Any delay by you in responding to us can jeopardize receiving all or part of your security deposit.

Thank you for your cooperation.

Sincerely,

Rental Manager

AGREEMENT TO CANCEL LEASE

This agreement is entered into on the following date: _____ , between _____ _____ (Resident), who leases the premises at the following address _____ and _____ (Owner).

Resident has asked for permission to break or cancel the rental agreement between the parties on short notice and/or prior to the expiration date of the agreement. Resident wishes to move out by the following date, _____ , even though he/she will not be able to give proper notice as required in the rental agreement. In exchange for Owner agreeing to cancel the agreement, Resident agrees to the following terms:

1. To provide Owner/Manager with written notice of intent to vacate.
2. To pay the current month's rent of $ _____ plus an additional amount of $ _____.
   These payments will be paid by the following date: _____.
3. To promptly return the keys to Owner and completely move and vacate the premises on or before the following date _____ , which shall be considered the cancellation date of this agreement.
4. To provide a forwarding address to Owner prior to vacating the apartment.
5. To leave the apartment in a clean condition and free of any and all damages.
6. To allow Owner to show the premises to any prospective resident with as little as one hour notice, anytime during the following hours _____ . If Resident can't be reached after Owner or Manager has made a good-faith effort to do so, Owner or Manager may enter and show the rental.
7. To hereby forever release any claims or causes of action that Resident may have or that shall arise in the future against Owner, its officers, directors, employees, or agents arising out of the rental agreement.
8. _____

If Resident fulfills the obligations agreed to above, Owner agrees to:

1. Release Resident from any further obligation to pay rent.
2. Not report any poor performance or unfavorable information regarding Resident to any credit or tenant reporting agencies.
3. Return the security deposit, provided that Resident has complied with the above terms, and provided that there are no unpaid outstanding charges of any kind due from Resident and that there are no damages to the property.

In the event Resident does not fulfill the terms above or is in default under any of the terms of the rental agreement, Owner shall have the right to keep and apply the aforesaid cancellation fee toward any damages arising as a result of such default.

Resident's Signature: _____ Date: _____

Resident's Signature: _____ Date: _____

Owner/Manager's Signature: _____ Date: _____

RELET AGREEMENT

Name: _____

Address: _____ Apt #: _____

City: _____State: _____ZIP: _____

Lease Expiration Date: _____

_____

The resident at the above address has requested permission to relet rental residence. The resident understands in order for the owner to consider granting permission for reletting the premises, the CURRENT RESIDENT must agree to and comply with the following terms:

1. The resident is responsible for any advertising costs incurred.
2. The resident is responsible to show the premises and find the new resident.
   However, the new prospective resident must complete a rental application and be approved by the owner. The owner has the sole right to accept or reject this resident per his/her current credit and selection criteria.
3. Until a new resident has been accepted, signed a rental agreement, paid the first month's rent for the premises plus a deposit, and accepted the keys, the current resident is not released from obligations according to the rental agreement. In addition, should a new resident be found, but for whatever reason cancels or not be able to fulfill the initial obligations required to move in, the current resident is still obligated to fulfill all responsibilities under his/her rental agreement.
4. If a new resident is accepted, the current resident agrees to have deducted from his/her deposit monies that may be necessary to clean or repair the premises and move out at least _____ days prior to the new resident's move-in date.
5. The current resident understands that he/she will be charged a reletting fee of $_____.
6. The current resident will turn in his/her keys and provide a forwarding address to the owner, and under no circumstances give a copy of any key to the new resident.
7. The current resident agrees to pay rent according to the terms of the agreement until the new resident's move-in date.
8. The current resident understands that the security deposit is refundable provided that the resident has complied with the terms herein, has no unpaid charges of any kind, and is not in violation of the rental agreement.

THE NEW RESIDENT, if accepted, must agree to the following terms:

1. Pay a full month's rent in advance and a security deposit.
2. Sign a rental agreement.
3. Accept the rental rate of $ _____ and accept the rental "as is" and agree that it is in satisfactory condition with no immediate repairs needed, unless stated _____.
4. Understand that the terms are a month-to-month agreement, and that the owner may change the terms of the agreement by providing a _____-day notice to the resident.

The above terms are accepted by the following parties:

Current Resident's Signature: _____Date: _____

New Resident's Signature: _____Date: _____

Owner/Manager's Signature: _____Date: _____

RIGHT TO REQUEST INITIAL MOVE-OUT INSPECTION

Date: _____

To: _____

_____

_____

Resident is advised that by signing, dating, and returning this form to Owner, Resident may request an initial inspection of the premises to be conducted by Owner, with or without Resident's presence, for the purpose of preparing an itemized statement of needed:

1) Cleaning

2) Damage repair

3) Personal property or appurtenances restoration, replacement, or return.

Such inspection will be performed by Landlord/Management after giving Resident 48 hours notice of the date and time of the proposed entry; Resident may be present for such inspection. Resident shall have the option to remedy any damage or uncleanliness in the premises, and to restore, replace, or return any personal property or appurtenances therein, as itemized by Landlord/Manager, up to the date or termination and, if Resident chooses to do so, Resident shall have the obligation to hire licensed and insured professionals, approved in writing, by Landlord/Manager in advance of any work done in the premises, to remedy any damage or uncleanliness and/or to restore, replace, or return any personal property or appurtenance in the premises.

To Landlord/Management: Resident requests an initial inspection of the premises. Please attempt to schedule a date and time with the undersigned to conduct the initial inspection. Resident realizes that Landlord/Management will provide a written notice to Resident at least 48 hours prior to any entry for such inspection and that if a mutually agreeable date and time cannot be agreed upon, the Owner/Management will conduct the inspection without the Resident's presence unless Resident previously withdraws his or her request for an inspection. An initial inspection statement will be prepared and delivered to Resident showing the items for which a security deposit deduction is proposed to be made.

___ By checking this paragraph, Resident(s) waives the right to have an initial inspection of the premises.

Resident's Signature _____ Date _____

Resident's Signature _____ Date _____

RECEIVE YOUR FULL DEPOSIT BACK WHEN YOU MOVE!

This list is provided at move-in and move-out so you are aware of the cost of property damage, and so you can avoid these expenses and do what is necessary to get all your deposit back.

Cleaning (not done by you)

Refrigerator	$35
Stove top or oven	$25–$50
Kitchen cabinet or countertop	$20
Kitchen or bathroom floor	$30
Bathtub/shower	$25
Toilet	$25
Carpet cleaning or deodorizing	$100–$150
Extensive cleaning	$75 per hour

Damages

Remove crayon marks	$25
Small/large nail hole repair	$10–$35
Replace interior/exterior door	$150–$250
Replace sliding glass door	$200
Replace faucets	$50
Replace bathroom mirror or cabinet	$50–$75
Replace shower heads	$15
Replace toilet	$175
Replace garbage disposal	$100
Replace countertop	$250–$450
Repair window pane	$75–$150
Replace blinds	$75
Replace tile/linoleum	$300–450

Missing Items

Replace light bulb	$1.50
Light fixture globe	$15
Light fixture	$50
Electrical outlet/switch	$5
Electrical cover plate	$2
Replace key	$2
Replace shower curtain	$10
Replace refrigerator shelve	$25
Replace oven knob	$8
Replace window screen	$25

Additional Charges

Replace door lock	$25
Replace curtain rod or towel bars	$20
Replace smoke detector	$40
Remove junk and debris	$75
Fumigate for fleas	$150
Replace fire extinguisher	$40
Replace thermostat	$75
Remove wallpaper	$150
Repaint wall	$25
Vacuum entire unit	$50
Clear drain stoppage	$75
Fence replacement	$25 per foot

Resident agrees that subject to the conditions above, the deposit will be refunded in full within _____ days after vacating premises. It's understood that the above amounts are minimum charges.

Resident(s): _____   Date: _____

SECURITY DEPOSIT REFUND REQUIREMENTS

From: _____

_____

_____

Date: _____

To: _____

Dear _____:

To insure you receive your full deposit, use this checklist:

____ 1. 30-day notice given.

____ 2. All walls, floors, and ceilings thoroughly cleaned.

____ 3. All appliances cleaned (e.g., stove, oven, refrigerator).

____ 4. Refrigerator unplugged and left open.

____ 5. All trash picked up and removed from house.

____ 6. Carpets cleaned by the following manner _____.

____ 7. Any draperies and blinds present at move-in hung back in place.

____ 8. All windows and doors closed and locked.

____ 9. Any damages to the property reported to our office at least two weeks before move-out.

____ 10. Grass cut and raked.

____ 11. All keys returned.

____ 12. _____

____ 13. _____

____ 14. _____

____ 15. _____

Deposit will be refunded within _____ days after you move to the forwarding address you must provide us.

Thanks for your cooperation.

Rental Manager

MOVE-OUT AND REMINDER LETTER

From: _____

Date: _____

To: _____

_____

_____

Dear _____:

   We have received your Intent to Vacate Notice, and we appreciate you are following the steps necessary so you can be entitled to receive as much security deposit as possible refunded back to you. As part of the requirements to have your deposit refunded, this letter is sent to remind you your rental agreement requires the premises be left clean and undamaged. Not only would we like to refund your deposit, but we would also like to give an additional $50 bonus if, with your cooperation, we get a new resident who signs a rental agreement to begin renting the premises within 48 hours after you vacate. To let you know how you can best cooperate with us and to make the cleaning requirement as clear as possible, we have provided the following checklist:

- Remove any unwanted items from the building and set them outside for trash pickup on the appropriate day prior to your final move-out. Please note that you may need to contact the appropriate sanitation office at the following number, _____, to make special arrangements for removal of large items. If you leave any items in the premises or outside that have not been removed after you vacate, the owner will have items removed and you will be held responsible for the cost of removal, which will be deducted from your security deposit.
- Please have the property looking clean and neat several days before you vacate, so that it looks presentable when we show it to prospective residents. We ask for your complete cooperation in allowing us to show the property. If we attempt to contact you for a showing and can't reach you, we ask for permission to enter the premises.
- Feel free to recommend any persons you know who may wish to move into the premises you are vacating. Have them call us at the following number: _____.
- Remove all food and items from the cabinets and the refrigerator.
- Clean all the appliances, including the stove, oven, and refrigerator.
- Replace any missing or burned-out light bulbs.
- Remove all items from the walls and sweep or vacuum all floors.
- Lock all doors and windows when you vacate and leave/bring the keys to the following location:

_____.

We will inspect the property after you have alerted us that the property has been vacated. We will check to ensure that it has been left clean and undamaged. If we have to hire someone to clean or repair damages, you will be notified of any charges to your deposit. Hopefully that will not be necessary.

Thank you for your cooperation.

Rental Manager

RESIDENT EXIT SURVEY

We received your request to vacate the premises you are now living in, located at _____.
We appreciate the opportunity you have given us to meet your housing needs. We will be glad to provide you with a reference for future landlords. Please include your forwarding address below. This is also the same address where we will send the security deposit due you. We would also like to ask if you could take just a couple of minutes to respond to our resident exit survey.

What is the reason for your move? Please check one:

_____ Need a larger house
_____ Need a less expensive dwelling (rent is too high)
_____ Buying a house
_____ Want to move closer to _____
_____ Want a place that included all utilities
_____ Want to move into a newer apartment building
_____ New job, work relocation, or military transfer
_____ Want a feature not available at current home _____
_____ No longer like this area because of _____
_____ Moving completely out of the area
_____ Need a place that accepts pets
_____ Death in the family
_____ Other _____

What feature, upgrade, or amenity in your current home did you like the most?
_____

What aspect of your rental home or neighborhood did you like the least?
_____

What was your favorite neighborhood store, restaurant, or hangout?
_____

Was there anything promised in your rental that was never done?
_____

How did you find out about the new residence you are moving to?
_____

Please give us the name and phone number of one person you know who is looking for a new home.
_____

Would you like us to provide you a reference letter that you can give your next landlord?
_____

If so, please include your forwarding address below. This is also the address where we will send the security deposit due you.
_____

Thanks for taking the time to complete our survey. Please mail this completed survey to the following address:
_____

We wish you the best of success in your next residence.

ITEMIZATION OF SECURITY DEPOSIT RETURN

Date: _____

To: _____

    This letter is to notify you of the itemization of the security deposit returned to you for the property you occupied at: _____.

    You rented these premises between _____ and _____ and officially vacated (keys returned, etc.) on the following date: _____.

Amount of security deposit: _____

Interest on deposit (if applicable or required by law):   _____

The following deductions were applied: Amount

_____   _____

_____   _____

_____   _____

_____   _____

_____   _____

_____   _____

_____   _____

Total amount deducted: _____

Balance of deposit returned: _____

Amount resident owes owner: _____

Please contact us at the following number, _____, if you have any questions or to arrange to pay balance due to prevent damage to your credit history.

VACANT UNITS CHECKLIST

Vacancies	Address 1	Address 2	Address 3	Address 4	Address 5	Address 6
Number of Bedrooms?						
Rental Rate?						
Cleaned?						
Carpets Cleaned?						
Partial Paint Needed?						
Complete Paint Needed?						
Make Over Complete?						
Locks Changed?						
Have Application?						
Have Deposit?						
Move-In Date						

Prepared by: _____ Date _____

CLEANING MAKE READY—RENTAL UNIT PREPARATION
(Please use this cleaning checklist to prevent oversights.)

Address: _____ Unit #: _____

City: _____ State: _____ ZIP: _____

Kitchen

___ stove/hood	___ countertops	___ cabinets
___ refrigerator	___ dishwasher	___ pantries
___ hardware	___ light fixtures	___ windows
___ sinks	___ walls/woodwork	___ floors

Bathroom

___ tub/shower	___ mirrors	___ tile
___ toilets	___ medicine cabinets	___ windows
___ cabinets	___ walls/woodwork	___ exhaust fan
___ countertops	___ floor/baseboards	___ hardware

Living room

___ walls/woodwork	___ closets/shelves	___ wall plates
___ floor/carpet	___ curtains/blinds	___ doors
___ ceilings	___ light fixtures	___ windows

Bedroom #1

___ walls/woodwork	___ closets/shelves	___ wall plates
___ floor/carpet	___ curtains/blinds	___ doors
___ ceilings	___ light fixtures	___ windows

Bedroom #2

___ walls/woodwork	___ closets/shelves	___ wall plates
___ floor/carpet	___ curtains/blinds	___ doors
___ ceilings	___ light fixtures	___ windows

Bedroom #3/Other _____

___ walls/woodwork	___ closets/shelves	___ wall plates
___ floor/carpet	___ curtains/blinds	___ doors
___ ceilings	___ light fixtures	___ windows

Additional Areas/Items

___ washer/dryer area	___ water heater area	___ fireplace
___ furnace/vents	___ staircases/steps	___ balcony/patio

Work done by: _____

Date started: _____ Date completed: _____

Time started: _____ Time completed: _____ Total hrs: _____

Signature: _____ Date: _____

VACANCY MAKEOVER CHECKLIST

_____ Check and test all wall receptacles and switches. One faulty switch may cause a new resident to question overall safety of the electrical system.

_____ Turn on and off all faucets. Check for leaks; also check around tub, showerheads, and under sinks.

_____ Flush toilets. Make sure they're functioning properly: No leaks around bottoms, maintain proper water level, and shut off properly.

_____ Close and open all doors, exterior, interior, sliding, and closets. Check doorstops, closet rods, and shelves.

_____ If drapes or mini-blinds are provided, clean or order replacements.

_____ Exterminate for all pests, and put air fresheners in place.

_____ Replace light bulbs. Good lighting helps in showing vacant units.

_____ Clean and check all appliances (including cleaning in and behind them).

_____ Make sure all kitchen countertops, drawers, and cabinets are clean. Remove old shelf paper. Check to see if all hardware and knobs are in place.

_____ Make bathrooms shine, including tubs (remove any decals), toilets, tile, cabinets, mirror, towel bars, toilet paper holders, and soap dishes (are all in place). Paint walls if needed.

_____ Check condition of paint on all interior walls and ceilings. Paint if necessary; fill in any holes.

_____ Clean and shine all vinyl floorings. Clean and deodorize all carpets and rugs.

_____ Clean all windows and mirrors. Replace any broken or scratched windows. Check to see if all screens are in place. Are they torn?

_____ Check heating units and air-conditioners, including replacing filters.

_____ Remove all trash, debris, or personal items left behind.

_____ Test smoke alarms.

_____ Sweep entryways and wash off front of building. Does front porch need a paint touch up?

_____ Check stairs, handrails, porches, and/or balconies.

_____ Rekey all locks and ensure all are working properly. See if any window locks are needed.

_____ Is exterior of premises clean and neat? Does grass need cutting or other landscaping needs?

_____ Any special welcome touches: _____

Checklist complete: _____ Date: _____

RENTAL MARKET SURVEY
(To compare your rental/prices with other properties in the area)

Area _____

Address _____

City _____ State _____ ZIP _____

Rent amount _____

Deposit required _____ App. fee _____

Bedrooms _____ # Bathrooms _____

Appliances _____

Utilities paid _____

Garage/storage _____ Extra cost _____

Do you allow pets? _____ Any extras? _____

How long been available? _____

Website _____

Area _____

Address _____

City _____ State _____ ZIP _____

Rent amount _____

Deposit required _____ App. fee _____

Bedrooms _____ # Bathrooms _____

Bedrooms _____ # Bathrooms _____

Utilities paid _____

Garage/storage _____ Extra cost _____

Do you allow pets? _____ Any extras? _____

How long been available? _____

Website _____

Area _____

Address _____

City _____ State _____ ZIP _____

Rent amount _____

Deposit required _____ App. fee _____

Bedrooms _____ # Bathrooms _____

Appliances _____

Utilities paid _____

Garage/storage _____ Extra cost _____

Do you allow pets? _____ Any extras? _____

How long been available? _____

Website _____

Area _____

Address _____

City _____ State _____ ZIP _____

Rent amount _____

Deposit required _____ App. fee _____

Bedrooms _____ # Bathrooms _____

Bedrooms _____ # Bathrooms _____

Utilities paid _____

Garage/storage _____ Extra cost _____

Do you allow pets? _____ Any extras? _____

How long been available? _____

Website _____

Area _____

Address _____

City _____ State _____ ZIP _____

Rent amount _____

Deposit required _____ App. fee _____

Bedrooms _____ # Bathrooms _____

Appliances _____

Utilities paid _____

Garage/storage _____ Extra cost _____

Do you allow pets? _____ Any extras? _____

How long been available? _____

Website _____

Area _____

Address _____

City _____ State _____ ZIP _____

Rent amount _____

Deposit required _____ App. fee _____

Bedrooms _____ # Bathrooms _____

Bedrooms _____ # Bathrooms _____

Utilities paid _____

Garage/storage _____ Extra cost _____

Do you allow pets? _____ Any extras? _____

How long been available? _____

Website _____

FOR RENT!

In the Following Area(s)

_____

Houses, Duplexes, Apartments

1, 2, and 3 Bedrooms

Rooms Also Available

Prices start as low as $ _____ per month

* Discount off your first month's rent
* Smaller deposits for those who qualify
* Some apartments include _____
* Open house to be held _____

CALL TODAY!

_____

To apply and get more information about the available rentals,
call and ask for _____

Leave your name and number and we'll call you back.

Visit our website: _____.

Bring This Flyer with You for a Discount Off First Month's Rent.

RESIDENT REFERRAL POLICY AGREEMENT
Receive up to $100 cash bonus!

It is the policy of _____ to pay current residents a referral fee (where state law permits) for telling new GOOD tenants about our rental properties. Because these people may become your neighbors, we wish to ensure that only qualified residents are accepted. Towards this end we are paying the referring resident a bounty of $100, subject to the following three conditions:

1. All incoming prospective residents are subject to the normal screening process. We appreciate your assistance in referring someone, but understand that the ultimate selection of any new resident is at the sole discretion of the landlord or a designated representative. The screening process consists of a rental application, a nonrefundable $ _____ screening fee, and a background check. All residents are screened for previous evictions, criminal history, and a credit check.

2. The new resident must pay on time for six months. This means the payment is to be to the landlord by the due date EVERY month. There must be no neighbor complaints of record against the new tenant.

3. The referring resident must be current with his or her rent at the time of the referral and must be current during the same six months as the new tenant. There must be no neighbor complaints of record against the referring resident.

The payment will be paid to the referring resident in the following manner: $50 paid immediately after the new resident is approved and moves in to our property. At the end of the first six-month period of occupancy by the new resident, an additional $50 will be delivered to the referring resident if all conditions have been met. If conditions have not been met, the referring resident will owe the landlord a refund for the first $50 of the bonus previously given.

THE EASIEST $100 YOU'VE EVER MADE!

Everyone likes a little extra CASH during and after the holidays. Wouldn't you agree?
But most of the time it requires working overtime, or picking up a second job.

I don't know about you, but I'm too busy as it is, and a second job is out of the question. But still, I'd appreciate a couple of extra hundred dollars for those unexpected expenses that always seem to pop up during and after the holidays.

What could you do with some extra spending money?

Maybe you could buy that special someone in your life a really nice gift this year. Or perhaps there is a particular piece of electronic equipment you've had your eyes on...

Whatever your reason... we'd like to make you an offer that would benefit both of us.
The homes/apartments we manage will have a couple of openings in the upcoming months, located at
_____. Instead of throwing the money away on ads in the
local paper, we thought we'd give it to our residents.

Show me the MONEY!

Here's the deal. If you refer someone to us, and they mention your name as who referred them, and they rent from us
during the upcoming month(s) of _____, we'll pay you $100 per referral! Normally we
pay $50 dollars referral, but since it's the holiday season, we're doubling our referral reward.

Now, how's that for easy money? If you live near the homes or apartments becoming available, you may know some
of the good points about the property or the neighborhood, with it's easy convenience to:
_____.

You should also know about the nice features of the properties, which include:
_____.

Okay, but what do I have to do?

All you have to do is keep your ears and eyes open. Surely you know a friend, relative, or co-worker that is looking for a great place to live. We're looking for a few great residents like you. And besides, wouldn't you rather pick your neighbors? Simply give them our phone number, _____, and tell them what you like most about living in your home. We'll do the rest.

Sincerely,

Owner/Management

HELLO, NEIGHBOR LETTER

Dear Neighbors,

I'm sending you this letter to introduce myself or simply give a friendly reminder that our company, _____, owns or manages the house located near you at
_____.

As you may or may not know, our present resident is in the process of moving out of our house and we are presently looking for new residents. We would like to work with neighbors like yourself to select residents who have pride in the neighborhood and who will keep the property and the neighborhood in good condition. If you know of any relatives, friends, or coworkers who will take pride in the neighborhood and who would like to move to this area, please have them call us at _____. We give to anyone who tells someone about our house and that person moves in _____.

Here is a brief description of our house: _____
_____
_____
_____
_____

We may even be willing to give an option to purchase the house to someone with good credit history and employment.

We are holding an open house to view the property on the following date and time:
_____.

If you have any questions you would like to ask about the house, just give us a call. Our phone number is
_____.

Also, if you ever have a problem with someone who moves in, or you see any wrong-doing, please do not hesitate to call, so we can clear up any problems quickly. Like you, we want the neighborhood to stay safe for everyone. Thank you for any assistance you can give.

Sincerely,

Rental Manager

PS: Our company also buys and leases homes on a long-term basis from owners who are moving out of the area or who want a guaranteed rent check and no more maintenance or resident calls. Give me a call and I'll be glad to talk with you and tell you how much our company would be willing to pay you to buy or lease your house.

STUDENT HOUSING LETTER

To: College/University Student Housing Director

From: _____   Date: _____

_____

_____

Dear Housing Director:

   I would like to introduce myself to you. My name is _____.
I own/manage rental homes conveniently located in a neighborhood surrounding your school only _____
miles from your campus. Your students, faculty, and staff who are new to your school and/or the area or transferring
or relocating will find our well-maintained homes and/or apartments also offer easy access to the major highways,
bus lines, and shopping. I am pleased to let you know we offer a $ _____ donation to your
school's housing department anytime we rent to one of your faculty members, staff, or students.

   I am writing this letter to ask if you would please include my contact information below on your list of housing
choices for your graduate students, international students, staff, and faculty. I've also enclosed a flyer(s) and/or index
card(s) describing our rental property that can be posted on appropriate bulletin boards. Our rental homes offer
many amenities options, including: _____.

   We can also offer furnished rentals. We offer a wide range of rental rates ranging from _____.
In addition, rent payments can be arranged to coincide with each semester. Quarterly, monthly, and biweekly payment plans are available.

   We offer rental terms for the academic year as well as short-term leases, and our unique two-year term for graduate students is available and very popular. Plus, we offer lease-to-buy programs in which your long-term staff or faculty may be interested. *Any person, student, or faculty member who presents a copy of this letter or a college I.D. will
receive $_____ credit toward the first month's rent or a free property upgrade.* Rent credit is subject to the
resident being otherwise qualified to rent as evidenced by an executed lease.

   I look forward to working with students who are relocating and seeking alternative housing choices. Let us know if
you need more. We will be glad to provide additional information if needed. You may call _____
if you have questions or if I can be of any help to your faculty, staff, or students. Please register my name and property in housing information you provide for students, staff, and faculty and use the following contact information.

Owner/Manager: _____   Phone: _____

Property Address: _____

Website Address: _____

Email Address: _____

Sincerely,

Rental Manager

CORPORATE VIP HOUSING

FROM: _____

_____

_____

Date: _____

Dear: _____

We want to offer and provide a housing service for your company that is needed from time to time for your important clients and/or employees. It is our understanding that you often work with clients arriving from out of town, or those staying in the area for a short-term basis. Some of these clients will be in need of temporary housing.

Our company owns and manages home rentals that are available for short-term periods. Our homes and/or apartments can provide needed temporary housing for out- of-town clients staying in the area for a designated time period, and also for employees who are relocating or here for short-term job assignments or training. Most landlords, local apartment managers and home rental agents avoid short-term leasing agreements. However, we provide quality homes and apartments on a weekly or monthly basis, completely furnished if needed, and conveniently located near _____. (At one-half the rate of local hotels.)

Please call our office for further information, or to reserve specific dates. We also know that in some cases, as with a client or employee arriving on short notice, you have no way of reserving space in advance. When that occurs, you must search for and locate suitable housing quickly. Often, the only short-term housing available on short-notice is at the more expensive hotel rates.

We offer one other option to you. We will allow any corporation or company to reserve a home (keep on hold) for their exclusive use and their clients. The home can be held for only one-half our normal rate ($_____ per day). Then, when the need arises for a client to occupy, our normal discounted rate goes into effect. This gives you the assurance of being able to meet the needs of your clients quickly, without them, or you, having the time-consuming and frustrating task of searching for adequate housing at double our cost. This can also be an extra selling point for your company to potential clients who will need a place to stay. Once again, please call if we can be of help in reserving a "VIP" home for your company, your clients, or your employees.

Our phone number is _____.

Sincerely,

Corporate Housing Manager

MARKETING LETTER TO LOCAL BUSINESSES

Personnel or Relocation Director

_____

_____

_____

_____

Date: _____

Dear _____ :

    Thanks for permitting me to talk briefly with you over the phone about the rental homes or apartment building our company, _____ , manages that are located near your company. Your employees would greatly appreciate and benefit from the nearness of our rental to your business location. Studies have found employees who live near where they work will be more likely to stay at their place of employment longer and be more productive at work. Our rental is only _____ miles from your company.

    We are glad you will include our rental on your listing of housing choices available for employees and personnel moving into the area. As we may have mentioned over the phone, anytime one of your employees rents from us, we donate $100 to your company or to the charity of your choice. The type of rental we presently have available is a _____. Included in the rental, we offer _____. Rental rates, depending on amenity preferences, start at $ _____ per month. Short-term company leases can also be arranged. We work with both large and small companies with just a few employees. We can provide furnished rentals complete with linens and small appliances.

    Any employee who presents a copy of one of the letters we've enclosed when applying for our rental will receive a $ _____ credit toward the first month's rent, if accepted. Along with letters to distribute directly to employees, we have also enclosed a flyer that you can post on employee bulletin boards. Please feel free to call our office at _____ if you have any questions, to request additional letters or flyers, or to set up an appointment to view our rental. I'll follow up with you as well to see if it's possible to set up a time when I can briefly address your employees directly, in a group setting, about our available housing.

Sincerely,

Rental Manager

MARKETING LETTER TO BROKERS

From: _____

_____

_____

Date: _____

Dear _____ :

I would like to introduce myself. My name is _____. I own and manage rental properties located in the following neighborhood(s) _____ _____.

I would like to develop a mutually beneficial business relationship with your company. I wanted to ask if you would consider referring individuals who may be interested in renting my properties. I would be glad to pay a half-month rent referral fee when a client of yours signs a rental agreement for one of my properties. I just ask that you, or the client, inform us before or at the time of application that he or she was referred by you. If you offer additional marketing or leasing assistance that can help me find suitable residents, I'd very much like to hear what services you offer.

A rental property I currently have available for rent, (or will be vacant soon), is located at _____ _____. The following is a description of the property: _____. The rental rate price range is _____.

I welcome the opportunity to discuss your possible assistance and give you more information about my properties or discuss any questions you may have about the rentals I own and manage. Again, I'm looking for assistance in finding suitable residents through any referrals you may send or by directly marketing and leasing my available rental. Though I'm not currently looking for a company to handle all management responsibilities, I may need such assistance in the future. Please call me at _____.

Sincerely,

Rental Manager

MARKETING RESEARCH FROM EACH APPLICANT
(Also can be used as a telephone pre-screening checklist)

Date: _____

Name of prospective resident?_____Phone?_____

Email address?_____ Have you seen our website?_____

1) How did you find out about us? (Advertising source?):

☐ Newspaper? Which one? _____ Day of the week it appeared _____

☐ For Rent Sign?

☐ Referral (From whom)? _____

☐ Website (Which one)? _____

☐ Flyer (Posted at what at location)? _____

☐ Letter (Received in mail or given by whom)? _____

☐ Agency or Rental Guide? _____

☐ Other Source? _____

2) Day of the week you received applicant's call?_____

3) Any other contact information of applicant? (Work? Cell? Fax? Email address?)_____

4) What size home or numbers of bedrooms are you looking for? Any special features you desire?_____
_____

5) How many total persons will occupy your next residence, including relatives or friends who may stay for even a short period? And how many pets do you have?_____

6) About how much are you looking to spend on the next home or apartment that meets your needs?_____

7) By what date will you need to be moved?_____

8) How much advance notice have you given your current landlord about your move?_____

9) Where are you currently living?_____

10) What is one thing you do not like about the property or management where you are presently residing? What is the reason you are moving?_____

11) Where are you presently working? How close would you like your work to be to your home?_____
_____

12) Do you have any favorite shops or stores in the area?_____

13) Which of the following special extras or upgrade items would you like included in your rental? (For example, ceiling fan, Internet access, TV, computer, washer or dryer, etc.)_____

14) Are you available for next showing appointment? (Which will be a group showing.) Or what is the reason for not wishing to visit rental? _____

NOTICE OF SALE OF PROPERTY—TRANSFER OF OWNERSHIP

From: _____

_____

_____

Date: _____

To: _____

_____

_____

Dear _____:

This letter is to notify you the property where you are currently living, _____ _____, has transferred ownership. The name of the new owner is _____. The new owner, or a representative, should be contacting you shortly, if they have not already done so. Please be advised from this point forward any and all concerns regarding your property should be directed to the new owner or to whomever the owner designates. This includes directing all rental payments, inquiries, requests, or questions to them. The new owner and or management has provided me with the following phone number and/or address to give to you. Use this information to contact the new owners and for where to send payments: _____ _____ _____

We have greatly appreciated the opportunity to provide housing for you. Though we are no longer managing the property you currently reside in, we will continue to manage other properties or work with home builders and real estate brokers in the area. If we can be of any assistance to you in the future regarding renting or buying a home, please contact us at _____.

Sincerely,

Rental Manager

CERTIFICATE OF

PROFESSIONAL DESIGNATION

"C.P.L."

Certified Professional Landlord

is awarded to

_____

FOR COMMITMENT TO CONTINUED LEARNING
IN THE FIELD OF LANDLORDING

From: Mr. Landlord Inc./MrLandlord.com

Signature: *Jeffrey E. Taylor, C.P.L.* (Founder, MrLandlord.com)

Date Received: _____

FINAL COMMENTS AND CHALLENGE

I want to share with you just a few concluding thoughts and a couple of bonus tips on how to best use the forms enclosed in this book. And equally important, I want to challenge you to continue to develop your professionalism and knowledge in the area of landlording and property management.

PERSONALIZE YOUR RENTAL FORMS

■ *Tip Number* **60**
Send forms and letters with your resident's name.

It's a nice touch and your communication is more effective when you send forms, letters, or notices to residents with their actual name. Avoid sending generic-looking forms that simply say "Dear Resident." Take a few moments to include the resident's name. To make this task easier and so that you can always send out personalized forms, we recommend our forms CD software program that includes the forms featured in this book. There is a special half-price offer for the forms software that is available to all those who purchased this book (see the following pages).

KNOWLEDGE IS POWER

■ *Tip Number* **61**
Always continue to learn. Take advantage of all the educational resources and services available to you.

Congratulations on taking steps to improve your management success by using the forms in this book. You will continue to face challenges that can bring many financial rewards, but you will also face risks that can cause financial disaster. That is why it is critical that you always continue to educate yourself and update yourself on the latest challenges facing landlords.

We recommend the following, if you have not done so already:

- Join a local real estate association. To find an association near you from among the hundreds of associations in throughout the United States, go to <www.realestateassociations.com>.

- Consult daily the MrLandlord.com Web site, specifically the most popular section for both new and long-term rental owners, which is the National Landlord Question & Answer Forum. We strongly suggest that all landlords take advantage of this resource where you can ask questions and receive free feedback from experienced rental owners and managers nationwide <www.landlordingadvice.com>

- Review for yourself the landlord-tenant laws for your specific state. Become very familiar with your rights and responsibilities as a landlord. Access our Landlord Law pages for all 50 states. Go to <www.landlordstatelaws.com>

- Screen all prospective residents carefully. The largest percentage of the problems landlords face are directly or indirectly the results of resident selection. You can make your life and landlording far more enjoyable and rental properties more profitable if you use the forms included in this book and always request a tenant credit report to weed out applicants who are most likely to cause you headaches. It's now easier than ever for individual landlords to run credit reports online <www.tenantcreditchecks.com>

- Purchase additional landlord books. The number one book recommendation for readers of this publication is the companion guide to The Landlord's Kit, titled: ___The Landlord's Survival Guide___. That publication fully discusses all the business principles and innovative landlording and management concepts that are interwoven into the forms of this publication. Some other excellent landlord books are available and can be found at <www.landlordbooks.com>.

- Subscribe to the Mr. Landlord Newsletter and *Rental Owner* email newsletter. Stay updated on new laws affecting rental owners nationwide, new challenges facing landlords, and additional educational resources available to you. As a purchaser of this book, you are entitled to a free subscription to the Mr. Landlord newsletter, plus six free special real estate reports to add to your success (see pages 257 and 258).

Index

Special Half-Price Offer for Buyers of This Book!

MrLandlord.com Rental Forms Software

MrLandlord.com Rental Forms CD Software. If you are planning to use the forms in this book, we also suggest that you get the CD program that includes all the featured forms. This Forms CD will allow you to:

- Easily create customized rental documents in minutes.
- Enter resident information and print professional looking documents fast!
- Edit, personalize, and print any of the 180 recommended rental forms.
- Create and save additional rental forms, letters, and notices.
- Add some of your favorite forms to the program

This Forms CD program is easy to use. Using the CD program, you can change any of the following aspects of any letter: font (letter) style, letter size, and line spacing. You can edit, delete, or customize and save any of the wording on the forms. You can even add some of your favorite forms to the program. And, of course, you can print any of the forms in minutes and produce professional-looking forms for your residents any time throughout the year, personalized with your or your company's name.

In addition, when you order the Forms CD program, as part of this special offer, you'll also receive a **Recordkeeping CD** with over 50 Recordkeeping Forms to record and keep track of vital aspects of the "administrative" side of your rental business. To add to the Forms CD, which includes forms to communicate effectively and professionally with residents and others, the Recordkeeping Forms are for "your eyes only," or for those helping you with management of the property. Most landlords (especially the majority who only do it on a part-time basis), try diligently to stay on top of the various challenges of rental properties. Often, however, there is not enough time in the day to handle full-time jobs, landlording duties, and also keep track of the "administrative" side of the business. Even staying on top of the recordkeeping for one or a few rentals can become overwhelming, if you don't have a simple system for maintaining your files and records. The Recordkeeping Forms will provide you that simple system to record, file, track, and maintain all your rental records, including property records, resident records, maintenance records, and income and expense records, so that you can stay in control of your rental business.

To order both the Forms CD and Recordkeeping Forms CD, call toll-free 1-800-950-2250, 24 hours a day. Or you can fill out this form, tear it out, and mail to Mr. Landlord, Box 64442, Virginia Beach, VA 23467.

____ **Yes! I want the Rental Forms CD with 180 forms, plus the set of Recordkeeping Forms on CD** (combined set is regularly priced at $199) for the special half-price offer of only $99.50.

Name: _____ Phone_____

Address: _____

City: _____ State: _____ ZIP: _____

☐ Visa ☐ MC ☐ Amex ☐ Discover Credit Card #: _____

Exp. Date: _____ Signature: _____

Date ordered _____ Total $_____ Check enclosed _____

E-mail address: _____

You may also fax your request by calling 1-757-436-2608 - 24 hours a day - You get an extra $5.00 discount for fax orders.

Special Free Offer for Buyers of This Book

**Receive Free a 6-Month Subscription (24 issues)
to our Mr. Landlord Newsletter
Plus 6 Free Special Reports
(Bonus value of $100)**

The six free special reports (guaranteed to help you be more successful as a real estate investor) you will receive:

1. *How to Get Rents on Time, Every Time*
2. *How to Collect Money Due You from Former Residents*
3. *Dozens of Rental Clauses to Cover You in Varied Situations*
4. *17 Costly Mistakes Almost Every Landlord Makes, Reducing Cash Flow by Thousands*
5. *How to Find and Select Residents, 100 Marketing and Screening Tips*
6. *Favorite Forms from Mr. Landlord Subscribers and Other Landlord Kit Readers*

The six money-making management newsletter issues you receive includes updated information about access to:

- Two free tenant credit checks
- Free additional updated rental forms
- Free preview of state-specific legal forms
- Free book and CD giveaways
- Free management software
- Free landlording tips
- Free real estate reports
- Free landlord calculators
- Free trial of direct rent deposit service
- Real estate laws affecting rental owners nationwide

_____ **Yes! Send me a free six-month subscription to the Mr. Landlord Newsletter**, so I will get many money-making management ideas, **plus access to the free items and services listed above** for rental owners. **Plus, send me the six free special reports** with tons of tips to help me be more successful as a real estate investor (total of $100 in bonus value).

The newsletters are sent by regular mail and the special reports are normally sent by email. Not on the Web yet? No problem, we will mail you the free six-month subscription to our popular *Mr. Landlord newsletter* (the most popular printed publication for landlords nationwide for 22+ years) and send the six free special reports.

Tear out this form and mail it to Mr. Landlord, Box 64442, Virginia Beach, VA 23467:

Name: _____

Email address: _____

Address: _____

City: _____ State: _____ ZIP: _____

Thanks for letting us be part of your real estate success team!